Round The Year

Ninety-nine stories for the primary school assembly

Jeanne L. Jackson

RELIGIOUS AND MORAL EDUCATION PRESS

Dedicated to Cobden Children – past, present and future.

Acknowledgements

Thank you to the staff and children of Cobden Primary School, for sharing these assemblies with me, and for continuing to be a source of inspiration and joy.

Thank you to Pete Johnson, for helping me to see the light through 'Windows', and without whom I would still be in the dark!

Thank you to Val Pennington, for your support and friendship, and for all your help in researching material for the book.

Religious and Moral Education Press
A division of SCM-Canterbury Press Ltd
A wholly owned subsidiary of Hymns Ancient & Modern Ltd
St Mary's Works, St Mary's Plain
Norwich, Norfolk NR3 3BH

First published 2000 by Leopard Learning Ltd, Bath

This edition first published by Religious and Moral Education Press 2003

Reprinted 2003

ISBN 1 85175 265 X

Typeset by Leopard Learning Ltd
Cover design by Topics – The Creative Partnership, Exeter

Printed in Great Britain by Bath Press Ltd, Bath for SCM-Canterbury Press Ltd, Norwich

Contents

Introduction v

September

Theme 1 Beginnings 1
Theme 2 Ourselves 7
Theme 3 Working together 12

October

Theme 1 Sharing 19
Theme 2 Harvest 26
Theme 3 Tricks and treats 33

November

Theme 1 Remember, remember 40
Theme 2 Myths 47
Theme 3 Legends 54

December

Theme 1 Awe and wonder 61
Theme 2 Star stories 69
Theme 3 Christmas 76

January

Theme 1 Three millennia 82
Theme 2 Messages 90
Theme 3 Rules 97

February

Theme 1 Friendship 103
Theme 2 Feelings 110
Theme 3 Power 116

March

Theme 1 Care of animals 123
Theme 2 Environment 130
Theme 3 Easter 136

April
Theme 1 Choices 143
Theme 2 Different perspectives 148
Theme 3 Fables 154

May
Theme 1 Doing your best 162
Theme 2 Campaigners for change 169
Theme 3 Speaking and listening 177

June
Theme 1 Revenge 184
Theme 2 Rights and responsibilities 191
Theme 3 Wealth, valuables and riches 198

July
Theme 1 Bravery 206
Theme 2 Achievements 214
Theme 3 Journeys 221

Alphabetical index of stories 229

Story source index 232

Thematic index 235

Introduction

Round the Year is a new collection of 99 stories for the primary school assembly, arranged as the title suggests, to follow the school year.

This arrangement, I believe, helps bring unity and continuity to the school. The stories are intended to be thought-provoking, stimulating and above all enjoyable, and it is my hope that they will stir the imagination of both children and staff, so that the themes they carry will be taken from the assembly into the classroom and will infiltrate other work already planned, making the theme a part of the thinking of the school and the assembly a meaningful and purposeful focal point in the school day.

Round the Year is designed to be as user-friendly as possible; I well understand the difficulty of finding time to search for material for collective worship day in and day out throughout the year. The book is therefore planned in weekly themes – three to each month, throughout the eleven months of the academic year. Each theme contains three stories – enough material for one school year, bearing in mind that schools will all have their own chosen means of filling the remaining two acts of collective worship required each week under the 1988 Education Reform Act. In line with the Act, the majority of the stories are "wholly or mainly of a broadly Christian character" and they reflect the "broad traditions of Christian belief, without being distinctive of any particular Christian denomination". However, many of the stories have been successfully told to groups of children of mixed ethnic background. The stories appeal to children of whatever background or personal belief, and do not presume a level of religious commitment. They retell equally well to small groups, or large assemblies, of children, although obviously the smaller the group, the easier it is to elicit comment, response and opinion. The stories have also been successfully used across the full primary school age range. Purists may ask about differentiation, but I believe that a good story can be told to an assembly of people with a wide age and ability range; each listener hears the story from his or her own standpoint, and can interpret it at their own level, from the purely superficial, to one where every nuance is understood, as is the tradition in story-telling.

The themes in *Round the Year* are all listed clearly in the contents, but each story is also cross referenced in a thematic index at the back of the book, thus making it as straightforward as possible for the busy teacher to find a story suitable for a theme being followed in school, which might not be one of the main themes in this book. *Round the Year* therefore can be used systematically throughout the year or as a dip-in resource.

The stories are gathered from a wide variety of sources, from local news items to myths thousands of years old, and the collection includes much original, specially-written material. I have included a story source index which I hope will be useful for those teachers looking for a particular type of story, as opposed to a theme.

Each story begins and ends in a conversational style which is easily adapted by the narrator. Each story ends with an optional prayer, but I have not added hymn suggestions, as I find that all schools have their own repertoire of well-used and well-loved hymns and songs.

I intend and hope that *Round the Year* will meet a need in primary schools, and that the stories will be enjoyed by both children and staff.

September

Theme 1: Beginnings

Mr Storten builds a house

Happy new school year everyone!

Beginnings are exciting! Here we are at the beginning of a brand-new school year and the start of lots of new projects. You're all in a new class with a new teacher; you have new books, new work, new goals and new challenges. During this year you'll learn new things and maybe make new friends. Yes, beginnings are exciting!

But it's important to remember that middles and endings matter, too. It's good to begin things, but the beginning is not much use if you don't see it through to the end. In today's story, someone was very good at starting things, but not much good at finishing them.

Mrs Storten looked out of her kitchen window onto the tiny concrete backyard and the busy street beyond.

'I wish we lived on a farm,' she said to her husband. 'It would be lovely to look out over green fields instead of all these houses. And wouldn't it be nice to have lots of animals to look after and a big farmhouse to live in.'

'Well, it's funny you should say that,' said Mr Storten, who was a builder, 'because I've seen an old derelict farmhouse that needs doing up and I thought we might buy it. There's lots of land with the house so we could get some animals.'

'Then let's buy it!' said Mrs Storten. So they did.

The farmhouse was too tumbledown for them to live in until it was rebuilt, so they bought a caravan and put it in the field next to the house. Mr Storten started work on the farmhouse as soon as it was theirs, and was full of enthusiasm about how he would renovate it and the improvements he would make.

The work progressed quickly. Mr Storten had to knock most of the old house down first, then he remade the foundations and started to rebuild the walls. Soon the doors and downstairs windows were in place, and then the upstairs window-frames were fitted. It seemed no time at all before the roof joists were in place, and then Mr Storten began to fit tiles on the roof.

But whilst he was up on the roof putting the last of the tiles on, Mr Storten noticed that the roof of the old barn was in a poor state of repair.

'I think I'll start on the barn next,' he said to Mrs Storten.

'But what about all the jobs there are to finish inside the house?' she said. 'There's all the plastering to do, and all the electrical work, all the plumbing and all the decorating!'

'Oh, I'll do all that later,' he said. 'I want to start on the barn next, then we can get some animals – a goat or two, and maybe a donkey.'

So Mr Storten started work on the barn. But he'd only got about half-way through the work, when he noticed the stables needed repairing.

'I think I'll start on the stables tomorrow,' he said to Mrs Storten.

'But what about the work that's still to do in the house?' she said. 'And the barn isn't finished yet. We can't get any animals until the barn is finished.'

'We can go ahead and get a goat and a donkey,' said Mr Storten.

'They can live in the field and if the weather's bad we can pop them into the house.'

So Mrs Storten was sent to market to buy a goat and a donkey, and Mr Storten started work on the stables. He rebuilt the walls and put in new stable doors and windows. He was just about to begin work on the roof, when he realised he'd not built a garage for the car.

'I think I'll do the garage next,' he said to Mrs Storten. 'We'll need a garage before the winter comes. We don't want the car standing out in all weathers.'

'But what about the jobs in the house that need finishing?' asked Mrs Storten. 'And what about the barn and the stable you've started but not finished.'

'Oh, don't worry about those,' answered Mr Storten. 'I'll finish those later,' and with that he started work on the garage.

The garage walls were about half-built when the police came to see him.

'Are these your animals?' they asked, leading a goat and a donkey behind them on a length of rope.

'Yes?' said Mr Storten. 'What are you doing with them?'

'They've escaped through your broken-down fence,' said the police. 'You need to get that fence mended. Now!'

'I will,' said Mr Storten, and he left work on the garage and started to repair the fence all round the farm.

He'd repaired about half of it, when the postman arrived with some mail.

'Look at these!' he said, showing Mr Storten some advertising leaflets with photos of beautiful conservatories. 'One of these would look really nice on the side of your house!'

'It would,' said Mr Storten. 'I'll build one!' And he went out straightaway and bought the wood and the stones and cement he would need to build a conservatory.

'But what about finishing the house and the barn and the stable and the garage and the fence,' cried Mrs Storten.

'Oh, don't worry. I'll finish them later. I must get started on this first!' And Mr Storten hurried off to begin digging out the foundations and building the framework for the conservatory.

As he worked, he was thinking about the glass he'd need to buy for the conservatory, and that set him thinking about a greenhouse.

'If we had a greenhouse, we could grow our own tomatoes and cucumbers,' he thought. 'I'll build a greenhouse with the spare wood that's left over from the conservatory,' and without consulting Mrs Storten, he began to work on the greenhouse, leaving the conservatory to finish later.

But half-way through building the greenhouse, he began to think about the garden.

'Wouldn't it be nice to have a garden pond, with goldfish, and lovely water plants?' he said to his wife. 'I could build a rockery and a stream with a waterfall. I could build a little bridge over the stream and a seat next to it, and in the summer we'll be able to sit and watch the fish. What do you think?'

'I think you should finish the house and the barn and the stable and the garage and the fence and the conservatory and the greenhouse, before you start on the garden!' wept Mrs Storten.

'No, I think I should start the garden before the winter sets in and the ground gets too hard to dig,' said Mr Storten. 'In fact, I'll go and start it now!'

'NO!' cried Mrs Storten. 'It's always the same. You start things and never finish them. Well now it's my turn. I'm going to start something. I'm going to start a holiday. And by the time I come back, EVERYTHING had better be finished!'

'But...but... where will you go?' spluttered Mr Storten.

'Disneyland!' shouted Mrs Storten. 'And if this house and barn and stable and garage and fence and conservatory and greenhouse and garden and pond and stream and waterfall and bridge, not to mention my tea, are not ready by the time I get back... I shall go again... and LIVE there!' and with that she went to pack her bags ready for the holiday.

I wonder what happened next? Do you think she went to Disneyland? More to the point, do you think she came back? And do you think Mr Storten had finished all those jobs he started? He was very enthusiastic about starting projects, wasn't he? But not so keen to finish them!

At the start of this new school year, I hope you're going to enthusiastically start lots of new projects; but I hope you'll do better than Mr Storten, because I hope you'll have the perseverance to see them through and to finish what you start.

Beginnings are important. But endings matter, too.

Dear God, please help us at the start of this new school year to be enthusiastic about its beginning. Help us to work hard, to do our best in everything, and to finish what we start. Help us to know that endings, just as much as beginnings, are important. Amen

How Coyote made the first people

One of the most exciting things about beginnings, is that you don't know quite how they're going to turn out. Beginnings are a bit like adventures; they lead you into new territory, and introduce you to new things.

Today, I have a story for you which the North American Indians tell, about the beginning of the world, and the first people. Stories like this are called creation stories; they are stories which people told to try and explain how the world began.

The Coyote had almost finished getting the world ready. He had put the earth and sky in position, he had built the mountains, scooped out the lakes and planted the forests. The animals watched him.

Then the Coyote set the world in motion; up until then everything had been still. He swirled the snow over the mountains, and tossed the wind across the plains. He stirred up the rivers, drizzled the rain on the lakes, and poured the waterfalls over the cliffs. He howled at the moon until it began to move across the sky and push the sun out of the way. He stared at the stars until they, too, shifted in the sky. The animals watched him, and told him how clever he was.

The Coyote basked in their praise. 'Yes, I am clever,' he said. 'That is why the Great Spirit Chief asked me to finish making the world. All I have to do now, is make the People. I shall do that tomorrow, but now it is bedtime and I must sleep,' and with that the Coyote left the animals and went to sleep, so as to be ready to make People the next day.

'People!' said the animals. 'I wonder what they will be like?'

'Well, they need to be big and strong and stand on two legs like me,' said the bear.

'No,' said the mouse. 'They need to be small and quiet, like me.'

'They should be able to run as fast as the wind, like me,' said the deer.

'I think they should be quiet and not make any trouble, like me,' said the sheep.

'No!' said the eagle. 'They should be brave and have sharp eyes like me.'

'They should be able to live in water and on land, like me,' said the otter.

'No! Like me!' said the owl. 'Able to turn their heads and see everywhere.'

'They should be like me,' said the fox. 'Cunning and quick.'

'No, like me,' said the beaver. 'No, me,' said the wolf.

And so it went on, each animal insisting that the new People should be just like them. They were still arguing when dawn broke, and the new day began. The animals set off to find the Coyote.

'Wake up Coyote!' they called. 'We have things to tell you. When you make the new People today, we want you to make them like…' And the argument started all over again.

'QUIET!' shouted Coyote. 'There's no point in making the new People like the animals we already have. If I do that I might just as well make some more bears or owls or eagles or foxes. No, I have already decided that the new People will be cleverer and more cunning than any of you.'

'Like you, you mean?' said the fox.

'Yes!' said the Coyote. 'Like me.'

'But that's not fair,' said the fox. 'You've already said that there's no point in making the new People the same as the animals we already have. I think we should all have a say in what the new People will be like.'

'Oh all right,' said the Coyote. 'Why don't you each make a model of what you think the new People should look like, and I'll choose whichever is the best and make the new People like that.' The animals agreed that this was an excellent idea, and they all went away to the riverbank to gather mud and clay with which to make their models. Then for the rest of the day, there wasn't a sound to be heard, as each animal worked at shaping a model of their ideal People.

The mouse made a model of small People with long tails. The bear made big People with strong sharp claws. The owl and eagle and hawk all made their People with wings. The salmon gave his People fins and a strong fish's tail. And so on. Each animal making a model of People like themselves. Only the Coyote made People that were different from himself. He made a man and a woman.

That evening, as the animals finished their models, they set them down on the riverbank to dry. Then, feeling very tired after all their hard work, they all went home to bed. Only the Coyote stayed awake.

When he was sure that every animal had left, the Coyote crept down to the riverbank. He filled a large empty shell with water and poured it over all the models except his own. He filled the shell again and poured more water on the models. Then more and more, again and again, until all the shapes disappeared and all that was left were some lumps of muddy clay on the riverbank. Then the Coyote picked up his small clay man and woman. He breathed life into their noses and set them down again, gently on the grass.

In the morning, the animals came to the riverbank to see which model Coyote would choose, and to watch him make the new People. But there was no sign of Coyote. Instead, looking out across the river and watching the sun rise, were two People; ready to begin their new lives on earth.

The story ends there, so we don't know what the animals thought about the new People who suddenly appeared overnight, and we don't know if they found out about the Coyote cheating and destroying their models.

The new People were ready to begin an interesting and exciting new life, just as you are ready to begin, what I hope is going to be, an interesting and exciting new school year. I wonder what happened to the People during their first year on earth? I wonder what new things they learned and what they achieved? And I wonder what new things you'll learn this year, and what you'll achieve? It'll be interesting to look back at the end of the school year, and see. I hope you will all do your best this year, and be happy and successful.

Thank you God, for the start of a new school year. Help us to do our best in everything we do, and help us to work together, play together and get along together, so that we and our school are happy and successful. Amen

The Wotsis

I wonder how far back you can remember? I wonder what your earliest memory is? Most people can remember being very small children, but not many people can remember being a baby. Yet we were all babies once, when we first began our lives.

Can you think of some of the things you needed when you were a baby? You needed cots and feeding bottles, baby walkers and playpens. But of course you don't need any of those things now. As we grow up we need different things; now you need reading books and school bags, children's toys and school uniform. But one day you won't need those things either, you'll have grown out of them just as you have grown out of your baby things.

Now that you're not a baby any more, you probably think that babies are very small, unimportant people, but listen to this story that the North American Indians tell!

Glooscap was a mighty warrior; the bravest and fiercest of them all. He had travelled everywhere and had battled with armies, wild animals, ghosts and goblins, monsters, spirits and witches. He had beaten them all.

'It's time I went home,' thought Glooscap one day. 'It's a long time since I've been back. It's time I went to see how everything is.' So Glooscap travelled home.

But when he got there, and walked in through the flap of the tent, he saw the strangest creature crawling about on the floor. It was small, light brown, had a very red face, and was making enough noise to make the sky fall in.

'Whatever is it?' called Glooscap to his wife.

She came hurrying in from outside, looking flustered and busy and tired and cross.

'It's a Wotsis,' she said. 'And don't you go upsetting it! If you upset the Wotsis, we'll never hear the last of it. As it is, I have to run about after it all day long. I've never had a minute's peace since it came.'

'Well, I wouldn't stand for it,' said Glooscap. 'You wouldn't find me being a servant to whatever-it-is.'

'You'd have no choice,' said Glooscap's wife. 'The Wotsis is the most powerful creature on earth. He is the past and he is the future. He is in charge of the world!'

'He's not in charge of me!' said Glooscap, and he stared at the Wotsis.

The Wotsis stopped its noise and stared back at Glooscap.

'I'm not scared of you!' shouted Glooscap. 'I've fought with men and beasts and bogies. I'm not scared of you!'

'Goo!' said the Wotsis.

'I am the strongest in the world,' yelled Glooscap.

'Goo, goo!' said the Wotsis.

'I am the most powerful,' thundered Glooscap.

'Goo!' And then 'Waaaah!' said the Wotsis, as it started its terrible screaming again.

Glooscap covered his ears and told the Wotsis to stop. He begged the Wotsis to be quiet. He pleaded with him to stop. But the Wotsis continued howling.

Glooscap tried to distract the Wotsis. He knelt down on the floor in front of him and pulled faces. The Wotsis cried louder. Glooscap stood up and did his ghost-scaring dance. The Wotsis screamed and shrieked. Glooscap sat down and sang his monster-scaring song. The Wotsis hollered and howled.

Glooscap sang all the songs and danced all the dances he knew, but still the Wotsis screeched and wailed and yowled and yelped and roared and bellowed and hooted. Glooscap tried to pick the Wotsis up, but it wriggled and jiggled until he had to put it down again. He gave it a stick to play with, but the Wotsis started to eat the stick and Glooscap had to take it away again.

'I told you!' said Glooscap's wife. 'There's never a minute's peace here now. And it doesn't matter how strong you are, you're no match for the Wotsis.'

'You're right,' said Glooscap. 'I've travelled the world and beaten every kind of creature I've fought, but I can't beat this one,' and he collapsed on the floor in a heap, exhausted with trying to quieten the Wotsis.

The Wotsis watched. It stopped its noise, and it smiled, first a small smile, and then a smile as big as the world.

'There, there!' said the Wotsis' mother, as she picked him up and cuddled him.

Glooscap was beaten by a …? Yes, the Wotsis was a baby. If you have a baby in your family you'll probably know just how Glooscap felt!

But babies grow up, just as you did. Their needs change, just as yours did.

In the future, your needs will change again. When you're grown up you won't need your school books, or even your teachers. You won't even need your parents in the same way you need them now. But, people always need people, and even when you're grown up, you'll always need your friends.

Dear God, help us always to care for people who are younger than us. Help us to remember how we felt when we were small, and never to hurt or bully those weaker than us. Help us to know that we always need friends in our lives. Amen

Theme 2: Ourselves

How much is he worth?

(Price cards and objects need to be prepared in advance. The objects don't necessarily have to be the same as these; whatever is easily accessible and meaningful to the children will suffice, but they need to have a wide range of value, and a child needs to be included in the line-up. It may be necessary to explain the meaning of worthless and priceless.)

You will see that I have a variety of things out here at the front, including a Year 6 child! Let's have a look at what's here.

There's a shell, a packet of crisps, a packet of biscuits, a plastic toy, a teddy bear, a bottle of champagne, a bike, a diamond ring, and a person. I also have some cards with prices written on. Here they are:

worthless	30p	80p	£2	£5	£15	£200	£1000	priceless

I now need two volunteers who would like to come and put the price labels on the objects. *(Ask the children to do this and then discuss with everyone why they decided on each individual price.)*

I wonder if the rest of you agree with what these two children have done. I wonder if any of you would have priced things differently. *(Discuss)*

I would definitely have put the 'priceless' label on our year 6 child(!). There is no way that you can put a price on a person. How could you begin to decide how much someone is worth?

A few weeks ago, there was a news item on the radio. It went like this.

One day, a mother and father and their eleven year old son were on their way home after a day out in the car, when they noticed that they were very low on petrol. They pulled into the nearest garage but realised that not one of them had any money. They'd spent all their cash whilst they were out, and neither of the two adults had their cheque books or credit cards with them.

The boy's father explained their problem to the woman at the garage pay desk, and asked if she could let them have a couple of pounds worth of petrol just to get them to a friend's house.

'If you could do that, I can borrow some money from my friend, then come back and pay you.'

'No, I'm sorry,' said the woman. 'I can't let you have any petrol if you can't pay for it now.'

'But the tank is nearly empty,' said the boy's dad. 'If I don't put some petrol in we're not going to be able to go anywhere.'

'Sorry!' said the woman. 'There's nothing I can do to help.'

Then the boy's mother had an idea.

'Look,' she said to the cashier. 'I have a gold watch. I'll leave this with you until we've been to our friend's house to borrow some money. Then you'll know we're coming back to pay you. And even if we didn't come back, you'd have more than the value of two pounds of petrol, because the watch is worth much more than that.'

'No. I'm sorry,' said the cashier again.

'Well look. Take my diamond engagement ring as well as the watch,' said the boy's mother. 'Surely you could take those two pieces of jewelry as security against a bit of petrol?'

'Sorry,' said the woman. 'You might not come back and how do I know that the jewelry is real. It might be fake for all I know.'

And then the boy had an idea.

'I'll be the security,' he said. 'You let my mum and dad have two pounds worth of petrol. Then they can drive to their friend's house to borrow the money, and I'll stay here with you until they come back.'

'OK,' said the garage cashier, and she knew that the mother and father would come back if their son stayed behind at the garage.

I wonder what you think about that story. Do you think the garage cashier did the right thing in saying no when the family wanted petrol? Do you think the parents did the right thing in letting their son wait at the garage for them whilst they went to borrow some money? The story raises lots of questions, but one thing it's very sure about is that you can't put a price on a person. Everyone is unique and everyone is beyond price because everyone is special.

Help us to understand, Lord, that each of us is special. Help us to know that everyone in the world is unique and everyone is valuable. Help us to remember that everyone is good at something. Help us to be tolerant when people seem different from us. Amen

Vital difference

Have you noticed how everyone is different and yet everyone is the same? Each of us is an individual and each of us is unique. There's not another you anywhere in the world, and yet we're all human beings and we're all so much alike.

Sometimes people are grouped together and everyone thinks of them as one unit. For example, if I'm talking to someone about all of you I talk about 'our school'. I don't mention you all individually by name, even though I know that each one of you is an individual.

In today's story, a merchant needed some help in understanding about individuality.

There was once a merchant who became very rich by trading in silks and spices. He travelled all over the world buying and selling beautiful cloth and strange foods. He went to Africa and India, to Russia and to China, to Persia and Peru. And everywhere he went he mixed with the rich and famous. He spoke to kings and queens and princes; he ate with emperors and czars; he stayed with sultans and with chieftains.

But everywhere he went, in every country he visited, the merchant noticed that some people were poor, others were hungry, some were homeless, some were ill or lonely or sad or old. And the merchant worried about them.

As the merchant became more and more wealthy, the poverty and suffering in the world worried him more and more. And at last he decided he would do something to help. But what? There were so many needy people in the world. He was a rich man, but even he didn't have enough wealth to solve all the world's problems. What could he do?

He went to consult a wise man that he'd met whilst travelling in Japan. As far as he knew, this was the oldest man in the world.

'If he's lived longer than everyone else, he must be wiser than everyone else,' reasoned the merchant.

'I need your help,' he said to the wise man. 'I want to help the poor people of the world, but there are so many of them I don't know where to start. I feel that it will be a waste of time because I will only be able to help a few. What shall I do?'

The wise old man looked at the merchant and said, 'Let me tell you a story. Sit down and listen.'

The merchant sat down and the old man began.

'There was once an old man who went for a walk on the beach early one morning just as the sun was rising. He walked at the very edge of the sea, and at first he thought he was all alone on the beach, but then he noticed a young boy up ahead of him.

'The boy was picking up starfish that were stranded on the sand, and he was throwing them back into the water. The old man caught up with the boy and said, "What are you doing?"

"I'm helping the starfish," said the boy. "The tide is going out and the starfish will die if they are left stranded on the beach in the heat of the sun."

"But the beach goes on for miles!" exclaimed the old man. "And there are millions of starfish. You cannot hope to help them all. How can your efforts make any difference?"

'The boy looked at the one small starfish in his hand, and he said, "It makes a difference to this one." Then he threw it to safety in the sea.'

After he had finished his story, the old man stayed silent for several minutes. Then he said, 'The old man learned something from the child that day. He learned that when you cannot help everyone, it is better to help someone. To the someone the help will be welcome.'

And the merchant understood the story, and knew that the world is made up of individual people and that each one is unique.

After his visit to the old man, the merchant spent some of his money on helping others. He couldn't help everyone, but his money made a difference to the people that he could help.

It's important to remember that every group of people is made up of individuals. And it's important to remember that every individual is unique and special and valuable. And remember, if you can't help *everyone*, then try to help *someone*.

Thank you God, for making each one of us different and unique. Help us to understand that the differences are not better... or worse... they're just different. Help us to know that everyone is of value, and everyone has an important part to play in the journey of life. Amen

What's in a name?

Just imagine how you would feel if your friends and family started to call you by a completely different name from the one you have. You might begin to feel you were someone else instead of you! Our names are an important part of who we are. Did you know that hundreds of years ago people didn't like telling other people their name? They felt they were giving part of themselves away if they said who they were.

I wonder why you're called what you are? Perhaps you're named after someone in your family, or even after someone famous. Or maybe your parents just liked the sound of your name – that's a good reason for choosing one.

Writers sometimes have difficulty in finding just the right name for their characters, and so they sometimes make up a name. Do you know the book 'Charlie and the Chocolate Factory' by Roald Dahl? If you do you'll have met the Oompa Loompas. Roald Dahl named them after the city of Kuala Lumpur. He liked the sound of it.

And do you know the story of Peter Pan? When J. M. Barrie wrote it in 1904, he put three children in the story, apart from Peter. He called the boys Michael and John, but he couldn't find the right name for their sister. Here's how he found it in the end.

J. M. Barrie's friend had a small daughter called Margaret. For some reason, no-one ever quite knew why, Margaret never called her father's friend Mr Barrie, or James (the J. M. stands for James Matthew). She didn't call him Uncle Barrie or Mr James, or even J. M. She always called him Friend.

'He's my father's friend, so he's called Friend,' she used to say.

One day J. M. Barrie was at his friend's house, talking, when Margaret burst in.

'Hello Friend,' she said. 'Will you tell me a story?'

'I'll tell you the story of my new play,' said J. M. Barrie. 'Are you ready?' And Margaret settled down to listen.

'It's all about a family with three children,' began J. M. Barrie.

'There are two brothers called Michael and John, and their older sister.

'One night, a boy named Peter Pan, flies in through their bedroom window, with a strange invisible fairy called Tinker Bell. Peter Pan tells the children that he has run away from home because he has overheard his parents talking about what he will be like when he grows up. "I don't want to grow up," says Peter Pan. "I never want to grow up." You see, Peter wants always to stay as a boy so that he can have fun. He thinks that grown-ups don't have fun!

'Peter, who is magic of course, teaches the children to fly and they fly away together, out of the bedroom window, to a wonderful place called Never-Never-Land. And here they meet the Crocodile, Tiger Lily, and Captain Hook and the pirates! Captain Hook is the wicked pirate chief and he hates boys. He tries to poison Peter Pan, but Tinker Bell (she's the invisible fairy, remember?), saves Peter by drinking the poison herself.

'Poor Tinker Bell is dying. She can only be saved if children believe in fairies.'

'I believe in fairies!' interrupted Margaret.

'That's good,' said J. M. Barrie. 'Then Tinker Bell will be saved. She won't die.'

'What happens next?' Margaret asked.

'Well, after all their adventures, the children and Peter Pan fly home, and the children's mother, Mrs Darling, offers to adopt Peter so that he can stay and be one of the family. But Peter says no. "I always want to be a little boy and have fun," he says, and he flies away again.'

'Does he ever come back?' asked Margaret.

'I haven't written that part of the story yet,' answered J.M.Barrie.

'But I think he will. I think he'll come back when the children are grown up, and perhaps when the girl has some children of her own.'

'What's the girl called,' asked Margaret.

'Well, that's the problem,' said J.M.Barrie. 'At the moment she hasn't got a name. I haven't found the right one for her.'

'Oh Friendy-Wendy,' said Margaret. 'That's not fair!'

'That's it!' said J.M.Barrie. 'You've just solved my problem. That's the name I've been looking for.'

'What?' said Margaret, looking puzzled.

'Wendy!' said J.M.Barrie.

'But Wendy's not a girl's name,' she said.

'It is now!' he said, and J.M.Barrie hurried home to write the new name in his play.

Margaret was right, Wendy wasn't a girl's name at the time she called J.M.Barrie 'Friendy-Wendy,' but as soon as the play of Peter Pan was staged, lots of parents chose it as a girl's name and it became very popular.

I wonder what the most popular names will be when you're old enough to have children. And which is the most popular name in our school just now? You could do a survey! One hundred years ago the most popular names were William, John, Florence and Mary. Last year the most popular were Jack and Daniel, Sophie and Jessica.

Have you ever wondered how many people have the same name as you? There may even be people somewhere with the same first name and surname as you. But even though people might have the same name, they're each individual and different. It's one of the most special things about people; everyone is so much like everyone else in lots of ways, yet everyone has their own personality and is unique.

Thank you God, for our names. Thank you for making each one of us different and special. Help us to remember that everyone is important, everyone is valuable, and everyone is good at something. Help us not to use name-calling to hurt or upset people. Amen

Theme 3: Working together

The cross-Channel ferry

It's amazing what people can do when they work together. You've probably already found this out. Perhaps you've been in a sports team, or joined in a class assembly; maybe you've been involved in a project with your friends, or perhaps you've helped when your school has been having a fund-raising activity, and you've discovered how successful it is when everyone helps. Things that are impossible for people to do on their own, can become perfectly possible when everyone works together.

In today's story, thousands of people worked together to help one man. Some people did a great deal to help, and others only did a little, but the important thing was that *everyone* helped in some way. If they hadn't done, the story would probably have had a very different ending.

Portsmouth was busy. It was always a busy city, with lots of people, lots of traffic, and always lots of ships, but on this particular day it was busier than ever.

It was a Saturday in summer. Hundreds of people were on their way to the huge ferries which would carry them and their cars across the English Channel to France. Hundreds more people were travelling back from their holidays in France and other countries in Europe.

And still hundreds more people were visiting Portsmouth because today was Navy Day; a special celebration day in the town. All kinds of activities and displays had been arranged. You could go and look round the ships – the war ships, the aircraft carriers and the big old-fashioned sailing ships. You could go for rides on some of the smaller boats and you could watch the air-sea rescue displays, the helicopter displays, and even a fly-past by the Red Arrows team. The sun was shining and everyone was having a wonderful time.

At just after one o'clock, one of the huge car ferries, called the Pride of Cherbourg, began taking on board its passengers and their cars. The ferry held 600 cars and almost 1400 passengers, and today the ship was full. The loading was successfully completed, the ship was secured for sea and it slowly moved away from the quayside. Most of the passengers were on the outside decks watching everything there was to see. There would be plenty of time later to go inside and sit down; the crossing to France was going to take about 5 hours.

But one man was lying down in his cabin. He didn't feel very well. He thought that he'd probably feel a bit better after a sleep, so he settled down in his bunk.

The Pride of Cherbourg continued her journey away from the harbour and down the long river estuary into the open sea.

When the ship had been travelling for about an hour and a half, the man who was feeling ill began to feel really poorly. He rang for one of the stewards, who sent for the ship's nurse. She took one look at him and knew he was very ill indeed.

The nurse went to find the captain and told him how ill the man was.

'He needs a doctor. He's too ill for me to be able to help him,' she said.

The captain sent out a message to all the passengers over the loudspeaker system. 'Is there a doctor on board?' he said. 'We have someone who is very ill and we need a doctor.' Luckily, one of the passengers was a doctor. He heard the message and hurried to see what he could do to help.

'We need to get this man to hospital,' the doctor said, when he'd examined the man. 'And we need to get him there as quickly as possible. How long will it take us to get to France?'

'We're one and a half hours into the journey,' said the captain. 'We have three and a half hours still to go.'

'That's too long,' said the doctor. 'He needs to go to hospital immediately.'

'I could radio for a helicopter to come and airlift him from the ship and take him back to Portsmouth,' said the captain. 'But it's going to take at least two hours to do that.'

'And the journey would be very stressful for him,' said the doctor.

'Then there's only one thing for me to do,' said the captain. 'I must turn the ship round and go back to Portsmouth full-steam-ahead.'

The captain knew that this was an important decision to make. Ferries hardly ever turned back once they had set off. They had timetables to keep to. The other passengers would be expecting to get to France on time. He was going to delay 1400 people for the sake of one man. But the captain realised how ill that one man was, and he hoped the other passengers would understand why he had taken the decision to turn back.

He put out another message over the loudspeaker system.

'Ladies and Gentlemen, this is your captain speaking. I have to inform you that we have a very ill passenger on board, and I have just taken the decision to turn the ship round and go back to Portsmouth as quickly as possible. This will mean that our arrival in France will be very much delayed, but I hope you will understand.'

The captain and the crew expected that many passengers would complain. But not one single person grumbled out of the 1400 on board. No-one complained.

When the ship reached the entrance to Portsmouth harbour, the captain had to radio to the harbourmaster to get permission to go in.

'There's no ship allowed in the harbour just now,' said the harbourmaster. 'There's a naval display just about to begin. All sea traffic has been stopped.'

'But I have an ill man on board,' said the captain. 'I need to have entry clearance straight away.'

'If it's an emergency, that's different,' said the harbourmaster, and he radioed the people in charge of the naval display to make arrangements to postpone it for one hour, to give the Pride of Cherbourg time to enter the harbour and tie up at the quayside. He then contacted Portsmouth hospital and arranged for an ambulance to be on the quayside as soon as the ship arrived.

From then on everything happened very quickly. The Pride of Cherbourg was given priority clearance, and everything else in the harbour stopped to let her through. The ship was quickly secured to the quay and the waiting ambulance with its team of doctors rushed the ill man to hospital.

By now the passengers on the Pride of Cherbourg were over three hours late and they were back in England; the naval display had been postponed; and all other sea traffic wanting to come in or out of the harbour was delayed. But no-one complained! Thousands of people were inconvenienced, but no-one grumbled. Everyone co-operated, and no-one criticised. Everyone worked together and no-one objected.

Eventually, everything got back to normal. The naval display went ahead, the Pride of Cherbourg set off again, five hours late, and the harbour was open to the ships that needed to use it.

And the man who was ill? He had an emergency operation in hospital and was soon well again.

The story had a happy ending because everyone worked together. The steward and nurse, the captain and the passenger who was a doctor, the harbourmaster and the people in charge of the naval display, all worked together as a team. The 1400 passengers helped by not complaining and by understanding why the ship needed to turn back. And the hundreds of people waiting to watch the display in Portsmouth also helped by being patient about the delay and by not grumbling. I wonder if the man who was ill ever knew just how many people had worked together that day to help him. I don't suppose he did.

Dear God, help us to understand the importance of working together. Help us to remember that everyone has a part to play, and that everyone's contribution is valuable. Help us to know that we are part of a team in our family, our school, our community and our world. Amen

The giant chopsticks

Working together enables us to do many things we just couldn't do alone. Imagine trying to play tennis on your own – I suppose you could use a wall to bounce the ball against, but it isn't quite the same. Imagine a game of chess or snakes and ladders – you can't play these games properly on your own, you need two people to work together.

There's even a saying which goes "Two heads are better than one". It means that if two people are working on something, there'll be more ideas than if there's only one person. Co-operating with other people, working together with them, is usually successful.

The Chinese people have a story about this.

There was once a Chinese Emperor who wanted to rule his people wisely and well, so he went to see the Old Man of the Mountains to ask for his advice.

'I want to understand my people,' he said to the old man. 'So I want you to tell me what is the worst about people and what is the best.'

'I can do better than that,' said the old man, who was also a magician. 'I can show you,' and he took down from his wall a picture in a bamboo frame. He handed the picture to the Emperor.

'Look at that,' he said. 'And you will see the worst in people.'

The Emperor looked at the picture and saw a huge table covered with every kind of food he had ever seen or tasted. It looked delicious. There was meat and soup and fish. There were sandwiches and sausages, pies and pasta, puddings and pastries and flans. There was fruit and bread, biscuits and chocolate, ice cream and jellies and jams. There was butterscotch pudding and toffee meringue; there was custard and yogourt and cream. There was . . . well there was every kind of food that anyone could ever think of.

But the Emperor didn't understand.

'Why are you showing me a picture of all this food?' he asked the Old Man of the Mountains. 'How is this going to help me understand my people?'

'Look again,' said the old man.

The Emperor looked again at the picture, and this time, to his surprise, he could see people moving greedily towards the table. But the people looked thin and gaunt and ill.

'How can they look so hungry when there is so much food?' said the Emperor.

'Look again,' said the old man.

The Emperor looked again and saw that each person had a pair of huge chopsticks. The chopsticks were over a metre long, and the people were trying to pick up food from the table and eat with them, but it was almost impossible. As they tried to pick up the food they dropped it, or they bumped into the person next to them and made them drop theirs. This caused arguments and even fights to start. The Emperor had never seen such a sorry looking group of people in all his life.

'They have to use the chopsticks,' explained the old man. 'And they have to hold the chopsticks at the end. They're not allowed to eat the food any other way. But you can see they are greedy people, each out for what he can get, little knowing that each can get very little because they are selfish and uncooperative people.'

The Emperor looked again and saw how the people were pushing each other to get to the table. He saw how they struggled to pick up the food with the giant chopsticks, and how impossible it was for them to eat the food.

'I don't want to look at them any more,' said the Emperor. 'It's too depressing. I can see that they are the worst of people. Show me the best of people, so that I can compare the two.'

The Old Man of the Mountains reached to the wall again and took down a second picture in a bamboo frame. He handed the picture to the Emperor.

'Look at that,' he said. 'And you will see the best in people.'

The Emperor looked at the picture and saw a huge table covered with every kind of food you could think of. It looked delicious. There was meat and soup and fish. There were sandwiches and sausages, pies and pasta, puddings and pastries and flans. There was fruit and bread, biscuits and chocolate, ice cream and jellies and jams. There was butterscotch pudding and toffee meringue; there was custard and yogourt and cream. There was... well, there was every kind of food that anyone could ever think of.

'But this is the same as the picture you have just shown me,' he said. 'I don't understand.'

'Look again,' said the old man of the mountains.

The Emperor looked again, and saw people moving towards the table, but this time the people looked happy and contented, cheerful and well-fed.

'Ah,' said the Emperor. 'These people don't have to use those long chopsticks, do they?'

'Oh yes they do,' said the old man. 'The rules are just the same as for the others. They are only allowed to eat the food with the chopsticks, and they have to hold them at the end. But look again.'

The Emperor looked again. He saw each person standing with another. He saw them look at the food together and choose what they wanted to eat. Then he saw the first person pick up the food with the chopsticks, and feed the second person. After a short time they changed over, and the second person fed the first with the giant chopsticks. By helping each other and working together, the long and awkward chopsticks became easier to manage. By helping each other, no-one went hungry.

'So you see,' said the Old Man of the Mountains, 'the best of people are thoughtful and kind and helpful, and they are prepared to work together. If you can encourage the people in your empire to work together, you will have the strongest empire in the land.'

'And the happiest,' added the Emperor.

I wonder if you've already discovered for yourself that being happy in what you do, usually goes with being helpful and co-operative. When we work together there's no knowing how successful we can be. Try it! And see what you and your friends can achieve!

Dear God, please help us to cooperate with our family and friends. Help us to have our own ideas, but to listen to other people's, too. Help us to learn to 'give and take,' and help us to be able to work alongside, and with, other people. Amen

The obstacle course

In today's assembly I'm not going to tell you a story, I'm going to show you something. I've set out a small obstacle course here at the front of the hall. Look! You have to:

- bounce this ball twice

- climb through the hoop
- throw and catch the beanbag twice
- skip 5 times with this rope
- put these two quoits on the skittle.

Sounds easy? Who'd like to try it? *(Choose a child.)*

There's just one thing I forgot to tell you – you have to do the obstacle course blindfold! *(Blindfold child and let him/her attempt the course.)*

It's not easy is it? Let's see if we can make it less difficult. I'd like another volunteer. *(Choose another child.)*

I'm going to ask A to try the obstacle course again, but this time B is allowed to help. B can talk to A and give him instructions. But he has to stand over here, he's not allowed to help in any other way. Let's see how it goes. *(Ask the two children to try the course again, one giving instructions, the other following the course.)*

Well, A is doing better than last time; it's surprising what a difference it makes when there's someone to help. But let's try to make the obstacle course even easier. I need another volunteer. *(Choose another child.)*

I'm going to ask A to try the obstacle course again, but this time B and C are both allowed to help. B can talk and give instructions like he did before, and C is allowed to touch the obstacles, and to touch A, though he can't actually do the tasks for him. Let's try again. *(Ask the three children to try the course again, one giving instructions, and one physically helping the child following the course.)*

Well, what a difference! How much easier it is when people help each other and show each other what to do.

Let's ask A how he felt when he was doing the course on his own, and how he felt when the others were helping him. *(Discuss with child.)*

When we help each other, when we co-operate with each other and work together, we can make difficult tasks much easier. When we have people helping us, we usually feel better and more encouraged to go on.

Lord, help us to be generous of spirit and prepared to give our time to help other people. Help us to work together co-operatively with the people in our families, in our school, and in our community. Amen

October

Theme 1: Sharing

Autumn leaves

All over the world, in different countries and different cultures, people believe that it is good to share. Sharing with others is a way of helping others, and helping others is something we should all try to do.

Today's story is a North American Indian myth; a myth is a story which helped people to understand the world about them, in the days before people knew about science. The story is about Autumn, but it's also about sharing.

Once upon a time when the earth was very new, the Earthmaker decided to make winter. Up until then there had only been summer, and sunshine and warmth.

The Earthmaker decided that a contrast was needed, a season to be the exact opposite of summer, so he made the winter. First he made the wind blow cold, then he added a bit of sleet. But he wasn't very impressed with that so he invented snow crystals and snow flakes. He whirled them through the sky in a blizzard and piled them high on the earth. Then he made ice. He covered rivers and pools with sheets of ice, and he even froze the sea. And he made frost. He made sparkling, glittering patterns of frost on the ice, and on the trees. He festooned the cobwebs with frost and dusted the leaves with it.

When the Earthmaker had finished making winter he stood back and looked at it. 'It's very beautiful,' he said.

'It might be very beautiful,' said the two legged creatures amongst themselves. 'But it's uncomfortably cold.'

'It's certainly very beautiful,' said the four legged creatures amongst themselves. 'But it's making us shiver.'

'We've never seen anything so beautiful,' said the six legged creatures. 'But it's making us ill.'

And all the other creatures – those with eight legs, those with many legs, and those with no legs, were all so cold they couldn't say anything at all.

The Earthmaker had decided that the winter was to last for many months. After all, there was no point in inventing it if it was to be over in a flash. But the creatures were unhappy. 'We can't go on like this,' they said. 'It's so cold that some of us are dying. Someone must go and see the Earthmaker and ask him to change things back as they were.'

So a woman was chosen to go and speak to the Earthmaker.

'The winter is very cold,' she said. 'We are very uncomfortable in it. Could you please give us the summer back again?'

'No, I can't do that,' said the Earthmaker. 'But I will teach you how to

make fire, and then you will be warm whilst the winter is here.'
And the woman went back to the others with the knowledge of how to make fire.

'Well that's all very well for you humans,' said a rabbit. 'But what about us? We can't make fire. I'm going to see the Earthmaker myself.' And the rabbit went off to speak to the Earthmaker.

'The winter is very cold,' said the rabbit. 'And we are very uncomfortable in it. Could you please give us the summer back again?'

'No, I can't do that,' said the Earthmaker. 'But I will give you thick fur, and I will teach those of you who want to sleep through the winter, how to hibernate, then you will be warm.'

And the rabbit went back to the others with the Earthmaker's promise.

'Well that's all very well for you animals,' said a goose. 'But what about us? We can't have thick fur and sleep through the winter. I'm going to see the Earthmaker myself,' and the goose went off to speak to the Earthmaker.

'The winter is very cold,' he said. 'And we are very uncomfortable in it. Could you please give us the summer back again?'

'No, I can't do that,' said the Earthmaker. 'But I will give you the power to fly south to warmer countries, and then you can escape the cold if you want to.'

The goose went back to the others with the news of what the Earthmaker was going to do to help.

'Well that's all very well for all you big guys,' said a tiny black beetle. 'But what about us? We can't fly all the way to the warm countries. I'm going to see the Earthmaker myself.' And the beetle went off to see the Earthmaker.

'The winter is very cold…' he began.

'Oh no, not again,' said the Earthmaker. 'It's no use asking me for ways to keep you warm. I've run out of ideas. You'll just have to manage as you are.'

The tiny black beetle crept back to tell the others what had been said.

'But that's just not fair,' said the birch and the beech and the maple trees, and they put their branches together and whispered amongst themselves.

'We've decided to help you,' they said. 'We'll share our leaves with you. When the winter comes we will take them off and spread them on the ground like a blanket, so that all the tiny scuttling creatures can shelter under them and keep warm and dry.'

The Earthmaker heard what they were saying, and was impressed by their generosity.

'How kind you are,' he said to the trees. 'I will reward you for your kindness. Before you take off all your leaves, I will change their colours to reds and golds so that everyone will know how good you are.'

And ever since then, the trees have changed colour in the Autumn, as a thank you from the Earthmaker for sharing their leaves with the smallest creatures.

Giving something of yours to someone else is what sharing is all about. You can share toys and sweets and food, but you can also share things that you can't see, like your time, or your skills. But whatever you share, it shows you are thinking about someone else, and caring about them.

Thank you God, for Autumn. Thank you for the colours of Autumn, the sights and sounds and smells of Autumn. Help us to find something this Autumn that we can share with someone else. Amen

Soup from a stone

Sometimes it's quite hard to share what we have with others. Sometimes we want to keep what's ours for ourselves. In today's story, some people didn't want to share what they had with visitors to their village. But a young man managed to persuade them to help him. Some of you might even think he tricked them?

There was once a young man who was travelling round the world. One evening he arrived at a village and thought he would ask someone to give him a meal. But just as he was about to enter the village, another traveller was leaving.

'You'll get nothing here,' said the other traveller. 'For one thing they've got nothing, and for another they wouldn't give it away even if they had! I've never known such a mean and miserable and selfish place.'

'I only want something to eat,' said the young man.

'Well, you won't get it here!' said the other traveller, as he trudged down the road.

'We'll see,' said the young man. And he made his way to the centre of the village where he looked around for a bit of spare land. Then he gathered a few sticks of wood and built a fire, searched on the ground for a nice fat round smooth pebble, and went to knock on the nearest door.

'What do you want?' said a woman who answered the door. 'I hope you're not asking for anything, because we've nothing to give you!'

'No, I don't want anything from you; in fact I want to *give* you something,' said the young man. 'I'm just about to make some stone soup which I'm going to share with everyone in the village when it's cooked, but I'd like to borrow a big cooking pot, please.'

'Well, I suppose I can lend you one,' said the woman, and she went into her kitchen and came back with an enormous metal cooking pot.

'That's perfect,' said the young man. 'I'll go and get the soup started, then do come and join me, won't you, and tell all your neighbours to come as well. There'll be plenty of soup for everyone.'

The young man strode off towards his fire. He filled the cooking pot with water from the well and put it on the fire to boil. When it began to bubble he dropped the nice fat round smooth pebble into the pot and began to stir it.

By now he had a small group of villagers gathered round him, watching to see what he was going to do. They were talking amongst themselves.

'He says he's going to make stone soup,' said one.

'I've never heard of stone soup, have you?' said another.

'He's borrowed my cooking pot; said he wanted a big one,' said the woman who'd lent him the pot.

'I don't think stone soup will taste very nice, do you?' said someone else.

The young man suddenly looked up from stirring the pot.

'It'll taste good,' he said. 'But it would taste even better with an onion in it. Unfortunately, I'm right out of onions just now.'

'I've got an onion,' said one of the bystanders, and she went to her house to get it.

The young man chopped the onion and dropped it into the soup. Then he took a large ladle out of his knapsack and tasted the soup. Everyone watched.

'Mm, not bad,' said the young man. 'But it would taste even better with a carrot or two. Unfortunately, I'm right out of carrots just now.'

'I've got some carrots,' said a man in the crowd, and he hurried to his garden to pull them up.

The young man chopped the carrots and dropped them into the soup. Then he held his nose over the cooking pot and sniffed.

'Mm, coming along,' he said. 'But it would do even better with a couple of leeks in it. Unfortunately I'm right out of leeks just now.'

'I've got some leeks,' said the woman who'd lent him the cooking pot, and she hurried to her pantry to get them.

The young man sliced the leeks and dropped them into the soup. Then he stirred it and said, 'Mm, cooking nicely, but it would cook even better with a bit of barley and a few peas. Unfortunately I'm right out of barley and peas just now.'

'There's some in my mum's kitchen,' said a small girl, and she ran home to get them.

The young man dropped the pearl barley and the fresh green peas into soup and dipped the ladle into it again. He offered the ladle to a woman standing near and asked her what she thought of the soup so far.

'Quite good,' she said. 'But not tasty enough for me. I like a bit of chicken in my soup.'

'I know what you mean,' said the young man. 'It would be much improved with a bit of chicken. Unfortunately I'm right out of chicken just now.'

'I've got a chicken in my larder,' said the woman, and she hurried away to get it.

The young man chopped up the chicken and dropped it in, then let the soup simmer. After a while he tasted it again. 'It could do with a handful of herbs, he said. 'Unfortunately...'

'I know, I know,' said one of the men. 'You're right out of herbs just now! Never mind, I've got some,' and he went to his house to get them.

By now the soup smelled wonderful. The young man offered a taste to one of the men. 'What do you think?' he said.

'It's nearly there,' said the man. 'Nearly there! But it could just do with a little bit of pepper and a pinch or two of salt. Unfortunately I haven't any...'

'But I have,' said his neighbour, and she went to her house to get the pepper and salt.

The young man shook a little bit of pepper and a pinch or two of salt into the soup, then stirred it again, then gazed deep into the pot.

'Isn't it a pity...' he said. 'Isn't it a pity... that we haven't any dumplings. Wouldn't a few dumplings just make this soup perfect? I love dumplings, don't you?' and he turned and looked straight at the woman who'd lent him the cooking pot.

'Oh, all right. I'll go and make a few dumplings,' she said. She was back in a few minutes and the young man dropped the dumplings into the soup. And in twelve and a half minutes the soup was ready. They all had some and it was delicious. In fact that soup was the talk of the village for years to come.

'Do you remember?' the villagers used to say. 'When that young man came to our village and made soup from a stone? Just fancy! Soup from a stone! Who would have believed it!'

I don't suppose the villagers would have given the young man food if he'd simply asked for it, but by offering to share something with them, they all helped with contributions for the soup.

Do you think the young man tricked the villagers? Did he really make soup from a stone? Did they know he was making them contribute to the soup?

I think the young man had learned on his travels round the world that people behave towards you in the same way that you behave towards them. If you are kind and friendly to others, they'll usually be kind and friendly to you. If you offer to share what you have with others, they'll usually share what they have with you.

Dear God, help us to understand that there are people in the world with far less than we have. Help us to share what we have with others. Help us not to want everything for ourselves. Help us not to be greedy and selfish. Amen

Shoeboxes

Sharing things with our friends and family is fairly easy because we see them almost every day. But sharing things with people we don't know, or people who live in other parts of the world is much more difficult, yet we know it's the right thing to do. So how can we do it?

A few years ago, a man called Dave Cooke and his friends came up with a brilliant idea of children helping children. Here's how it happened.

One day, just before Christmas 1990, Dave Cooke was at home in North Wales, when he happened to see a TV programme about orphaned children in Romania. The children were living in huge freezing-cold buildings, with outside toilets, no medical supplies, and no toys or games. Many of them were dying of starvation and illness. There were a few nurses looking after the children, but there were so many children and so few carers that there was no time for any cuddles or hugs, and many of the children spent every day tied to their beds, to stop them running about or getting in the way.

Dave Cooke was so moved by what he saw that he decided to do something to help, and he asked some of his friends to help him raise some money for supplies and medicines. They set a target of £5000 and decided to try and send two trucks of supplies in time for Christmas.

Dave Cooke went on local television and appealed for help. He thought that a few people would respond, but he wasn't ready for the deluge of help that started to arrive almost straight away. Other people had seen the original TV programme too, and wanted to help. They sent food and blankets, medicines, toys and games, medical equipment and even x-ray machines. More and more people sent in supplies and money, and even the local schools became involved in helping.

And then someone, (no-one quite remembers who), said, 'Why don't we ask all the children to fill a shoe box with things another child would like, and seal it with a Christmas message. That way, lots of children will receive a Christmas present specially for them on Christmas Day.'

And so 'Operation Christmas Child' was born. Thousands of shoe boxes began to pour in. A van went round doing nothing else but visiting schools collecting even more shoeboxes.

But by now Operation Christmas Child had problems! Dave Cooke had wanted to fill two trucks with supplies, but they already had enough for ten! He'd set the original target at £5000, but now he changed it to £50,000! And still the gifts poured in.

People offered practical help too. Someone offered Operation Christmas Child an empty factory to use as a warehouse. Some more people gave their time to work as secretaries, completing all the mountains of paperwork that were necessary for the trucks' journey to Romania.

At last, on December 12th, Operation Christmas Child was ready to go. The ten trucks were loaded. The drivers were ready. There was just one more last job to do. The trucks needed decorating! Those huge freight lorries were wrapped in tinsel and lights so that they looked like enormous versions of the Christmas gifts they were carrying.

Hundreds of school children – the shoe box army, who had made Operation Christmas Child such a success – lined the road and cheered as the convoy set off. And still everyone helped. The motorway police accompanied the convoy to Dover. The trucks were allowed through the Dartford Tunnel without having to pay the toll. P & O Ferries carried the trucks over the Channel to France for free, and an entire army of commercial truck drivers waved and cheered and hooted and tooted at the convoy to help it along its way on the roads of

France, Belgium, Germany, Austria, Hungary and finally, Romania... and the first problems!

The border guards wouldn't let the trucks into Romania. First they said the papers were not in order, even though Dave Cooke insisted that they were. Then they said that *they* would deliver the presents to the orphanage; but the truck drivers knew the parcels would never get to the children if they handed them over.

'We have to deliver the parcels personally,' said one of the drivers. Then the guards said the trucks couldn't go over the border because of all the tinsel and decorations on them! 'You can have the decorations to keep, if you want,' said Dave Cooke, and he began unwrapping the tinsel and lights. This seemed to work, and when the border guards had been given all the decorations from the vehicles, they let them through the border control.

By now it was dark and snow was beginning to fall. The convoy edged carefully along the bumpy, unlit, narrow roads. There was no other traffic about; just an occasional horse and cart on the road, but up ahead was another problem. The first truck had stopped at a bridge over the road. It was much too low for the trucks to get under.

'We can't go this way,' said the driver. 'We'll have to go back.'

'But we can't turn the trucks round on these narrow roads,' said another driver. Just then a patrolman on a motor bike came along the road. He was amazed to see ten huge trucks parked on the road. Trucks like these never came to this part of Romania!

The drivers explained the problem, and the man helped them to back up the trucks on the narrow road in the dark, and then he led them to the town of Oradea and the orphanage.

The convoy arrived at first light the next morning, and drove up to the front doors of the huge grey brick building. Suddenly, hundreds of children appeared behind the bars of the windows, anxiously looking out wondering what was happening.

Dave Cooke and the drivers went into the building and were unable to speak because of what they saw. These children were living in dark filthy rooms, with no heating and no glass in the windows. The rooms had no furniture, no toys, no pictures, no curtains. Some of the rooms hadn't even any beds and the children slept on dirty blankets on the floor. There was no hot water, and only one toilet for nearly two hundred children.

The drivers went back outside to the trucks, many of them in tears. They began to unload the Christmas shoeboxes and took them inside to the children. And then it was as if the children suddenly came to life, as if they'd been given some sort of Christmas sparkle along with the gifts. They suddenly began to talk and to laugh. They hugged the drivers and thanked them for their presents. One child said 'I've never had a present before.' It was the very first time that anyone had ever given him anything.

The drivers stayed and played with the children and promised them that they'd come back. Then they left to deliver equipment and supplies to the nearby hospital. All too soon it was time for Dave Cooke and the drivers to set off on the long journey back to Wales. This time there were no delays, and they arrived home in just a few days.

The trip had been happy and sad at the same time. It gave the drivers plenty to think about, but they all had just one question to ask. 'What next?' They knew that Operation Christmas Child must continue.

Operation Christmas Child is now an international registered charity. It gives long term help to eastern European countries, and sends out doctors, nurses and teachers, as well as medicines, supplies and equipment. It works to get rid of the huge orphanages and builds small family homes to replace them. And every year it sends shoeboxes of presents to children who otherwise wouldn't have anything for Christmas. It delivers hope to children who have nothing. Operation Christmas Child does all this because one man wanted to do something to help, and lots of other people joined in.

Since 1993, Operation Christmas Child has hand-delivered more than 18.5 million shoebox gifts to needy children in 120 countries. The shoeboxes have been given to children in refugee camps, hospitals, orphanages and schools. And every gift has been carefully packed, with love, for Christmas.

Perhaps *you'd* like to send a shoebox to Operation Christmas Child, so that a child somewhere could receive it on Christmas Day.

(Further information, together with details of what to put in the boxes and where to send them, can be obtained from occ@melksham.org.uk or www.melksham.org.uk.)

Help us, Lord, to know that there are people in our world who have far less than we have. Help us to share what we have with others whenever we can. Help us to learn to share the resources of the world fairly, so that everyone in every country has what they need. And help us to know the difference between what we need, and what we want. Amen

Theme 2: Harvest

Harvest anagram

Harvest is the time of year when we think about saying thank you to God for all our food. In the olden days in Britain, saying thank you for the harvest meant saying thank you for the fruit and vegetables, and especially the corn, that people grew on their own land in order to stay alive.

Nowadays, we don't have to grow our own food. The shops are full of delicious foods from all over the world that we can go out and buy whenever we want. But it's still important to say thank you to God for all the food that our earth provides.

I'm going to need some help in our assembly today. I have some cards here with letters on them, and I need seven volunteers to hold them.

(Choose seven children to hold the large pre-prepared cards.)

[H] [A] [R] [V] [E] [S] [T]

What word do we have when the cards are arranged like this? Yes, it says harvest. Now, I need some more helpers who would like to come out and rearrange all, or some, of the letters to spell some new words. Who'd like to help?

(Choose another couple of children to rearrange the letters. They are likely to come up with any of some sixty anagrams which you can then comment on, within the theme of harvest. There is, to my knowledge, only one unsuitable word! The children of course, can be 'helped' to present the words you want.)

EAT	Something we like to do! Here in Britain we have lots of different foods to choose from, and although we sometimes say we're hungry, there's always something for us to eat.
EARTH	We need to look after our planet Earth. It provides us with everything we need in life.
EARS	We all have ears! But do you know that stalks of wheat are called ears? Wheat is the grain we use to make our bread.
EAST	In eastern countries, like China and Japan, they eat quite different foods from us here in Britain. But they usually have enough to go round.
HAVE	Here in Britain we have plenty of food. But do you know that two out of every three people in our world don't have enough to eat?
HEART	Something we all have. Our hearts pump blood round our bodies and keep us alive. But we also think of our hearts in terms of caring for others. We need to care about everyone on our Earth.
REST	We have lots to eat, so we could say 'I'm all right Jack!' But what about the rest of the people in the world who don't have enough to eat? Perhaps we could think of ways of helping them.
SHARE	Although two out of three people in our world don't have enough to eat, there is enough food to go round if we share it. The trouble is, we in the western world have too much food, and the people in the developing countries – the third world – don't have enough.
STAR	In the Christmas story, a star led the Wise Men to Bethlehem and the new king born in a stable. Christians believe that Jesus teaches us to look after everyone in our world, and to share what we have with others.
STARVE	Starve means dying of hunger. Sometime we say we're starving when we mean we fancy something to eat. But some people in the

	world have nothing to eat for days and weeks on end. Those people are starving.
TEA	Everyone here knows that tea can mean a drink or a meal. But in some countries, the people don't have either.
TEARS	Just try to imagine what it would be like to have nothing at all to eat. Think what it would be like to see people in your family die of starvation.
VEST	Our earth provides not only our food, but all our clothes as well. Think of wool and cotton and silk and leather which are all natural fabrics. Even our man-made materials come from natural products to begin with. We all have plenty to wear, but other people are not so fortunate, and don't have enough.

Harvest time is a time of thanksgiving and sharing. It's a time to say thank you to God for all the food the earth provides us with. But it's also a time for thinking about others who don't have as much food as we do. It's a time for trying to do something to help other people; a time for sharing with other people.

Thank you Lord, for all the earth provides. Help us to know that the earth can provide enough food for us all, if we learn to share it. Amen

How corn came to America

How many of you like pop-corn? And how many of you have ever eaten corn-flakes or corn-on-the-cob? Most of you I should think. I suppose you all know that pop-corn, corn-flakes and corn-on-the-cob all come from the same plant. It's called maize or Indian corn, and although it grows now in our country, it started off in South America where it's been an important food for the American Indians for thousands of years.

Here's the story of how Indian corn came to America in the first place.

Once upon a time when the world was still new, there lived a poor family of Indians, deep in the south of America.

In those days, the Indians lived off the land and ate animals they hunted with bow and arrows, and fish they caught with hook and line. Food was plentiful and the Indians did not go hungry. But the father of one family was a poor hunter and an even worse fisherman. He always did his best, but no matter how hard he tried to provide for his family, he was never able to bring home enough food for his wife and children.

He tried to teach his eldest son, Wotek, to hunt and fish, but since he was so poor at it himself, he was a poor teacher for the boy. The family grew thinner and hungrier.

One day Wotek decided that since he was the eldest boy and now nearly a man, it was his duty to leave home and fend for himself, and then there would be one less mouth to feed and one less person to worry about. He told his parents of his plans and set off. His father went with him to the edge of the Great Forest, and there they said goodbye.

Wotek walked for another few miles, across the edge of the Great Plain and into the Unknown Forest. Here he stopped and made himself a shelter of sticks and leaves under the branch of a large tree. He had nothing to eat, but drank from a clear stream which ran through the forest. Then, tired after his journey, he lay down to sleep in his shelter. He dreamed he was fighting with a strange tall thin green ghost with yellow hair.

In the morning Wotek built a fire and tried to catch a fish for his breakfast, but although there were fish a-plenty in the stream, he had no luck in catching one.

He next tried to snare a rabbit. He made a trap of twigs and string and sat patiently waiting for a rabbit to be caught. He waited one, then two, then three hours, but although there were rabbits a-plenty in the Unknown Forest, none came into his trap.

Wotek then took his bow and arrow and went to the edge of the Great Plain. He hid in the undergrowth and waited for the deer to come. He could see them in the distance. Slowly the herd moved closer to him. Wotek stayed quite still. The deer moved closer. Wotek fitted an arrow to his bow and took aim. The arrow flew into the air and landed short of the deer. Its movement frightened the herd and they galloped away.

Wotek went back to his shelter. He sat on the ground and called to the Great Spirit to help him.

'I cannot hunt. My family cannot hunt. How can we live if we have no food? Teach me how to provide for my family now that I am nearly a man.'

The Great Spirit heard his prayer and sent a strange tall thin green ghost with yellow hair, who asked Wotek to fight with him.

'I saw you in my dream,' said Wotek. 'But why are you here? How can you help me by fighting with me?'

'Just do as I say,' said the strange thin ghost, and he began to wrestle Wotek to the ground. They struggled and rolled over and over on the soft earth. But Wotek was weak with hunger and soon lost the struggle. He lay exhausted on the soil.

'Fight me again,' said the yellow-haired ghost. 'Fight me and kill me!'

'I can't do that,' said Wotek.

'You must,' said the tall green ghost. 'And then you will be able to provide food for your family.'

'I don't understand,' answered Wotek. 'We can't eat you.'

'That's right,' said the ghost. 'But I am only the spirit. Listen to what you must do. First you must kill me in the fight. Then you must clear a patch of ground of stones and weeds, and dig a deep hole. Bury me in the hole then go back to your family. Every time there is a new moon you must come back and visit my grave. Sprinkle water on it each time you come, and make sure it is kept free of weeds. In time you will see my children, and my grandchildren and my great-grandchildren, and they will feed your family forever.'

Wotek still did not understand the strange spirit, but there was no time to ask more questions because the fight began anew. But this time the ghost grew pale and weak and, Wotek was able to kill him easily.

He did as he had been told and cleared the stones and weeds from a patch of ground then dug a hole. He buried the ghost and covered him with earth. Then Wotek went back to his family and told them all that had happened since he left the village.

At the time of the new moon, Wotek and his father returned to the place where Wotek had buried the ghost. Everything looked just as it had before, but Wotek sprinkled the earth with water and pulled up a few weeds which had appeared. At the next new moon they went back again, and this time were surprised to see a tall thin green plant beginning to grow. And by the next new moon the plant was taller than either Wotek or his father. They noticed that it had yellow feathery tassels near the top, and long green oval shapes further down.

'What shall we do with it?' asked Wotek's father.

'Let's leave it and see what happens next,' said Wotek.

When they returned at the time of the next new moon, the strange plant was heavy with golden corn cobs. Wotek tasted the corn.

'It's good,' he said. 'And now I know what to do. We must plant some and eat some. The corn we plant will grow again, and when it ripens we can plant some and eat some. We can do that forever. We'll never have to go hunting again, but we'll always have food. We must thank the Great Spirit for helping us.'

So Wotek planted some of the corn and harvested it the following year. Then he planted more and gave some to his neighbours. They harvested it and planted more and gave some away. And so it was that Indian corn came to America all those years ago. All because a family didn't know how to hunt and the Great Spirit helped them find food they could grow.

This type of story is called a 'myth'. It's a story that people made up a long long time ago to try to explain how and why something is there in the world. Perhaps you could remember Wotek's story next time you eat pop-corn or corn-flakes or corn-on-the-cob. And you might just think about how many people there are all over the world who are eating some kind of corn at the same time as you!

Thank you God, for the food we eat. Thank you for the food that keeps us alive, and thank you for the fun-food we have. Help us to remember that not everyone has enough food to keep them alive, and many people have no fun-food at all. Help our world leaders to share the earth's food fairly. Amen

Kimoto and the rice harvest

Harvest time is a time for thanksgiving and for sharing. In today's story from Japan, the villagers were having a festival to say thank you for their rice harvest. One of the villagers shared his harvest in a quite extraordinary and unselfish way.

Kimoto had lived for many years on the island of Japan. He was a rice farmer and his farm of paddy fields was in steps up the side of a hill overlooking the sea.

From the topmost rice field, Kimoto could see for miles. He could see the long sweep of yellow beach at the bottom of the hill, the village nestling halfway up the hill, several other neighbouring farms dotted on the hillside, and of course the sea. Always the sea. Wherever he looked it was always in view.

Kimoto sometimes thought he would have liked to have been a fisherman instead of a rice farmer, but when he looked at the sea when it was rough and churning and angry, he was glad he earned his living from the land.

One day, at harvest time, Kimoto was standing in the top field looking at his stacks of rice waiting for threshing. The harvest had been excellent that year, there was more rice than Kimoto could remember ever having grown before.

'It won't make me rich,' he said to himself. 'But it'll do very nicely, thank you!'

He looked across the hillside at some of his neighbours' farms. They, too, had had good crops this year. There would be plenty to celebrate at this year's Harvest Festival. Down in the village, preparations were already well under way for it. Lanterns were being hung in the streets and banners and flags fluttered from nearly every window. On the beach the huge bonfire was almost built, and people were already gathering round it ready for the lighting ceremony and the dancing that would follow. Other people were setting up long trestle tables ready for the food to be set out upon it. Things were almost ready for the Harvest Festival and there was a feeling of excitement and expectancy in the air.

Kimoto was just about to leave his top field and join the others on the beach, when he felt the earth tremble and shift beneath his feet. He knew straight away what it was. Earthquake! They happened often in this part of the world. Kimoto had seen plenty of them to recognise this one. Sometimes they were quite minor and caused little or no damage. But even though the houses were built to withstand earthquakes, sometimes the movement was so great that whole villages and even towns were destroyed.

The first tremble had stopped now, and Kimoto waited to see if it would be followed by another, as often happened. But no. The earth stayed firm.

But as he waited, Kimoto glanced across to the sea and was horrified at what he could see. The earth's movement had caused the sea to run away from the beach and the villagers gathered on the beach were standing watching this strange event.

From their position, down at sea level, they had no way of seeing what was happening in the distance. But Kimoto could see. He could see the water gathering way over on the horizon. He knew that in only a matter of minutes, all the water now running away from the beach, would suddenly come surging back towards it. The sea, with all the power of a tidal wave, would engulf the beach and all his friends and neighbours would surely be swept away and drowned.

He had to warn them. But how? He had to let them know immediately to come away. But there was no time. No time to run down to tell them. Too far to call or shout. The seconds ticked by. The tide was about to turn and come surging back towards the land.

'I have to make them leave the beach. I have to force them to come away. I have to do something!' said Kimoto out loud, and even as he asked himself what to do, he knew the answer.

He quickly ran to his house. He picked up a burning log from the fire and ran back to the field. He set fire to first one, then another, and another, of his rice stacks. They were tinder dry and burst into flame straight away. Soon all his precious rice stacks were burning. The smoke and flames rose high into the sky and someone down on the beach noticed.

'Hey! Fire!'

The others turned to look.

'It's Kimoto's. It's on fire. Quick. We must go and help him.' And without another thought for the strangely disappearing sea, or the Harvest Festival, or the bonfire or tables or food, they all ran up the hillside to help Kimoto put out the fire on his farm.

No sooner had the people left the beach than the tidal wave swept in and surged up the beach and even into the streets of the village. The strength of the water damaged houses and shops. It pulled down the lanterns and banners. On its way back to the sea bed it washed away the giant bonfire and the tables on the beach. It even swept away the golden yellow sand leaving bare rock in its place. There was no doubt that anyone in its way would have been swept out to sea and drowned. But in climbing the hill to put out the fire, Kimoto's friends and neighbours were saved.

They were of course, too late to save Kimoto's rice crop. It was completely destroyed. But Kimoto knew that the lives of the people were more important than his rice harvest.

I wonder what happened next? I wonder how Kimoto managed for the rest of the year without any rice. What would you have done if you'd been there?

Thank you Lord, for the harvest. Help us to be generous enough to share what we have with others. Help us to know that the earth can provide enough food for everyone if we share what is available. Amen

Theme 3: Tricks and treats

The trickster tricked

There are many stories told all over the world about tricksters; people or animals who try to trick others into doing something. The trickster is often lazy and mischievous, he usually wants something for nothing, or perhaps he just wants to be naughty; but one thing you can depend upon, is that the trickster always gets found out in the end!

Some of the best known trickster stories are the Anansi stories from West Africa. Anansi is a spider. He's great fun and very lovable; he's very clever, extremely naughty, and is always playing tricks on people, so as you can imagine, he's always in trouble. But somehow, no-one can ever stay cross with Anansi for long.

Anansi likes eating, but he doesn't like work, as this story shows.

Once upon a time there lived a very hard-working fisherman. He was always up with the sun, setting his nets in the river, or off with the tide to the deep waters of the sea. In the evening, after he'd taken the fish to market and eaten his tea, the fisherman would sit outside his house mending nets, or would go down to the harbour to clean or repair his boat. He was always busy.

Anansi watched him. He saw how hard the fisherman worked, but he also noticed the fine fat fish that the fisherman brought home to his wife and family every day. Fish that his wife would bake or fry, poach or steam or make into delicious soups or stews or pies.

Anansi's mouth watered at the thought of all that fish. He liked fish. He especially liked thick white fish, dipped in batter, and fried until it was soft and juicy inside its crispy crunchy coating.

Suddenly, Anansi had an idea. 'I know what I'll do,' he said to himself. 'I'll offer to work for the fisherman, then he'll give me some fish for helping him.' But Anansi had no intention of doing any work. He was going to trick the fisherman into giving him all the fish he wanted.

Anansi strolled down to the harbour. The tide was out and the fisherman was scraping barnacles from the underside of his boat.

'Would you like some help?' called Anansi. 'Would you like me to work for you? We could be a good team, you and me!'

The fisherman looked up from his work. He knew Anansi of old! He knew his ways and his tricks, but the fisherman had a few tricks up his sleeve, too!

'Why not?' he called to Anansi. 'I shall be pleased to have you aboard. I could do with a bit of help. You can start tomorrow.'

The people standing watching said, 'What a fool you are, fisherman. Anansi will trick you! He'll make you do all the work and he'll get all the fish. You'll see!'

'Yes! We'll see!' answered the fisherman.

Early the next morning Anansi presented himself for work.

'Now, we need to sort out who's going to do what,' said the fisherman. 'And as I see it, somebody has to do the work, and somebody has to get tired. So, we'll take it in turns, shall we? This morning I will do all the work and you can get tired, then this afternoon we'll change over and you can do all the work and I'll get tired.'

Anansi looked puzzled. Things were not going quite as he planned.

'Shall we do that?' asked the fisherman. 'I'll do the work first and you can get tired?'

'No, no,' cried Anansi, who, above all else, hated to get tired. 'No, that's not a good idea at all. I'll do the work, and you can get tired.'

'Well, if that's what you want,' said the fisherman.

So Anansi pulled up the anchor and steered the boat out to sea. He put up the sails, he coiled the ropes, he let down the nets, he pulled in the fish and sorted them and graded them and gutted them and packed them in baskets. And the fisherman lay on his bunk and yawned and stretched and kept telling Anansi how tired he was. By the end of the morning Anansi was exhausted, but the fisherman said he was more tired.

'But don't worry,' said the fisherman. 'This afternoon we'll fish in the river and it'll be my turn to do all the work, whilst you get tired.'

'No, no,' cried Anansi, who, as you know, hated to get tired. 'No, that's not a good idea at all. *I'll* do the work, and *you* can get tired.'

So Anansi pulled up the anchor and steered the boat up the river. He put the traps over the side of the boat and lowered them one by one. All through the afternoon he lowered those traps and pulled them up again to take out the fish they had caught. And the fisherman sprawled on the bench in the boat and snoozed and nodded and snored.

By the end of the afternoon Anansi was exhausted, but the fisherman said he was so tired he hardly had the energy to go home and eat his tea.

'I'll pay you this evening, when we take the catch to market,' the fisherman said, and he staggered home for his tea, moaning and groaning and grumbling and grousing about how terribly tired he was.

Later that evening Anansi met the fisherman down by the harbour. The fisherman insisted that it was his turn to do the work of carrying the heavy baskets of fish to market, and Anansi's turn to get tired. After all, that was what they'd agreed. Taking turns was only fair.

'No, no,' cried Anansi in anguish, because above all else, he hated to get tired. 'No, no, you can't trick me. You're not going to make me get tired. I'll do the work and you can get tired.'

'Well, only if you're sure,' said the fisherman.

'I'm perfectly sure,' said Anansi, who was not at all sure how things had got to this state.

So Anansi carried all the heavy baskets of fish from the boat in the harbour, up the steep hill to the market, whilst the fisherman plodded along behind, huffing and puffing and blowing and gasping as though he were very tired indeed.

When they arrived at the market place, Anansi set the fish down under the trees, and the fisherman sat down on an upturned box next to them. The customers soon arrived and began to buy, and in no time at all, every single fish had been sold and the fisherman was jangling a bagful of money. He reached into the bag and pulled out three small coins which he gave to Anansi.

'One for this morning's work. One for this afternoon's, and one for this evening's,' he said.

And Anansi realised, that instead of tricking the fisherman as he'd planned, the fisherman had tricked him. Anansi had done all the work, yet had no fish and hardly any money. At first Anansi felt angry, but he was a good loser, so he laughed at himself and danced away into the trees, singing, 'There's always next time. I shall win next time!'

Anansi learned that if you play tricks on people, you have to be prepared for them to play tricks on you! And if you try to get out of doing the work, like Anansi thought he was going to do, you might end up doing twice as much.

Dear God, please help us to do our fair share of the work when something needs doing. Help us not to be greedy and not to trick people into doing things for us. Help us to be open and honest in our dealings with others. Amen

The People of Chelm

There are some wonderfully funny stories that Jewish people tell to their children, of the city of Chelm in Poland. The people of Chelm are friendly and hardworking, but they're not very clever although they think they are incredibly wise. The people of Chelm are easily tricked, and I'm sorry to say that there are people in the world who are happy to take advantage of them because tricking them seems so easy.

Here's the story of how it all started.

When God made the world, he thought it would be best if there were equal numbers of wise and foolish people everywhere, so he asked one of his angels to fly over the world with two sacks; one containing wisdom, and the other full of foolishness.

'Sprinkle a little of each wherever there are people,' said God. 'And then there will be wise and foolish people in every place, and that will be fair.'

So the angel set off and did what God asked. But unfortunately, as he flew over a certain high mountain at a place called Chelm, one of the sacks became caught in the top of a tree. The angel pulled the sack free, but as he did so it tore open and all the wisdom fell out onto the ground. (Or was it the foolishness that fell to the ground? I'll leave it for you to decide!)

Soon after that, the people who lived in the area decided to build themselves some better houses.

'We'll build the new houses with wood,' they said, for there were plenty of trees growing on the mountainside.

The Chelmites worked hard. They climbed the mountain every day to reach the tallest, straightest trees. They trimmed off the leaves and branches and cut down the trunks. And what trunks! It took ten men to carry each tree trunk down the mountainside to the valley where the houses were to be built.

One day whilst they were working, a traveller came by.

'Why are you wasting all your energy on carrying those heavy tree trunks down the mountainside?' he asked. 'Why don't you just roll the trunks down the mountain? They'll go down by themselves,' and he went on his way shaking his head at their foolishness.

The people of Chelm held a meeting to discuss the traveller's idea.

'Do you think it would work?' they asked each other.

'It would certainly save a lot of effort if it did,' they said, and after a great deal of debate and discussion and deliberation, the people of Chelm decided that it was a good idea, so they carried all the tree trunks back up the mountain so that they could push them down to the bottom without having to carry them.

'Brilliant! Wonderful! How clever!' they all said. 'How lucky we were that the traveller just happened to come this way and share that good idea with us!'

Work on the new houses progressed well, and soon they were almost finished. Another day's work, and they could all move in. Then, horror of horrors, someone noticed that they had forgotten to build the synagogue!

'How could we have forgotten?' they said. 'It's here on the plans in black and white. It's perfectly easy to see; right in the middle of the houses, in the place where the synagogue ought to be,' and they sat and cried at their forgetfulness.

Then someone spoke.

'Never mind,' he said. 'We can easily put things right. All we have to do is pull down all the houses, build the synagogue, then build all the houses again.'

'What a brilliant idea,' everyone said, suddenly becoming much more cheerful at the thought of the solution. 'And what a good thing that we're so clever and wise, otherwise we'd never have thought of the answer.'

So the people of Chelm pulled down all the carefully built houses, built the synagogue where the houses used to be, then rebuilt the houses round it. The trouble was, they'd now run out of space. The last of the houses were right up against the foot of the mountain. There was no room left in the valley.

'What shall we do when we want to make our city bigger?' they asked themselves. 'What happens when our children grow up and want houses of their own? What shall we do then? We have no more space to build.'

They thought about the problem and scratched their heads. They held a meeting and formed a committee. They made lists and plans and schedules. But they couldn't decide what to do about the problem. Then one Chelmite said, 'There's only one thing we can do. We'll have to move the mountain.'

'Of course,' they all agreed. 'How clever we are to think of such a brilliant and sensible solution. What a good thing it is that we're so wise and have so many good ideas.'

So the people of Chelm ran outside, and put their shoulders to the mountain. They pushed and heaved. They strained and shoved and thrust against the mountain. But it would not move.

They took off their coats and put them in a pile on the ground and had a rest. Then they tried again. This time everyone joined in; mothers, fathers, uncles, aunts, cousins, neighbours, grannies, babies, even the cats and the dogs joined in, to push the mountain back a bit so that there would be more room to build. And while they were busy doing this, three travellers came by, up to no good.

'What do you suppose they're doing?' said one.

'I don't know, but it looks mighty strange,' said another.

'They've left their coats in a heap. Look!' said the third.

The three travellers looked at each other, and without another word they picked up that pile of coats and made off with them. Meanwhile, the good people of Chelm struggled and strained against the mountain. Sweat poured from their foreheads and they grunted and groaned and wheezed and sighed with the exertion of it all. Suddenly, one of the Chelmites turned round.

'Hey, look!' he shouted excitedly, and everyone turned to see.

'Look! We've done it! We've moved the mountain! We've moved it not just a bit, but a *lot*! We've moved it so far we can't even see our pile of coats any more! We must have moved it *miles*!' And the people of Chelm burst into wild applause at their own cleverness in moving the mountain so far.

Later they had a party to celebrate their success. They talked of how lucky they were to be so wise, and how their city would grow and grow, probably until it filled the whole world. What fortunate people they were!

I don't suppose the tricksters who stole the coats had any idea that the people would think they'd moved the mountain when they saw the coats gone. The story had a funny ending, but I think it's sad that the coat thieves took advantage of the Chelmites when they were busy pushing the mountain, no matter how odd it seemed.

I hope you never try to take advantage of, or poke fun at, people you think are not as clever as you. Remember, right at the beginning of the story, God wanted there to be wise *and* foolish people in his world. There's room for everyone in the world, and remember, everyone is good at something. The Chelmites were good at being cheerful and positive; those two qualities are very important in life.

Help us Lord, to remember that everyone in the world is loved by you, that everyone is valuable, and that everyone is good at something. Help us to be kind and caring to people who need protecting, and to those who are younger or weaker than us. Amen

Katie-Lee's Treat

Have you noticed how there are two kinds of people in the world? There are those who are extremely selfish and never think about others, and there are those who are kind, generous and thoughtful and always concerned about other people. What sort of person are you?

It's an easy question for me to answer, because I know that everyone in our school is kind and caring and unselfish – most of the time! In fact, I think that most people in the world are basically caring towards one another. You only have to look in the newspapers and on TV to see that every day there are hundreds of people, from individuals to huge business concerns, trying to make life better in some way for others.

This is the true story of some of those people.

Several years ago, a group of people met together to try to do something to help children who were seriously ill with diseases they could die from.

'We can't give the children medical care, because they're already getting that from the doctors and nurses in hospital,' they said. 'We can't go out and buy loads of toys, because what is suitable for one child might not be suitable for another,' they said. 'But we'd like to give them some sort of treat. So what can we do to help these children?'

'Wouldn't it be wonderful if we could give every child a wish!' someone said. 'Each child could make a wish, and we would organise things to make the dream come true!'

'It's a brilliant idea,' said the others. So the 'Make-a-Wish Foundation' was started.

The children wished for all sorts of things, from computers, to trips to Lapland to see Father Christmas. Nothing was too difficult for the Make-a-Wish team to organise. Lots of children wanted to go to Disneyland in Florida, and Make-a-Wish planned dozens of visits. It wasn't just a question of raising the money to buy the tickets, though that was part of the Make-a-Wish job; no, they had to organise doctors and nurses and ambulances to go with the children as well, because some of the children were very ill indeed.

And then along came Katie-Lee.

Katie-Lee was seven and had cancer. She'd had to endure some very difficult chemotherapy and no-one knew whether the treatment was going to be successful. The people from Make-a-Wish asked her if there was something really special she'd like; something she'd always dreamed of, something she'd always wanted.

'I'd really like a twin pram,' she said. 'I wish I could have a pram to hold a boy doll and a girl doll.'

No-one had ever asked Make-a-Wish for a pram before.

I suppose it would have been easiest for the Make-a-Wish people to go to the local toyshop and buy a twin pram, maybe a mass-produced plastic one, but Katie-Lee was a special little girl and deserved a special pram, so Make-a-

Wish went to Yorkshire, to the Silver Cross factory that made beautiful full-size prams for babies.

'Could you make a one-off, very special, red twin pram for Katie-Lee?' they asked.

'We certainly can,' said the manager. 'It'll be very expensive, and it'll take at least four weeks to make.'

'Ah! That's a bit of a problem,' said the people from Make-a-Wish. 'We haven't any money, and we'd really like it by, say, the day after tomorrow? Katie-Lee is very ill you see.'

'Just a minute,' said the manager, and he went off to speak to the people in the factory who actually made the prams. In a few minutes he came back.

'Katie-Lee can have her pram,' he said. 'It'll be ready for you to collect the day after tomorrow. We'll help you to make her wish come true – oh, and you won't need to pay for it. We'll give it to Katie-Lee.'

So work started on the very special pram. Fifteen staff at the factory worked over, for no extra pay, so that the pram would be finished in two days instead of the usual four weeks. The two hand-stitched red hoods were fitted at either end of the pram. The shiny red body of the pram was painted with a smart silver trim, with Katie-Lee's name and with the Make-a-Wish logo of a silver wishbone. The lining was stitched into the pram, then the whole thing was fitted to the big curved brackets which fastened it to the white wheels.

'Well, we can't send the pram to Katie-Lee with nothing in it!' said one of the workers, so they all contributed towards buying two beautiful teddy bears, which they dressed as a boy and a girl. At last the pram, complete with twin teddies sitting in it, was ready.

Make-a-Wish could hardly believe their eyes when they went to the factory to collect the pram. It was beautiful. It was totally original – there wasn't another pram like it anywhere in the world. And it was already a collector's item, and worth a considerable amount of money.

'Thank you,' they said. 'Katie-Lee will love it. It's a very special present for a very special little girl.'

'You need to thank my workers,' said the factory manager. 'They made it! And we all hope that Katie-Lee will enjoy playing with it.'

Make-a-Wish took the pram to Katie-Lee, and it was exactly what she'd dreamed of. One little girl had made a wish and it had come true, thanks to a lot of people who were happy to give their time and skills and money to help someone they didn't even know.

Katie-Lee's wish came true because of the unselfishness of the people at Make-a-Wish, the Silver Cross factory, and the fifteen workers. One very ill little girl had a treat because other people wanted to do something to help.

Wouldn't it be lovely if everyone took the time and trouble to want to help other people? Wouldn't our world be a wonderful place? Perhaps we can start with our school, today. Let's see if each one of us can do something to help someone else, in some way, today.

Dear God, help us to be thoughtful and caring towards other people. Help us to be the sort of people who help others, and not the sort of people who play unkind tricks on others. Help us to be protective towards those who are ill or weak or in need. Amen

November

Theme 1: Remember, remember

Saint Nonmiricordo and the fish

November the first is All Saints' Day, a feast day when Christians remember all the forgotten, unknown or unrecognised saints who have ever lived, and who do not have a special feast day of their own. There is of course a difficulty with this, because how can you remember a saint who is forgotten or unknown? It's quite a problem!

But the idea behind the feast day is that it's an opportunity to think about all the good people who have ever lived, and to remember that good always wins over evil. Today's story is from Italy. It's about a saint that people can hardly remember. But although everyone has almost forgotten the saint, no-one has forgotten the fish!

The story goes that the saint went travelling in Italy. But the story is so old, and people's memories so dim, that no-one can remember his name. But they do remember that he was a small, round, friendly sort of person, and that he was very good at telling stories, especially stories from the bible. So good in fact that people for miles around would come to hear his stories when they knew he was in the area.

The saint, (he needs a name so we'll call him Saint Nonmiricordo), travelled all over Italy and managed very well until he came to a town called Cos'èquesto on the edge of the Adriatic Sea. And it was here that his problems began.

You see, the people of Cos'èquesto were not law-abiding citizens, they were a wild and rough set of people. They thought nothing of lying and cheating, swindling and stealing. It was a normal way of life for them. So when Saint Nonmiricordo came to town, they were not impressed, and no-one came to listen to him or his stories.

'Never mind!' said Saint Nonmiricordo to himself. 'I'll go to the church every day. They'll come in the end, if only out of curiosity, then I'll be there, ready and waiting for them, and I can tell them some of my stories and talk to them about God.'

But although Saint Nonmiricordo went to the church every day, no-one from the town came to see him. No-one was interested in listening to what he had to say.

'Never mind!' he said to himself again. 'If they won't come to me, then I'll go to them. I'll go to the market place every day instead. They'll all be there, and I can tell my stories in the market square just as well as anywhere else.'

So Saint Nonmiricordo went everyday to the market square. He sat in the middle of all the hustle and bustle and buying and selling and shouting and yelling, and he told his stories. But no-one listened. The people of Cos'èquesto simply ignored him and carried on with their lives.

'Well, this is a waste of time!' said Saint Nonmiricordo to himself after a while. 'I might just as well be talking to the fish in the sea, for all the notice these people are taking of me!' And that's when he had his idea.

He left the market square and made his way to the beach. Then he settled down on a large rock just where the waves were lapping on to the sand, and he started to tell his stories.

At first nothing happened. And then a small fish poked its head out of the water. It dived down into the waves again, and in two minutes several more fish had appeared, then more, and even more. Saint Nonmiricordo continued with his story.

The fish, now between two and three hundred of them, arranged themselves in orderly rows with the smallest fish at the front and the larger fish behind, looking for all the world like an assembly-full of children. They stood upright in the water with their heads poking out, listening intently to the words of Saint Nonmiricordo. He continued with his story.

A short distance away, a man from Cos'èquesto was fishing for his dinner. He gaped in astonishment when he saw the fish standing to attention in neat and tidy rows, listening to Saint Nonmiricordo tell his story; then he took to his heels and ran back to the town to tell everyone what he'd seen. No-one believed him of course.

'Then come and see for yourselves,' he shouted, as he ran back to the beach to watch.

A few minutes later, Saint Nonmiricordo was aware of a great crowd of people coming on to the beach. He took no notice and carried on with the story, as though talking to fish was the sort of thing he did every day. When the people of Cos'èquesto saw the fish listening so carefully and standing so still, they said, 'He must have something really important to say if even the fish will listen to him. Perhaps we'd better listen too,' and they all sat down quietly on the sand so that they could hear what he had to say.

When he had finished the story, Saint Nonmiricordo thanked the fish for listening, then turned and thanked the people and they all wondered why they hadn't listened to him before, because the story had been so good.

After that, the people of Cos'èquesto came to listen to Saint Nonmiricordo every day. Sometimes they gathered on the beach, sometimes in the market square and sometimes in the church. And slowly Saint Nonmiricordo began to teach the people to live better lives, to care for each other, and to understand that lying and cheating and swindling and stealing aren't the best way to live.

And as for the fish? Well, Saint Nonmiricordo went to the beach to tell them a story on the third Thursday of every month, because they had enjoyed the first one so much.

In our assembly, Saint Nonmiricordo can stand for all the forgotten and unknown saints. He's a good one to have to represent the rest, because he changed the people of Cos'èquesto for the better, and All Saints' Day is about remembering that good always wins over evil. *(Do you know what Saint Nonmiricordo's name means in Italian? [It means 'I don't remember']. Maybe you could find out?)*

Thank you, Lord, for all the saints who have ever lived. Thank you for all the people who have set an example to others by leading good lives. Help us to say no to lying and cheating and stealing when we are tempted to do those things. Amen

The firework maker

'Remember, remember the fifth of November
Is gunpowder, treason and plot.
I see no reason why gunpowder treason
Should ever be forgot.'

I think most of you will have heard that rhyme about Bonfire Night, before. It reminds us of Guy Fawkes, and the story of how he tried to blow up the Houses of Parliament. Nowadays, many people in Britain celebrate Guy Fawkes Night, or Bonfire Night, by having bonfire parties or by going to organised firework displays.

But I wonder if you've ever thought about who makes the fireworks for these big displays? There is only one company in Britain that makes display fireworks, and the man who started the company is called Ronald Lancaster. Mr Lancaster is also a vicar, and his nick-name is the "Master Blaster Pastor". It's a good name for a vicar who makes fireworks, isn't it!

Ronald Lancaster first became interested in making fireworks when he was 14. It was during the Second World War, and you couldn't buy fireworks, so he and his dad made their own. Ronald loved making fireworks. It was like a mixture of chemistry and cooking. The fireworks were exciting and had colour and life and movement, but Ronald knew how dangerous they were. He knew that they were made from explosives, and he and his dad were always careful to follow the safety rules.

After the war, when Ronald was grown up, he continued to make fireworks, but now he began to experiment. He made bigger, brighter, more colourful ones. He invented totally new fireworks that had never been seen before. He began to arrange huge firework displays so that hundreds of people could watch the fireworks safely. He had the fireworks all timed to go off at exactly the right moment in the display by having them electronically controlled.

He started his own factory; the only one in Britain making display fireworks. And all the time he was very very careful about safety. All the time he ensured that his factory was properly run, and that all the fireworks were properly tested so that they were safe when they became part of a display.

The smaller fireworks that were sold in shops were tested on a special sand pit. It was five metres in diameter, five metres across, and the sparks had to fall inside the sand circle for the fireworks to be declared safe. If the sparks went further than the sand circle the fireworks couldn't be sold. The bigger fireworks, for the displays, were tested on a helicopter pad at the local airfield. All the debris, the bits of firework that fall back to earth after they've gone off, were all carefully collected and then taken to the laboratory to be tested. Always, always, Ronald Lancaster was concerned about safety. He knew how important it was in dealing with fireworks.

And all the time that Mr Lancaster was testing fireworks and making displays, he carried on inventing new fireworks. He made the most amazing golden rain and silver snow. He made huge traffic lights that shot red, orange and green balls of light into the sky. He made rockets that went so high in the sky they could hardly be seen, and then they burst into showers of stars. He made red and green and orange and purple skyfizz and starbursts. And all the time, Ronald Lancaster made sure that every single firework was safe.

And then it happened! A flying saucer went out of control.

The flying saucer was a spectacular firework. First of all it spun like a Catherine wheel, giving off showers of coloured sparks. Then, still spinning, it rose vertically into the air and went higher and higher until it exploded in a burst of shimmering stars. The firework had been tested and it seemed perfectly safe.

But on this particular occasion, something went wrong.

The crowd was enormous. Everyone was having a wonderful time. The weather was good, it was dry and bright – just right for a firework display. Everything was going according to plan. The first part of the display was already over, and the flying saucer had just been electronically ignited.

It fizzed and spluttered and whizzed on its stalk, and sent out its showers of sparks.

'Oooh,' said the crowd.

Then the flying saucer left its stalk and began to climb up into the sky, just as it was supposed to do.

'Aaah,' said the crowd.

But then, for no apparent reason, the flying saucer suddenly changed direction. It started to go sideways. Straight in the direction of the crowd. Ronald Lancaster stood, horrified, and watched. There was nothing he could do to stop the out-of-control firework. He knew there would be serious injuries if the flying saucer went into the crowd, but luckily it skimmed over the heads of all the people. Then it changed direction again and headed for the beer tent. Again Ronald Lancaster stood, horrified, unable to do anything to stop it. Again, Ronald knew how serious the injuries could be if the firework set fire to the tent. He felt dreadful. He'd invented this firework; he'd made it. And he'd always taken such care about safety, but now this had happened.

But luckily the flying saucer changed direction once more. It flew in a diagonal line over the top of the beer tent, then exploded in a shower of stars and came down to earth again in the empty field behind the display area.

The people, completely unaware of how much danger they'd been in, thought the firework was supposed to fly in the way it had.

'Bravo!' they shouted, and they clapped and cheered. 'Well done!' they said to Ronald Lancaster. 'That was magnificent! How clever of you to make a firework do that! How ever did you manage it?'

'Oh, it was a one-off,' said Ronald Lancaster. 'It was a never-to-be-seen-again sort of firework,' he added.

The very next day, Ronald Lancaster withdrew the flying saucer from all the displays, because the most important thing for him was safety. He couldn't risk an accident happening. He knew how exciting fireworks were, but he also knew how dangerous they were, and he always put safety first.

Mr Lancaster's factory is still in production, and it is still the only factory making display fireworks in Britain today. If you see a big celebratory firework display on the television you can be sure it'll be one of Ronald Lancaster's, and if you go to a big firework display, you can be sure the fireworks will have come from Mr Lancaster's factory. The factory is still as concerned about safety as it always was. We need to be just as concerned about safety when we are near fireworks.

Dear God, thank you for the fun and excitement of fireworks. But help us to know that they can hurt or even kill people. Make us remember never to fool around with fireworks. Help us to have a safe and happy Bonfire Night. Amen

Remembrance Day

November the 11th is Remembrance Day. You will have seen remembrance poppies on sale, and you may have seen special remembrance services on the television. Many people have a two-minute silence at 11 o'clock on Remembrance Day, as a mark of respect for all the people who died in the wars for our country this and last century. Eleven o'clock on the eleventh day of the eleventh month is when the papers were signed which put an end to the First World War.

Hundreds of thousands of people died in that war, and this is the true story of just one of them. The letters in the story are real letters, which have been saved for over ninety years.

It was 1914 and Rose and Benjamin had been married for just over a year. They'd moved into a tiny cottage in the village in Yorkshire where Ben had grown up, and now they'd just had their first baby. It was a boy and they called him William Leslie. They should have been wonderfully happy, and in many ways they were, but they were also worried. England was at war with Germany, and young men all over the country were joining the army.

'You won't have to go away and fight, will you?' said Rose.

'I shouldn't think so,' said Ben. 'They say the war will be over by Christmas.'

But the war wasn't over by Christmas, and in the New Year a message arrived in Rose and Ben's village, to say that all the men who were fit and active had to join the army and fight for their country.

Rose was distraught. 'You can't leave me and the baby. He's so small. We need you to look after us.'

'I have to go,' said Ben. 'I have no choice in the matter. I'll write to you whenever I can, and you can write to me. I'll be home again in no time, you'll see,' but of course Ben didn't know then what was going to happen. He set off for the war with the seventeen other young men from the village.

For two weeks Rose heard nothing. No news of any kind. She didn't know where Ben was, or how he was, or what he was doing. There were no radios or televisions or telephones in those days. There were newspapers but they gave only limited information. The only thing to do was to wait for a letter to come through the post, but the postal service was unreliable because of the war.

Three weeks went by and still Rose heard nothing. Four weeks... and then a letter. It was from Ben, it was written on a scrap of paper with a bit of pencil, and was written in a hurry.

> "My dearest wife and baby," it said.
>
> "I am pleased to say we arrived safe and well but tired. We had a good send-off from Doncaster with bands and a guard of honour with rifles. It took twelve hours to get here to Salisbury Plain. The train comes right into the camp and you never saw such a sight in all your life. Huts as far as you can see and thousands of soldiers. One thousand motor wagons came in new yesterday morning, and as many this morning.
>
> There are twenty-five men to a hut and we have to cook our own food. You must not write to me here for I think we are leaving for Southampton on Sunday, and then on to France. We are going by road with the motor-wagons and then over the sea.
>
> I don't know when I shall be able to come home again, but don't worry about me, only think about when I shall come back.
>
> I will send you my address as soon as I know it, and then perhaps you could send me a parcel.
>
> I hope you and baby are well. I must close my letter now my darling,
>
> With love from your ever loving husband, Ben."

Rose saved the letter and read it over and over again. She looked forward to receiving Ben's next letter... perhaps there'd be an address next time so that she could write back. She didn't know then, of course, what the next letter was going to tell her.

One week went by... two weeks... three weeks... four... five weeks... then another letter, but this time not from Ben. Rose could see by the stamp on the envelope that it was from France, but she didn't recognise the writing. She tore open the envelope.

> "Madam
>
> I regret to inform you that your husband is very seriously injured. He was admitted to this hospital yesterday. I will write and let you know his condition in a few days.
>
> Yours Truly, Ward Sister, General Hospital, Rouen, France."

Rose didn't know what to think. She had no means of contacting the hospital, other than by letter and letters took such a long time. She didn't know how badly Ben was injured, or where or how it had happened.

The next day another letter arrived.

> "Dear Mrs Street
>
> I am so sorry not to be able to write you a more favourable report of your husband. His condition remains critical and the doctor gives little hope of his recovery. I will write again tomorrow."
>
> Yours Truly Sister Martin."

Again, all Rose could do was wait for the next letter. It came in two days' time.

> "Dear Mrs Street
>
> I deeply regret to inform you that your husband died this morning at 3.30am. His condition grew gradually worse last evening. He was conscious until the last and his one thought was for you and his child.
>
> With true sympathy, I remain yours sincerely Sister Martin."

Rose then received several more letters: one from the war office, confirming that Ben had died, a telegram from the war office with the same news, and a letter from the army chaplain telling her all about the funeral. Rose had to learn to live without Ben, and William Leslie grew up never having known his father. Ben was the first man from his village to die, but he wasn't the only one. Of the seventeen who went to war, only one came back.

Rose and Ben's story is only one of thousands of similar stories. Behind all the statistics of war there are real people who died to help their country.

Remembrance Day gives us the chance to remember those people and to thank them for giving their lives so that our country could be free.

"We will remember them."

At eleven o'clock, on the eleventh day of November – the eleventh month, a peace agreement was signed which put an end to the First World War. Today we remember all those who were killed or injured in that war, and in other wars this and last century. We pray that our world may learn to live in peace, so that people of all countries and backgrounds can settle their differences and live together in the world family. Amen

Theme 2: Myths

How fire learned to run

Hundreds and hundreds of years ago, before people understood the world as we know it today, people wondered about the sun and moon, the earth and sky, the rivers and rocks and mountains. They wondered how they got there and who made them. And in order to try to understand their world, those early people made up stories to explain the world's mysteries.

Those early people all over the world told the stories to their children and to their children's children, and so it went on, all down the years until today. Nowadays we call those stories myths, and although they are very old, many of them still contain messages which are just as useful to us as they were to those far off people long ago.

See if you can find the message in this story from Africa.

Once upon a time when the world was new, Fire lived by himself on an island in the middle of a lake. Sometimes he would lie still and smoulder quietly, and the animals who lived around the lake would say, 'Ssh! Fire is sleeping. Don't wake him for he might be bad-tempered when he wakes.' And other times Fire would leap up from sleep and crackle and flare and the animals would say, 'What is the matter with him? Why does he seem so cross?'

'I think he's cross because he's lonely,' said Leopard one day. 'I'm going to go and play with him.'

'Don't go,' said the other animals. 'It's not safe. He's sometimes wild and dangerous and not tame at all. Don't go!' But Leopard wouldn't listen and went to the edge of the lake and called across to Fire.

'Hello Fire. I want to come and visit you. I want to come and play.'

'You can't do that,' answered Fire. 'You can't come to my island, it's not safe. You must stay there, but you can talk to me if you want, I'd like that.'

So Leopard went to talk to Fire every day. He stood at the edge of the lake and Fire stayed on his island. Then one day Leopard said, 'I don't like having to shout at you across the water. I'm coming to see you.'

'No!' warned Fire. 'You mustn't come. It isn't safe. I'm not to be trusted with visitors.' But Leopard was already gathering stones to build a bridge. The lake was shallow and stone by stone Leopard made a causeway across to the island.

'No,' wept Fire. 'Don't come any closer. I'll have to hurt you if you come closer and I don't want to do that.' But Leopard wouldn't listen and continued to pile up the stones, one after the other until he was almost there.

Suddenly, Fire whooshed into life and flared into the sky. The air sizzled and hissed. Leopard felt the heat of Fire on his skin and he turned and ran back across the bridge of stones to safety.

'Now, stay away from me,' shouted Fire to his friend.

But Leopard wouldn't listen and ran back across the stones. There was now just a small stretch of water between him and Fire's island. Another few stones would easily bridge the gap. But Leopard knew now how fiercely hot Fire could be. So he sat on the stone bridge and talked to Fire from there.

'That's better,' said Fire. 'We're both safe if you stay there. But don't come any closer or you'll make me angry again.'

For the next few weeks all went well. Leopard visited Fire every day and talked to him from the end of the stone bridge. But soon, Leopard grew bored.

'It's not fair,' he grumbled. 'I come to visit you every day, but you never come to visit me.'

'You know I cannot leave my island,' said Fire. 'I have to stay here.'

'But I want you to come and see me,' insisted Leopard. 'Come tomorrow and we'll visit all my other friends.'

'I can't,' said Fire. 'I might get my feet wet and I shall be very put out if that happens! Anyway, if I come over there where there's all that space, I might learn to run. And if that happens, the world will never be the same again.

'You mean you can't run?' said Leopard in amazement. 'Well I can teach you. I can run fast.'

'You don't understand,' said Fire. 'I must not learn to run.'

'That's silly,' said Leopard. 'Running is fun,' and he ran backwards and forwards across the stone bridge to show Fire how easy it was.

'Go away, Leopard,' said Fire. 'Go away.'

Later that night, when Fire was quietly sleeping, Leopard finished the stone bridge. He stepped onto Fire's island. It felt hot around the edges. Leopard looked at his stone bridge and worried about Fire getting his feet wet on the smooth wet shiny stones. Suddenly he had an idea. He ran back across the bridge to the forest. He gathered as many dry leaves and twigs and branches as he could carry, and ran back to the bridge. He lay them on the stones like a carpet, then went back for more. By morning the bridge was dry as tinder, and there was no danger of Fire getting his feet wet.

'Look what I've done,' shouted Leopard as soon as the carpet was finished. 'You can come over here to see me now. We can play together in the forest. I'll teach you how to run!'

Fire woke with a start. He turned red with anger. He poured orange and yellow and white flares into the sky then roared and crackled across the bridge. He ran through the forest and thrust his fingers into the homes of the creatures who lived there. He killed the small creatures and singed the feathers of the birds. The larger animals fled in terror.

'You foolish Leopard,' he shouted, and his tongues of flame burned Leopard's fur as he spoke. 'Don't meddle with things you don't understand,' and he swept past Leopard, burning the forest as he went, and not stopping until he came to the sea, where he got his feet wet and drowned.

And ever since that day, Fire has been able to run, and Leopard has had spots to show where Fire burned him.

What a story! And what do you think is the message? I think the story is a warning about fire, and how dangerous and destructive it can be. I think there's also a message in the story about interfering, meddling, doing something you've been told not to do, and about being too insistent and pushy. Nowadays, we know that fire can be useful when it's controlled by people who know what they're doing. But if Fire is let loose to run about, it is just as dangerous now as it ever was.

Help us Lord, to understand the strength of fire. Help us to know how quickly it can get out of control, and how much damage and injury it can cause. Help us to know that fire can serve humankind, but only when it is kept under control by adults who know how to deal with it. Amen

The snow spirit

The early people of long ago made up stories and myths to try to explain the world around them. They also made up stories about the weather. At that time they didn't understand what caused thunder and lightening, earthquakes and avalanches, or even the rain and the wind; they thought there were spirits who controlled all the different kinds of weather.

Here's a myth from Japan, about the snow. It's an explanation of why a man died when he and his friend were caught in a blizzard, but the story goes on to talk about promises.

Once upon a time when the world was new, two friends were out walking in the high mountains of Japan. It was wintertime but the sun was bright in the sky and glistened on the sparkling snow. Then the clouds came. They were heavy with snow and they gathered together until they blotted out the sun and turned the day grey. Then they opened themselves and let the fat snowflakes fall to earth. The wind saw the snow falling and whipped it into a swirling blizzard. The path the men were travelling on disappeared under the snow and it was impossible to see the way ahead.

Suddenly they stumbled on an old disused hut that had once been used by shepherds caring for the mountain goats.

'We'll stay in here until the blizzard is past,' they said, and they huddled in the corner to keep warm.

But although they were out of the blizzard, the wind blew in through the cracks in the wall and the snow drifted in through the holes. It was bitterly bitterly cold. The older of the two men fell asleep and whilst he slept, the snow spirit came into the hut and breathed on him. Her breath turned to crystals of ice in the cold air. She turned to the younger man. He could see that she was young and beautiful with white hair and skin. She was dressed in a long white fur trimmed robe and she carried a white cloak. She seemed very gentle, but the younger man felt afraid of her.

'What do you want?' he asked.

'You know I am Yuki-onna, the snow woman,' she said. 'I breathe my icy breath on anyone who comes to my mountain in the snow. I keep them here with me for ever.'

'I don't want to stay here forever,' said the young man. 'I want to go home. Let me go. Don't breathe your ice crystal breath on me, please.'

Yuki-onna, the snow spirit, looked at the older man, now icy cold and as white as snow. Then she turned to the younger man.

'I have taken your friend, so I will let you go,' she said. 'But only on one condition. You must never ever tell anyone you have seen me.'

'I promise. I'll never tell anyone,' vowed the young man, and as he said that, the snow spirit drifted away from him and evaporated.

In the morning the blizzard had stopped and the young man set off down the mountain and went home. He told no-one of the strange snow woman he had seen that night; only that he and his older friend had become lost in the storm and that his friend had died in the blizzard.

Several years later, the young man met and married a beautiful and gracious young woman called Yuki. The name means snow in Japanese, but it was a common name for a girl in those times, and the young man thought nothing of it. The two of them were very happy together, and in time they had four lovely children. Yuki was a good wife and mother.

Then one evening when the children were in bed and Yuki and her husband were sitting together by the fire, the moon shone in through the window and its light fell on Yuki's face, turning it silver white like frost. The young man looked at his wife and said, 'You remind me of a woman I met many years ago. She too had skin as white as the moonlight.'

'Who was she?' asked Yuki.

'Her name was Yuki-onna,' answered the young man. 'It means snow woman.'

'Tell me about her,' said Yuki.

'I promised I would never tell a living soul what happened that night,' said the man. 'But it was all a long time ago. A friend and I were caught in a snow storm and took shelter in an old hut. During the night the snow spirit came. She breathed death on my companion but spared me when I promised never to tell I had seen her. I have told no-one until today.'

'And you think that your promise no longer stands because it was made a long time ago?' asked Yuki, harshly, and as she spoke her appearance changed.

She turned cold as ice and white as frost. She stood up and pointed a long finger at him, like a splinter of ice.

'If it were not for my children, I would kill you,' she said. 'Instead I shall leave. I cannot stay with someone who has broken a promise,' and Yuki-onna, the snow spirit, melted away until all that was left of her was a small pool of cold water on the floor.

The man never saw her again. He told no-one else of his snow spirit wife; afraid that she would breath her icy breath on him or his children if he did. And he wished, how he wished, that he had kept the promise made all those years before.

I suppose they would have all lived happily ever after if the man had kept his promise. I suppose he would never have known that his wife was the strange snow spirit from the mountain. There are lots of myths containing this theme of keeping your word, because it was as important to the people of long ago, as it is today. It matters that we have people we can trust, especially people who are close to us. And it matters that our family and friends can trust us.

Dear God, help us to keep our word when we have given it. Help us to be trustworthy to our friends and family. Help us to take care with our promises, and only to make those promises we know we can keep. Amen

How the jellyfish lost its bones

Have you ever seen a jellyfish? They are strange sea creatures with soft bodies that you sometimes find washed up on the beach. But if you find them in the sea you must take care because they can sting you. The Japanese people tell wonderful stories of sea creatures. They say that all the sea creatures and even the tides used to be ruled by a fierce Dragon King called Ryujin, who lived deep in the sea. Today's story is a myth telling why the jellyfish is the curious shape it is. But as with most myths, it contains a message about how to behave.

Once upon a time when the world was new and the animals were not all as they are today, the Dragon King of the Sea lived deep beneath the waves with the Dragon Queen, his wife. They ruled all the creatures of the underwater world; the fish and the dolphins, the sea snails and corals and sponges, the seals and the whales and the sharks. All the creatures served the Dragon King and obeyed his every command. If they didn't, the Dragon King would banish them from his kingdom and send them onto dry land where they would quickly die without the sea water to keep them alive.

One day, the Dragon Queen became very ill. The Dragon King ordered all kinds of special foods and delicacies to be given to the queen in order to make her well again, but nothing she was given could tempt her appetite.

'She needs to eat the liver of a live monkey,' said the old octopus, who knew about such things.

'And where would I get one of those from?' asked the Dragon King. 'There are no monkeys living in my kingdom. I believe they are land creatures, although I have never seen one for myself.'

'They live in the trees by the shore,' said the octopus, knowledgeably. 'I have seen them when I have had my head above the waves.'

'Then go and get me one,' said the Dragon King. 'Bring it here and I will arrange to have its liver removed and given to the queen. Then she will be well.'

So the octopus set off for the shore, but as he went he started to worry. 'I shall have to stay out of the water until I find a monkey, and if it takes me a long time to find one I might become too dry, and then I shall become ill, and then I might die.' As he was thinking these things, a jellyfish came running by. In those days jellyfish had bones in their bodies and even more feet than the octopus.

'Jellyfish, I have a job for you,' called octopus. 'The Dragon King wants you to find him a monkey. The queen is ill and needs to eat the liver of a live monkey in order to be well again. You are the one he has chosen to do this important job, because you are brave and strong. And anyway, you have a great many feet so you will be able to run ashore quickly, catch a monkey and bring it back to the king.'

The foolish jellyfish puffed up with pride at being chosen to go on an errand for the king. After all, he was brave and strong, and it was true he had a great many feet to run with. He set off straight away, and found a small monkey playing in the branches of a tree. He caught it by its arm, and invited it to come and see the wonders of the underwater world and meet the Dragon King.

'It sounds fun,' said the monkey. 'I've never been under the sea before. But how will I get there?'

'I'll show you how to swim,' said the jellyfish. So the monkey and the jellyfish set off together to the kingdom under the sea.

'How will I get back again?' asked the monkey when they were almost there.

'Ah, well, you won't be going back,' said the jellyfish, and he told the monkey about the Dragon Queen's illness and how she could only get better if she were to eat the liver of a live monkey.

'You mean I'm going to be eaten?' he asked, horrified.

'Well, I don't suppose she is going to eat all of you,' said the jellyfish. 'She only needs your liver!' but the monkey realised what danger he was in and quickly thought of a plan.

'Oh jellyfish, I am so glad you've told me why I am going to see the Dragon King. But you see, the visit will be a waste of time, because I do not have my liver with me. Oh no. I don't carry it about all the time. It's far too heavy. I normally leave it hanging in my tree back on the shore. We can either go and visit the Dragon King without it, or we could, I suppose, turn back and go and get it. What do you think?'

The jellyfish was quite sure that the Dragon King would be angry with him if he took back a monkey with no liver, so he agreed to swim back to shore with the monkey and collect the missing liver. They went back, and the monkey made a great to-do of searching in his tree.

'It's been stolen,' he shouted. 'Someone has stolen my liver. I left it right here in this tree and now it's gone!'

'What shall we do,' cried the jellyfish.

'You must go back and tell the Dragon King what's happened, and I shall stay here and search for my liver,' said the monkey. So that's what they did.

'You silly spineless cowardly creature,' shouted the Dragon King to the jellyfish who was shivering with fear. 'Can't you see you've been tricked? He told you that lost liver story so that you would take him back to shore and so that he could escape. You're as silly as a quivering jelly, no wonder they call you jellyfish. Well, squishy fishy! Since you are called a jelly, you can be a jelly,' and the Dragon King shook him and shook him until his bones turned to dust and his feet dropped off.

'And as for you!' shouted the Dragon King to the octopus, who was slinking away so that he wouldn't get into trouble. 'None of this would have happened if you'd done as I asked you, instead of trying to get someone else to do your work for you. Anyway, I should never have listened to you in the first place. The queen is well again now, so all that talk of live livers was rubbish. I shall never listen to your advice again,' and the Dragon King set the octopus's arms waving for the rest of time as a warning for other creatures not to listen to him.

And the monkey? Well he sat in his tree and chattered to the world about the day he narrowly escaped being taken to the kingdom of the Sea Dragon. In fact, his great great grandchildren still talk about it today!

Do you suppose the jellyfish was really shaken and shaken until its bones turned to dust and its feet dropped off? I don't think so either, but it makes a good story. Did you find the other messages in the story? What about the way the octopus tried to get someone else to do the work he was asked to do? And what do you think of the way the jellyfish gossiped to the monkey and told him of the Dragon King's plans? Do you think he was right to do that? And what do you think about the violent way the Dragon King punished the jellyfish and octopus?

Stories like these old myths are very thought-provoking – that means they make us think about the hidden messages. It's good to think things through and make up our own minds about what we believe.

Dear God, help us to be responsible and reliable when we are asked to do things at home and at school. Help us to do the jobs that are ours, even when we don't want to or when we would rather be doing something else. Help us always to do our best. Amen

Theme 3: Legends

The sword in the stone

Do you know what a legend is? It's a story that's been passed down through the years, of a person who might have lived at one time; a person who was kind or considerate or generous or helpful, or who had some other special qualities or strength of character.

Sometimes the stories can be a bit far-fetched, and often over the years the stories get mixed up with other stories, but in almost every legend there's at least one little bit of the story that's true. It's up to the listener to decide which bit!

Some of the best known legends are about King Arthur and the Knights of the Round Table. King Arthur is said to have lived about fifteen hundred years ago. He was brave and bold and stood up for truth and right. But the first of King Arthur's legends tells of someone else trying to become king, by lying and cheating.

Here's what happened.

The boy, Arthur, stood in front of the sword in the stone and wondered what to do. He looked around him. No-on was about, they were all at the tournament. He should be there too, but his older brother, Sir Kay, had sent Arthur back to the house for his sword, which he'd forgotten. But the house was locked; Arthur could not get his brother's sword. Maybe if he borrowed this one, his brother would be pleased with him. It didn't seem to belong to anyone, and it was a very beautiful sword. Arthur made up his mind. He quickly pulled the sword from the stone and ran back to find the others.

As soon as Sir Kay saw the sword, he knew it was the one from the stone in the churchyard. No-one knew where it had come from. It had suddenly appeared on the day that Merlin the dream-reader had called all the knights together to tell them that the old king, Uther Pendragon, was dead.
It was a strangely beautiful sword, but even stranger were the words written in gold on the stone underneath it. 'Whoever pulls this sword from the stone, is by right of birth the King of all England.'

Sir Kay knew that many knights had already tried to pull the sword from the stone, in the hope that they might become king, but so far none had succeeded. In fact the highlight of the tournament that afternoon was to be when all the brave and strong knights were to try again to pull out the sword. But Sir Kay saw that the prize could be his, with a bit of lying and cheating. He grabbed the beautiful jewelled sword and ran to Sir Ector, his father.
'Look Father!' he shouted, waving the sword up high. 'I have the sword from the stone. I pulled it out only a few minutes ago and I came straight to you to show you. I have the sword, so I must be the rightful King of all England.'

Sir Kay expected his father to be joyfully excited at the news of his eldest son becoming King of England, but Sir Ector turned pale.

'Did anyone see you draw the sword from the stone?' he asked.

'No Sir,' said Kay.

'Come with me,' said Sir Ector, and he led Kay and Arthur back to the churchyard and the stone that had held the sword.

'You must obey me and tell me truthfully how you came to have the sword,' he said to Kay.

'I came here and... No, I took hold... I mean I pulled the sword... and...' but Kay could not look his father in the eye and lie to him.

'I'm sorry,' he said. 'It wasn't me. My brother gave me the sword. It was Arthur who gave it to me.

'I didn't mean to steal it,' said Arthur, who was sure he was going to get into trouble. 'I only borrowed it. Kay left his sword in the house and sent me back to get it. The house was locked and I couldn't get in. I didn't want him to be without a sword for the tournament, so I borrowed this one. I was going to put it back, honestly!'

'Put it back now,' said Sir Ector, quietly.

Arthur did as he was asked.

'Kay, pull out the sword,' said Sir Ector to his son.

Kay took hold of the jewelled handle of the sword and pulled. He tugged with all his strength but he could not move the sword from the stone. Then Sir Ector tried to pull out the sword. He was unable to do so.

'Arthur, take the sword from the stone,' he said.

Arthur gripped the handle and pulled out the sword as easily as if it had been in its leather sheath. As he did so, Sir Ector and Sir Kay knelt on the ground before him.

'What are you doing?' asked Arthur. 'Why are you kneeling?'

'Because you are the king,' said Sir Ector. 'The sword is magic, and can only be pulled from the stone by the one who is rightfully King of England.'

'But I am not the King of England!' laughed Arthur. 'I am Arthur, your son, Kay's brother.'

'No,' said Sir Ector sadly. 'You are not my son. Until just now I did not know whose child you were. But now I understand. Your father was King Uther Pendragon, the king of all England. You are his son and the throne of England is yours by rights.'

'But I am *your* child,' protested Arthur.

'My child, but not by birth,' said Sir Ector. 'When you were a baby, Merlin the magician brought you to me and asked me to bring you up as my own child. He would not tell me who your real father was, only that it was unsafe for you to stay with him, and that one day everything would become clear. That day has come. You have drawn the sword Excalibur from the stone, and in doing so you have proved beyond doubt that you are the King of England.'

And so it was, that Arthur, still only a boy and not yet a knight, was declared King of all England, for, try as they might, no-one else could pull the magnificent sword from the stone.

Later, King Arthur, with his half-brother Sir Kay at his right hand, Merlin the dream-reader at his left, and his wife Queen Guinevere, began to bring peace to England. King Arthur founded the Knights of the Round Table in Camelot, and whenever a knight became worthy of a place there, Merlin the magician would make his name appear on his seat at the table. King Arthur and the famous knights Sir Galahad and Sir Lancelot, together with all the other knights, had many exciting adventures as they tried to bring peace and justice to England all those years ago.

I wonder what would have happened in the story if Kay had stuck to his lie about pulling out the sword himself? I suppose Arthur might never have been declared king, except that I think Merlin the magician, or even the magic sword itself might have brought the truth out some other way. That's the funny thing about truth, it usually comes out in the end, no matter how much you try to hide it. Have you noticed that?

It's interesting in the story to notice that Kay didn't get into trouble for trying to cheat about the sword. He was forgiven because he told the truth in the end, but I think he'd have got himself into much more serious trouble if he'd continued with the lie. What do you think?

Help us Lord, to be honest in word and deed. Help us not to lie to people, even if we think it's going to get us out of trouble. Help us to know that lying makes things worse. Help us not to cheat. Help us to listen to our conscience and to do what we know is right. Amen

Robin escapes

Do you ever think that things are unfair? Every so often life can seem to be unfair, no matter how fair we try to make things in our families and school and community. But if you think things are unfair now, you should have lived in Britain in the time of Robin Hood! In those days you could be thrown in prison or even hanged for just one small offence, especially if you were poor. The rich landowners, like the Sheriff of Nottingham, held all the power and they often tried to make sure that the poor people had no rights of any kind. They treated the poor very unfairly.

Robin Hood and his band of men, together with Maid Marian, stood up for the rights of the poor people. They became outlaws - they lived outside the law of the land - and they sometimes even stole from the rich to give to the poor.

Here's the legend of how Robin Hood became an outlaw.

Robin looked at the small brown dog.

'She's no good to me,' said the farmer. 'She's the last of the litter and too weak to live. Take her into the forest and leave her there to die.'

'Can I keep her?' asked Robin. 'I'll look after her and care for her until she's stronger. She won't be a nuisance, I promise.'

'All right,' said the farmer. 'But don't let her near the King's deer in the forest.'

Robin took the dog to the hut he lived in at the edge of the forest. Robin lived on his own there now, even though he was still just a boy. Up until a few months ago his father had been head gamekeeper of Sherwood Forest, but one day when he'd gone to complain about some unfairness to the Sheriff of Nottingham, the Sheriff had refused to listen and had him thrown into prison and then hanged. Soon afterwards, Robin's mother had died, leaving Robin to fend for himself.

Robin looked after the young dog well, and named her Trickett. She soon grew fit and strong and Robin and she became the best of friends.

One evening Robin and Trickett were walking along a track in the great forest when they saw some strangers coming the other way. Trickett stopped and stiffened, as though she sensed trouble.

'I see a way of making a bit of money here,' whispered one of the men to the others. 'Let's turn him in to the king's foresters and say he's been stealing deer. They'll reward us well for the information.'

The strangers approached Robin.

'Good Evening,' said the leader of the group. 'That's a good looking dog you've got there. It's a good hunter I'll bet?'

'She's fast and can hunt rabbits well,' agreed Robin, pleased that the men were admiring Trickett.

'If she can hunt rabbits, she can no doubt hunt deer,' said the stranger.

'No,' answered Robin. 'We never hunt deer.'

'Then what are you doing in the king's deer forest?' snapped the stranger.

'I live here,' said Robin, suddenly feeling afraid.

'You're stealing deer with your hunting dog,' snarled the man. 'You're coming with us, you and your dog; there's money in this for us!' and before Robin could do anything about it, the men had grabbed him and Trickett and dragged them off to see the foresters.

'Stealing the king's deer, eh?' said the forester. 'It's a crime punishable by death. You'll appear in court in ten days' time and tell your tale to the judge. For now, get out!' and he pushed Robin to the door. Robin reached for Trickett but the forester grabbed her first.

'The dog stays with me,' he said, and kicked her into the corner of the room where she lay, cowering.

Ten days later Robin went to the court which was set up in an old barn. The strangers were there, and the forester they'd taken Robin to see. He had tied a rope round Trickett's neck and was holding her tight. The judge was the chief forester, who listened to Robin's side of the story, then heard what the other foresters had to say.

'It's quite clear you're guilty,' he said. 'You were in the forest intending to steal the king's deer. But you will not steal from the king again. I sentence you to death. Neither will your dog steal the kings' deer again. It'll have its front paws cut off so that it can't run.'

'NO!' shouted Robin. And he leapt across the barn, grabbed Trickett and fled through the door before anyone had a chance to stop him.

'Seize him!' called the judge. The foresters and bystanders, strangers and onlookers poured through the barn door to catch Robin. And in that throng of people lay Robin's salvation, for whilst they were pushing and jostling to get through the door, he and Trickett were off and away, over the fields, into the forest, criss-crossing the streams so that no-one could pick up their scent. Eventually, they reached a disused Abbey church, where they hid until the hue and cry had died down.

'Well Trickett,' said Robin. 'The law is unfair and mean and unjust. We cannot live within the law, so we'll live without it! We'll be outlaws. But we'll do what we can to change the unfairness of the way they treat people like us.'

The next night, Robin and Trickett journeyed deep into the forest and met other outlaws, people like them who had been unfairly treated by the rich and powerful landowners. Together they lived in the great forest, taking no notice of the law, but always working to help the poor, the needy, the weak, and the people who had been treated unfairly.

Robin Hood and his Merry Men had many adventures in and around Sherwood Forest. The legends are so famous they've been turned into books and videos, films and television programmes.

But I wonder what you think of Robin! He lived as an outlaw, he lived like a highwayman. He sometimes stole from the rich to give to the poor. Stealing was as wrong then as it is now, so do you think he was right to do it? And I wonder what you think about the way he and Trickett were treated at the beginning of the story. It's a good legend, because it gives us lots to think about.

Dear Lord, help us to try to be fair in everything we do. Help us to listen to other people's points of view. Help us to care for those who are smaller, or weaker, or less advantaged than us. Amen

Oona McCool and the Giant Cahoolin

There are many Irish legends about giants who fought fierce and terrible battles with each other. But one of the legends is different from all the rest because it isn't about killing and slaughtering; it's about a giant's wife who wins the battle not by fighting but by thinking! Oona is by far the cleverest person in the story.

Oona McCool was brave and strong, exactly how a giant's wife should be, which was just as well since her husband Finn was as cowardly as custard, but she had also a good head on her shoulders, and she could think!

The Giant Cahoolin was a bully, and had already fought with and beaten every other giant in the whole of Ireland, and now there was only Finn McCool left to fight. But Finn was difficult to catch because he was always running away.

One day Finn was sitting outside his house on the top of the mountain when he heard a rumbling on the other side of Ireland. He ran inside, trembling.

'It's the Giant Cahoolin,' he cried to his wife. 'He's on his way to beat me up.'

'Stay cool!' said Oona McCool. 'It's brains not brawn that counts. We'll beat him, but not with fisticuffs. You just leave everything to me,' and she put her ear to the ground to find out how long they had until the Giant Cahoolin should arrive.

'An hour and a half and three strides,' she said. 'Time enough!' and she got out her baking things and started to make potato cakes. But what cakes! She made them as big as cartwheels, and she hid an iron baking griddle inside three of them. Then she baked them to perfection and set them on the windowsill to cool. Just then Oona McCool felt the ground shake.

'He's here,' she said. 'Quick, put these on and climb into the baby's cradle.'

She handed Finn a long white frilly nightie and a lacy bonnet, and picked the baby out of the cradle and hid him in the cupboard. 'Now pull the blankets up around you and don't say a word.' No sooner had Finn got into the cradle than there was a thunderous knock on the door.

'I know you're in there,' shouted the Giant Cahoolin. 'Come out and meet me like a giant, not a miserable mousy man.'

Oona McCool went to the door.

'To be sure there's no-one here but me and the baby,' she said, waving her arm in the direction of the cradle. 'But you can come in and take a cup of tea with me, if you'd like.' The Giant Cahoolin stepped into the house.

'That's a fine baby you have there, Mrs McCool,' he said. 'I wonder where I might find his father?'

'Oh, what a pity you've missed him,' said Oona McCool. 'He set out only this morning to look for a giant by the name of Cahoolin, and I wouldn't like to be in his shoes when my Finn finds him,' she added. 'For my Finn McCool is a giant and a half. Just look at his baby here. To be sure what a giant he is to have a baby like this one!'

The Giant Cahoolin looked into the cradle at the enormous baby squashed into it. He noticed the whiskers on the baby's chin and the gigantic fingers curled round the top of the blanket.

'Smile for the nice visitor,' cooed Oona McCool to the baby, and the baby obliged, showing its enormous teeth.

The Giant Cahoolin began to feel uneasy. If this was the baby, what indeed was the father like. Perhaps he'd been misinformed when he'd heard that Finn McCool was a shivering coward.

'Now, can I be offering you a pot of tea and some cake?' said Oona to the Giant Cahoolin. 'But I wonder if you would mind doing something for me first of all? Would you just be going outside to turn the house around to face the morning sun? Finn usually does that each morning, but he was in such a hurry to go out this morning and find Cahoolin, that he must have clean forgotten. I'll make the tea whilst you do that,' and she smiled at the Giant Cahoolin.

He went outside and tried to turn the house. What a struggle! Cahoolin heaved and pushed and pulled at the house. Bit by bit he managed to turn it on its foundations, but by the time the house was facing the sun, Cahoolin was exhausted. And to think that Finn McCool turned the house every day! He must surely be stronger than Cahoolin thought. Yet when Finn-in-the-cradle felt the house move, he shivered and shook with fright.

'If he can do that to the house, think what he can do to me,' he whispered to Oona.

'Stay cool, McCool!' said Oona. 'It's brains not brawn that counts. Lie still and don't talk.'

Whilst Cahoolin was busy turning the house, Oona was setting the table. Cups as big as barrels and spoons like spades. Plates as big as the moon for the potato cakes with the iron griddles inside.

She made the tea and called Cahoolin in.

'I'm sorry it was a struggle for you to move the house,' she said. 'You see my Finn does it so easily I never thought it might be difficult for you. But never mind. Sit you down and have a cake. They're Finn McCool's favourites.'

The potato cakes indeed smelled delicious, and the Giant Cahoolin was hungry. He opened his mouth wide and took a great bite of cake.

'Yeoww,' he howled as he spat out his two front teeth. 'Whatever is in this cake?'

'Well, upon my soul, it's potato and flour and a little bit of butter,' said Oona McCool. 'Don't tell me you don't like my potato cakes! Finn and the baby here love them,' and she gave a cake to Finn-in-the-cradle, and he gobbled it greedily.

'Here, try another,' she said to Cahoolin, who took another cake from the plate and bit into it.

'Yeoww,' he howled, and spat out two more teeth.

'Well to be sure, I don't understand it,' said Oona. 'You must have softer teeth than a baby. The little one here eats my cakes all day long. Here! You give him one to eat,' and she gave Cahoolin a potato cake to give to the baby.

Cahoolin carried it to the cradle. He held it out for the baby to eat... and Finn jumped out of the cradle snapping his teeth at the Giant Cahoolin, who ran out of the house and down the mountainside, declaring that he never ever wanted to meet Finn McCool, if that was just his baby.

Oona and Finn laughed and laughed and then took the griddles out of the cakes and ate them for dinner. After that, Finn was never scared of Cahoolin again, or at least, not really scared.

Oona was right when she said that it's brains not brawn that counts. She meant that thinking things out is much more important than using fists and feet to settle an argument.

I hope you sort out your difficulties by using your brains, and not by resorting to fighting.

Dear God, we know we will not always like everyone we meet, but help us to learn to get along with the people in our family and neighbourhood and school. When we have disagreements with people, help us to think of ways of putting things right; help us not to use fighting as a means of sorting out arguments. Amen

December

Theme 1: Awe and wonder

The rabbi and the emperor

When was the last time you looked at something in the natural world, and thought 'WOW!'?

I hope it was recently, but I bet it was a while ago. You see, we all get so wrapped up in our everyday lives, we are all so busy, that we forget to appreciate the spectacular world around us. And sometimes, we become so used to watching things on TV and video, that we forget to appreciate things in the real world.

What was the last thing you looked at that was amazing? My most recent things were:

- a beautiful red sky one morning when I was coming to school,
- a spectacular double rainbow that I saw when I was out in the country. It stretched from one side of a valley to the other,
- the sound of pebbles on a stony beach the last time I went to the seaside. When I walked on the pebbles they sounded hollow and they echoed as though they were hundreds of years deep.

Our world is full of amazing sights and sounds. In today's story, someone didn't know about God's power in the natural world.

There was once an emperor who went travelling through his empire to meet his people.

On his travels he met a rabbi, and they began to talk.

'I've heard about your God,' said the emperor. 'And I want to know more. Tell me about him! Is he as powerful as me? Does he have as much land in his kingdom as I have in mine?'

'Those questions are easy to answer,' said the rabbi. 'My God is more powerful than any man, even an emperor; and all the land there is, belongs to him.'

'That's impossible,' said the emperor. 'He doesn't own my land, and I own the biggest empire in the world! And I don't see how he can be more powerful than me. If I order something to be done, it is done immediately. For example, if I wanted that mountain moving over there, my servants would move it. Even if it took twenty years, it would be done because I ordered it.'

'You may be an emperor,' said the rabbi. 'But you are only a man. God is more powerful than any man.'

'I want to see your God for myself,' said the emperor. 'Take me to him and let me meet him. I have questions I want to ask him.'

'I can't do that,' said the rabbi. 'God is so powerful that no-one can see him. Not even the emperor of the biggest empire in the world. Not even you!'

At this the emperor grew angry.

'How dare you not obey me!' he said. 'I *order* you to take me to see your God!'

'I can't do that,' said the rabbi again. 'No-one can see God.'

'I *command* you to take me to your God,' shouted the emperor.

Again the rabbi said, 'I'm sorry. I can't do that.'

'Then I shall have you executed for not obeying my command,' said the emperor angrily, and he called for his soldiers to kill him.

But before the soldiers had chance to seize the rabbi, he asked the emperor for one last request before he died.

'I want to show you something,' said the rabbi. 'Will you come with me?'

'Is it a trick? Are you going to try to escape?' asked the emperor.

'No,' answered the rabbi. 'I just want you to come with me. Your soldiers can kill me when I've shown you something, if you still want them to.'

The rabbi took the emperor outside into the bright sunshine. He walked to the edge of the cliff where the sea was beating against the rocks.

'Look at the sea,' he said to the emperor. 'Can you see how powerful it is?'

'Of course,' said the emperor.

'Then show me its power,' said the rabbi.

'I can't do that!' said the emperor. 'No-one can see the power of the sea.'

'Well, if that's too difficult, just show me one single drop of water. Point one out to me. Go on!' said the rabbi.

'You know I can't do that,' said the emperor. 'No-one can point to just one drop of water in the whole sea.'

'Then look up there,' said the rabbi, and he pointed to the sky. 'Show me the wind.'

'You can't *see* the wind,' said the emperor. 'You can only see what the wind does, but you can't actually see it.'

'Then show me the stars,' said the rabbi.

'But it's the middle of the day!' said the emperor. 'You can't see the stars when it's sunny!'

'Well how do you know they're there?' asked the rabbi.

'Because you just *know*,' answered the emperor, who was beginning to get annoyed again because he couldn't understand why the rabbi was asking him these things.

'Can you see the sun?' asked the rabbi.

'Of course I can see the sun,' said the emperor. Then he added, 'But you can't look at it. If you look at the sun you could be blinded because the sun is so powerful.'

'Exactly!' said the rabbi, triumphantly. 'I knew you'd understand eventually!'

'Understand what?' asked the emperor, who didn't understand at all.

'There are all these things out here – the sea, the wind, the stars, the sun, they're all here yet you've not been able to show me anything that I've asked to see. But perhaps they're all too big! Let's try something smaller! Can you see that tiny beetle over there?'

'I can see one on that rock,' said the emperor.

'It doesn't matter which one,' said the rabbi. 'Any one will do. Show me its cells. Show me the genes that make it a beetle and not a mouse, or a lizard.'

'I can't do that, you know I can't,' said the emperor.

'And I can't show you God,' said the rabbi. 'All the things I have asked you to show me are only servants of God, so just imagine how powerful God is. He is so powerful that no-one can see him.'

'I think I am beginning to understand,' said the emperor. 'I'm sorry I ordered you to be killed – I thought you were disobeying me, but now I see that you were trying to make me understand how powerful God is,' and the emperor instructed his soldiers to leave.

The emperor realised that compared with God, he was not powerful at all. If you are lucky enough to see a huge waterfall, or the sea in bad weather, or a sunset when you're in a plane above the clouds, you, too, might begin to understand the power and wonder of the natural world.

Help us, Lord, to be aware of the wonderful world around us, and to find time to appreciate the beauty of the world. Help us to do what we can to look after the world, so that future generations can enjoy it too. Amen

Angel Falls

Have you ever seen a waterfall? They're amazing! All that water, gallons and gallons of it, pouring over the edge of a rock, never running out because there's always more. All that noise, as the water empties itself into the pool or river below. All that spray! Sometimes the spray is so heavy that you can't see through it; it's like looking into fog. But at other times, if the light is right, you see wonderful rainbows in the spray.

Powerful, spectacular, natural wonders like waterfalls, always set me thinking. Where does all that water come from? Why does it never run out? Why is it that there's so much water, yet you can't watch one bit of it and follow its journey to the bottom, because it's all moving so fast, so strongly, so fiercely. How did the waterfall get there in the first place? And what would happen to something that got swept over the edge of the waterfall?

In today's story, someone found a waterfall quite by chance, when he was looking for something else.

Jimmy Angel was an American airman. In 1935 he was flying his plane over the mountains of Venezuela, looking for gold. The mountains in this part of the world are rich in gold and diamonds, and the gold sometimes gets swept down from the mountains in the fast flowing rivers. But the area is so huge, and the rainforest so thick and dense, that in 1935 it was not possible to send expeditions by land to search for the gold. Air searches were more practical. Jimmy Angel and his crew used to fly over the mountains and the rainforest looking for the tell-tale signs of gold deposits on the river beds.

On this particular day, Jimmy Angel was flying over Devil Mountain. It was a huge, craggy, rocky mountain, named after the Devil because it was so dangerous and wild. Jimmy knew that the mountain was at least 65 million years old, and had been formed when the molten rock at the centre of the earth pushed its way to the earth's crust. He looked down at the mountain top which was worn and weathered with time. He could see deep cracks and crevices, fissures and pits. He could see huge pools of water which had collected in the cracks and pits, and in places the water spilled over the edge of the mountain in gigantic waterfalls. But Jimmy Angel couldn't see any gold.

He flew over the mountain again.

'Nothing doing!' he called to the crew. 'There's nothing here.'

'Just a minute!' shouted Bill above the noise of the engine. 'Down there. I think I saw something. Take her down a bit further.'

Jimmy flew the plane down the side of the mountain and circled it over the rainforest below.

'Down there!' said Bill again. 'Follow the line of the river. Go down a bit lower.'

'I can't take her down any lower. It's not safe,' said Jimmy.

'Just a bit lower. I think I saw gold in the riverbed.'

Jimmy edged the plane a little lower. The crew peered out of the windows.

'No!' said Bill. 'Sorry. It must have just been the sun glinting on the water. Take her up again.'

Jimmy pulled on the controls to bring the plane up and out of the mountain's shadow, but it was too late, they were too low, the climb was too steep. The engine sputtered and stalled. The plane crashed.

It lay in pieces strewn across the rainforest. Part of it landed in a swamp. The tail broke off and plunged to the forest floor. But somehow, amazingly, unbelievably, all the crew were alive.

The thick, impenetrable jungle lay all around them. Ahead of them sat the bulk of Devil Mountain, impossible to climb. To the right was the river, too deep, too fast-flowing to cross. They had only two choices. They either stayed where they were and died. Or they attempted to find their way out of the jungle and walk to safety.

'Well, there isn't a choice, is there?' said Jimmy Angel. 'Because we're not going to sit here and wait to die.'

They collected the things they thought they would need from the broken plane – a groundsheet, a waterproof cover, some chocolate bars, knives, rope, an axe. And they set off to walk through the rainforest. Trees and creepers blocked their way. There was no path, no way through. They had to cut a way through, with the axe and the knives. The air was hot and damp. The undergrowth was so dense that as soon as they had cut an opening big enough to crawl through, the jungle seemed to grow again and close in on them. It could take as long as a whole afternoon to move forward just a few metres. And all the time there were the cries of wild animals, the buzz and sting of insects and the slither of snakes.

At night they slept on the groundsheet on the forest floor, with a waterproof cover over them. They ate the chocolate, square by square to make it last. They struggled through the jungle for eleven days. And then they saw it. It was the most magnificent, spectacular, awe-inspiring sight any of them had ever seen. The memory of it would stay with them for the rest of their lives.

It was a waterfall, but a waterfall the like of which none of them had ever seen before. It spilled over the edge of Devil Mountain and cascaded down onto a rocky ledge over 800 metres below. Then it fizzed and bubbled into the air in a boiling frenzy before falling another 200 metres into a huge pool at the foot of the mountain. Over one thousand metres of waterfall, it was eighteen times higher than the world famous Niagara Falls.

The men stared at it. Words were not enough to express their feelings at seeing something so impressive, so extraordinary, so staggeringly remarkable. But each man was thinking his own thoughts about beauty and about God and about the wondrous world in which they lived. And the men knew that, even though they were lost, even though their lives were in danger, seeing this phenomenon was worth it. They knew that although they had not found gold, they had found something much more valuable and rare and special.

Eventually one of them spoke. 'Where is it? What is it? I don't remember seeing a fall like this marked on any map?'

'Have you thought that it's maybe not on any map?' said Jimmy. 'Have you thought that it's probably been here for millions of years and we are the first people, ever, to see it? Have you thought that up until now only God knew it was here?'

The men camped by the waterfall that night so that they could enjoy its splendour for as long as possible. Then they set off again to find their way out of the rainforest.

Jimmy Angel and his friends reached safety and told everyone of the amazing waterfall. He was right when he said it wasn't on any map. The wonderful waterfall didn't even have a name. The waterfall is marked on maps now though. It's called Angel Falls, after Jimmy and the men who discovered it. It's the world highest waterfall. It is still surrounded by impenetrable rain forest and can only be seen from the air, or sometimes from the river, during the few weeks of the year when a boat can navigate the water.

Jimmy Angel and his friends learned during their time in the rainforest, the jungle, that there are things is this world worth more than money or gold. They were able to appreciate something beautiful and remarkable even though their lives were in danger. They were able to understand a little of the awe and wonder in the natural world.

Dear God, please help us always to be ready to notice the wonders of our world. Help us to appreciate the glory and the value of the natural world. Help us never to harm our planet but to do what we can to keep it safe for the future. Amen

Planet Earth

I'm going to describe something to you, and I'd like you to see if you can guess what it is.

It's small and round like a marble, but the most beautiful marble you have ever seen. It sparkles blue like a jewel and is laced around with swirling white. It shimmers and shines and glitters and gleams like a fragile delicate Christmas tree ornament, and it hangs in the blackness of space.

What is it? Yes it's our Earth. It's the world. That's how our world looked to one of the American astronauts who saw it for the first time from his spacecraft. Just imagine seeing our world from the distance of space! Space travel is still very new, but perhaps as this millennium moves forward, mankind will travel much further into space and will begin to explore it, understand it, and make maps of it; just as people explored and mapped the Earth during the early part of the last millennium.

And who knows? You may be part of that exploration and discovery!

I wonder what it's like to travel into space? Today, I'd like us to travel there in our imagination. So, let's go on a space journey!

The preparations are finished and all our training is completed. We are fit and ready for our space journey. We walk slowly towards our spacecraft, looking round us. We don't want to miss anything so we notice everything around us very carefully. We see how green the grass is and how bright the flowers are. We feel the wind on our faces and we smell the air. It smells of a mixture of flowers and fresh air and fuel. We see the television crews and the spectators standing waving behind the barriers, and we wave back. We feel a little scared. After all, space travel is dangerous. We might not come back. This might be the last time we stand on our Earth.

We look at the rocket, and at the space module inside it that will be our home for the next few weeks. It looks so small. Can it really carry us safely round the moon and back?

There are people all around us, space engineers checking instruments and dials, making last minute adjustments, then suddenly it is time for them to leave and the hatch door clangs shut. We are alone. Completely alone in the spacecraft.

The countdown starts. Ten. Nine. Eight. We hear the power and vibration of the engines. Five. Four. Three. Two. One. Lift-off. And the rocket starts to move. Not with a great rush as we might expect, but slowly, majestically; technology overcoming the laws of gravity.

Suddenly, we are busy. There are jobs to be done. There's no time to talk or to gaze out of the window. We spend a lot of time unpacking things then packing them again, because in space, where it is weightless, everything must be tidied away in lockers or containers, otherwise things will float around and get in the way and be dangerous.

But we can't avoid looking out of the window.

We see swirls of white cloud and glimpses of land spread out like a map. And we see brilliant blue sea. So much sea that we think our planet should be called Water instead of Earth. Each time we look out, our blue planet is a little smaller, until eventually we have travelled so far and Earth is so small that we can hold up one thumb and make it disappear. We can obliterate it from space. That's how fragile our planet is.

Our spacecraft separates from the rocket. Our bodies can feel the roaring power of the rocket as it pushes our module into orbit round the moon. We accelerate to 25,000 miles an hour. We know that there are only the thin walls of the capsule separating us from the cold emptiness of space. We know that if anything goes wrong, we will die; but everything is going according to plan. And there is work to do. We must check the instruments, analyse the data and report back by computer link to Earth.

But we can't help looking out of the window.

It's still there. The beautiful blue sparkling spinning Earth, hanging in black space, with no strings or wires to hold it up. The space around our blue planet is deep black; blackness deeper than we've ever seen, yet at the same time bright with sunlight. But the sunlight falls into the blackness; there's nothing for it to light up – except our Earth which glitters and shines. It looks so round in the darkness. And so alone. And so small.

When we are on the Earth it seems so big. The distances between one place and another seem so great. A few hundred years ago people thought our planet was enormous. But now, looking at it from the distance of space, we realise in surprise and disbelief just how small and fragile it is.

When we first left Earth, we all pointed to our own countries as we saw them becoming smaller. Then we pointed out the five great continents. But now all we see is one Earth. One planet. One nation. The lines of the individual countries are invisible from up here. The scars of national boundaries are gone, and we are aware of only one Earth. A fragile Earth. An Earth we must care for and look after.

We realise that we all belong to that small blue planet. All the people who lived before, who live now, and who will live in the future; all the black people, white people, old people, young people, fat, thin, clever, rich, poor; all the people there could possibly ever be, all belong to that one family who live on the small blue planet.

But enough thinking and gazing and day-dreaming! There's work to be done. Check the instruments, fill in the data on the computer, report back to mission control.

But we just can't help looking out of the window.

The spacecraft rotates as it travels, and our window becomes like a cinema screen showing an ever changing picture. First there's darkness filled with stars, millions of stars, more than we've ever seen before. Then the sun glides past, then the moon swims by, then the earth sparkles past the window. And then the parade starts all over again, like an action replay on television; stars, sun, moon, earth, stars, sun, moon, earth. On and on for infinity.

We wonder where it all came from. Where it's all going. Why it's there. We don't know the answers, but we know that every time we look out of the spacecraft window, we feel awe and wonder, joy, curiosity and amazement. And we become aware of the power of God.

But, we're gazing again! Back to work!

All too soon it's time to start the preparations for our return to Earth.

The engines thrust us out of the moon's orbit. The Earth grows larger before our eyes. We enter the earth's atmosphere and hear the wind rushing past the windshield. The pressure grows and pushes us back into our seats. We look through the window and see orange threads of flame burning past. Then, as we enter the thicker layers of the atmosphere, the spacecraft bumps and jolts as though we're in a cart driving over cobblestones. We hear the engine for the soft landing start up; then thud, we hit the ground and roll over. The hatch opens and we see sky and human faces peering in at us, all talking at once.

We're home!

Our arms and legs and bodies feel heavy, as though the earth is sitting on our shoulders, weighing us down. But it's good to be back.

Hello Earth! You're looking big again! But we've seen how small and fragile you really are. We'll look after you and keep you safe.

Everyone who has ever been in space, feels the same about wanting to care for our earth, our small blue planet. And everyone who has ever been in space can only look in awe and wonder at our Earth, that provides us with everything we need. Because of course, in space there is nothing; no food, water, sound, smell, light, taste, nothing. I suppose that's why it's called space!

Dear Father God, thank you for the wonders of our world. Thank you for our planet Earth, which feeds us and clothes us and provides us with all we need. Help us to appreciate the beauty of the Earth, to care for it, and to do nothing that will harm it. Help us to know that our Earth is fragile and that we have a duty to look after it. Amen

Theme 2: Star stories

Orion

Have you looked up into the sky recently, when it's dark? What could you see? If you were lucky and it was a clear frosty night, you'd have been able to see hundreds and hundreds of stars. But bad luck if you picked a cloudy night and you couldn't see anything!

December is one of the best months for star-gazing. For one thing the nights are long – December 21st is the longest night of the year – and on clear frosty nights the stars are easy to see and they show up well against the dark sky. And for another, the two groups of stars that are easiest to recognise are clearly visible in the winter. They are Orion, which is high in the sky in the south in winter evenings, and Ursa Major, sometimes called the Great Bear, or the Plough, which is in the north east.

The stars are millions of miles away from us, and from each other, but from where we are they look as though they are arranged in groups. These groups of stars are called constellations, and over the years stories have been made up about them, to try to explain how they got there.

Today's story is about Orion, the hunter, and he's one of the easiest constellations to find.

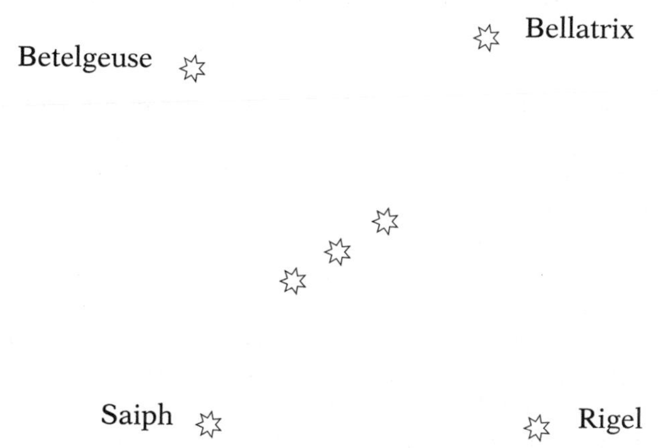

(I find it helpful to make a large plan of the positions of the stars, and refer to it as the story progresses. It's not necessary to go into detail about the individual stars' names, but many children are interested to know what they are, especially Betelgeuse, often pronounced Beetlejuice.)

Orion was one of the Gods of ancient Greece. He was a mighty hunter, and he was the most handsome God of the ancient world.

Orion had many friends, and his best friend was the Goddess Artemis, who loved him very much. The two of them were almost always together. But Orion also had enemies, and his worst enemy was Apollo, the Sun God. Apollo was the brother of Artemis and he was jealous of Orion. He was jealous of the way Orion and his sister got on so well, and he was jealous of the time that Orion and Artemis spent together. Apollo was so jealous of Orion that he spent a great deal of time planning how to get rid of him. And one day he found his chance.

Orion and Artemis went hunting on the island of Crete. Orion was the God of hunting, and Artemis was the Goddess of archery. She was incredibly skilled with a bow and arrow, and it was said that she could kill anything with an arrow, no matter how far away it was.

The day was very hot, and after Orion and Artemis had hunted some wild boar and some deer, Orion said he was too hot to do any more, and he wanted to go for a swim.

'Do you want to come with me?' he asked Artemis.

'No, I'll stay here on the beach,' said Artemis. 'You go on your own, and I'll see you after your swim.' So Orion went swimming, and Artemis started searching for shells on the beach. She didn't know that her brother, Apollo, was watching. She didn't know that he was planning a trick to get rid of Orion.

Apollo waited until Orion had swum well away from the shore. He waited until Orion was so far away from the shore that he could hardly be seen, then he walked towards Artemis.

'Hello!' he said.

'Hello,' said Artemis, somewhat surprised to see him. 'What are you doing here?'

'I thought I'd help you with some target practice,' he said. 'I bet you can't shoot an arrow to hit that pebble on the top of that rock,' and he pointed to a tiny stone on the top of a nearby cliff.

'Easy,' said Artemis, and she fitted an arrow to her bow, took aim and shot it straight and true towards the target. The pebble fell down the rock face.

'Well, yes, I suppose that was easy,' said Apollo. 'But it was easy because the pebble wasn't moving. I bet you couldn't hit a *moving* target.'

'Try me,' said Artemis, who couldn't resist a challenge.

Apollo looked around as though he was searching for something for Artemis to aim at. 'There!' he said suddenly. 'Out there on the sea. Look. There's a little black dot. You can just see it from here. I bet you can't hit *that*!'

Artemis looked. She could just make out a tiny dot almost on the horizon. There was no way she could have known it was Orion. There was no way she could see that the tiny black dot was Orion's head bobbing up above the waves as he swam.

'Easy!' she said, and she fitted an arrow to her bow. She carefully took aim. It was certainly much more difficult to hit a moving target, but she was sure she could do it. She pulled back the bow string as far as she could, carefully glanced along the sight line one more time, and shot the arrow straight and true towards the target. The tiny dot disappeared beneath the waves.

'Well done!' laughed Apollo. 'I knew you could do it. Well done!' and he left his sister and went home to gloat on his triumph.

Artemis put down her bow and arrow, and looked out to sea. She wondered where Orion was. He'd been swimming a long time now but he'd surely be back soon and she could tell him all about Apollo's challenge. Artemis waited and waited, but there was no sign of Orion. She began to feel worried. Where could he be? He was a strong swimmer, but he never stayed in the sea as long as this. She began to be really anxious.

The long afternoon wore on and still Artemis waited. Then, in the early evening, the tide turned, and the incoming waves brought with them the body of Orion.

'Oh no,' whispered Artemis, as she ran to the edge of the sea. And then her dismay turned to despair, and she saw her own arrow in Orion's head, and she realised what had happened.

She was beside herself with grief and with anger at Apollo for tricking her in the way he had. She shouted and cried, but nothing of course could bring Orion back to her.

'But I loved him.' She said to Apollo. And then she had an idea. 'I'll never let you forget how important Orion was to me,' she said. 'I'll make you remember every single day,' and she took the body of Orion up, up into the sky, and placed a star at each shoulder and another at each knee. She put three stars along his belt, and a cloud of stardust on his sword.

And there he has stayed ever since, as a reminder to everyone, and especially to Apollo, of how much Artemis loved Orion.

Perhaps you could try to find Orion in the sky on the next clear evening. But remember, never go out looking at the stars in the dark on your own, always go with an adult you trust.

When you look at the stars, you realise just how small our earth is, and how big the universe is. The night sky, with all those millions of stars, is truly spectacular. No wonder people through the ages have made up stories to try to understand it. Maybe you could try to make up a story for a star pattern you can see.

Thank you, Lord, for the beauty of the night sky. Thank you for the majesty and magnitude of it. Thank you for our planet earth, and help us to appreciate its beauty, and to do what we can to care for it. Amen

The Pleiades

If you look in the sky above and to the right of Orion's shoulder, you will see a small hazy patch, and when you look more carefully you'll see it's a cluster of stars. You can usually see seven stars – six quite bright ones and a much fainter one. This is the brightest and most famous star cluster in the sky and is called the Pleiades, or the Seven Sisters.

The story goes that the seven sisters lived in ancient Greece and were the daughters of the God Atlas, whose job it was to hold up the heavens on his shoulders.

The seven sisters were always together, and one day there were out walking when Orion saw them and began to follow them. At first it was a game and the girls laughed, but when he wouldn't stop chasing them they began to feel frightened. After all, Orion was the God of hunting and the seven sisters were afraid that he might kill them if he caught them. But the faster they ran away, the faster Orion ran after them, until, terrified, they called to the God Zeus to help them.

Zeus could see how scared they were. He could also see that Orion was just about to catch them and that there was nowhere for them to escape. So Zeus turned the seven sisters into seven white doves.

The doves flew up and up out of reach of Orion, then into the safety of the sky, but as soon as they were there Zeus turned them into seven stars. He turned the youngest sister into a pale star that could only just be seen; she was in love with an ordinary man, so couldn't be allowed to shine as brightly as her sisters, who were to marry Gods. Zeus himself was to marry the eldest of the seven sisters. Her name was Maia.

Soon after they married, Maia had a child. All new babies are special of course, but this baby was extra-special because he was a baby of the Gods. This baby was able to do the most extra-ordinary things... and this baby was naughty! He was called Hermes.

One day, when he was only just big enough to walk, he went outside by himself to play in the sunshine. He found an empty tortoise shell lying on the ground and laughed with pleasure at the sight of it. He picked it up, took it inside, drilled some holes round the edge of it, fastened some strings to the holes, and made a musical instrument. He had invented the first musical lyre, and beautiful music lay hidden inside it.

That night, when his mother was asleep, Hermes climbed out of his cradle and went out into the moonlight. He ran to the fields where Apollo's cattle were sleeping, and he stole fifty of the best animals. Then he threw his baby shoes into the river, and fastened tree bark to his feet so that no-one would be able to tell who had been walking on the soft soil. For the next hour or so, Hermes played with the cattle, driving this way and that until they were quite dizzy. Then he took them down the mountain and hid them in a cave. No-one would think of looking for them there, and no-one would know from the tracks whether they had gone up the mountain or down.

But, unbeknown to Hermes, a man working in his field by the light of the moon, saw this wonderful baby go by, driving a herd of cattle, and he could hardly believe his eyes. No-one else saw Hermes, and as soon as the sun began to rise, he ran home, slid in through the keyhole, climbed into his cradle, fell asleep, and looked as though he had been there all night.

In the morning, Apollo soon realised that fifty of his best cattle were missing. He happened to see a man working in a field and asked him if he'd seen anything.

'Yes,' said the man. 'I saw a baby wearing the strangest shoes, driving the cattle up and down, up and down, then I don't know where they went.'

As soon as he said this, Apollo knew that the baby must be Hermes. No other baby could possibly drive cattle up and down a mountainside in the middle of the night! Apollo looked at the ground to see whether the tracks gave any clue as to where the cattle might be; but they didn't.

Apollo went to Maia's house and demanded to see the baby. Maia asked him in. There lay Hermes in his cradle, fast asleep.

'You see, he can't possibly have stolen your cattle!' said Maia.

'Cattle?' said Hermes innocently, waking up at the sound of their voices. 'What's cattle? I don't know what cattle means. I've only just learned to talk and I've never heard that word before!' But Apollo didn't believe him, and insisted that they go to see Jupiter to sort it all out.

When Hermes stood in front of Jupiter's throne, he said he'd never seen any cattle, and in any case, he didn't know what they were. But as he said this, he gave Jupiter such a mischievous wink, that the great God couldn't help but laugh. Then Hermes suddenly pulled out his musical lyre from underneath his coat, and began to play such wonderful music on it that all the Gods in Olympus stopped to listen.

When Hermes had finished playing, Apollo said that the music was so good, he would forgive Hermes for stealing the cattle, and he could keep them if he wanted to. Hermes was so pleased that he gave Apollo the lyre to keep, and the two of them were the best of friends for the rest of time.

Zeus gave Hermes the job of being his messenger, to keep him out of further trouble, and he made Maia into the brightest of the group of seven sisters, so that she would always be remembered.

The Ancient Greeks were not the only people to name the star clusters and constellations, the Ancient Chinese and Japanese people made maps and named the stars too, but it is the Greek names that have been handed down to us and that are still used even today.

It's amazing to think that the same constellations were being looked at and studied all those thousands of years ago. Even stars, of course, don't live forever; they are formed and eventually they die, but in between they exist for millions of years. The next time you look at a star, just think about how long it's been there.

And speaking of time, do you realise that the stars we see now, are the same stars that the Wise Men saw in the sky when they travelled to Bethlehem that first Christmas, two thousand years ago? It's quite a thought, isn't it?

We praise you, Lord, for the stars and the planets. Help us to appreciate the size and age of the universe, and to know how small we are in comparison. We thank you for all the astronomers through the ages, who have helped us to understand the night sky. Amen.

Ursa Major

The other constellation which is easy to find in the winter sky, is The Great Bear. It has other names too; it's sometimes called the Plough, or Ursa Major. There's a smaller constellation nearby with a very similar pattern to The Great Bear, and that's called The Little Bear, or Ursa Minor.

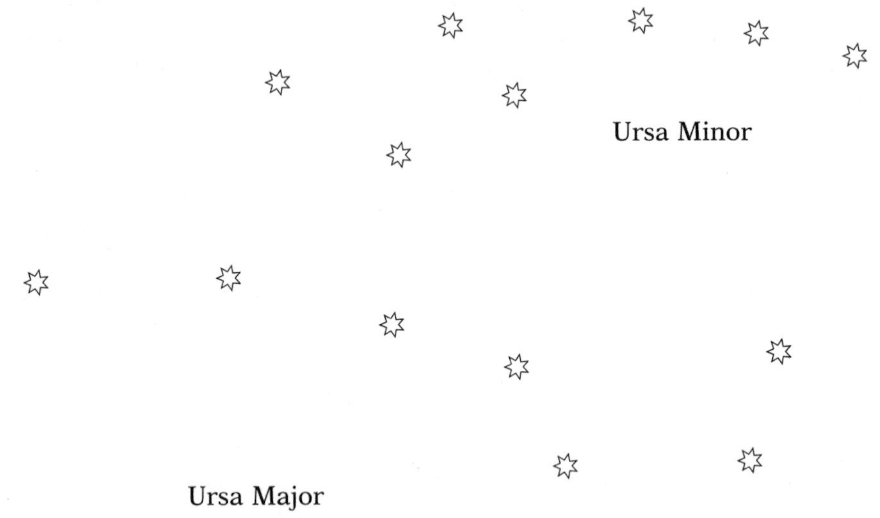

Here's the story of how they got there.

In the days of Ancient Greece, when the Gods and Goddesses lived on Mount Olympus and ruled the world, there was a Goddess called Artemis. She was a beautiful creature, shining and silver like the moon. She was the Goddess of hunting and always carried a silver bow and arrow that she could use with deadly accuracy. She never missed her target! Artemis was always accompanied by three beautiful silver-coloured hunting dogs, who could kill any animal with one snap of their jaws if Artemis ordered them to do so.

Artemis had many friends to whom she was very loyal... as long as they did what she wanted! But she was merciless and cruel if any of them angered her, and she would do anything to get her own back if they displeased her.

One day Artemis decided that she didn't want any of her friends to fall in love with any of the Gods. So when her friend Callisto fell in love with Zeus, Artemis was beside herself with rage.

'You're not to see him any more,' she shouted at Callisto. 'I forbid you to fall in love with him!'

But Callisto laughed at her. 'I shall fall in love with whom I choose,' she said. 'It has nothing to do with you! Anyway, Zeus and I already have a baby,' she added.

This news made Artemis even more angry, and she was determined to have the last word.

'I shall teach you to disobey me!' she shouted. 'I shall turn you into a bear and then you will be so ugly that no-one will love you.' And she pushed Callisto to the ground.

Callisto didn't believe her and tried to stand up, but as she did so she saw that her fingers were turning into the claws of a bear. She held up her arms to Artemis and tried to speak, to plead with her not to do this, but she could only utter a long low unhappy growl. Within minutes she had changed completely into a large brown bear, and she slunk away to hide herself in the trees.

'There!' called Artemis after her. 'He won't love you now!' and she set her silver hunting dogs to chase after Callisto.

Callisto ran and ran to escape from the dogs. She hid in a cave for the rest of that night, and by morning the dogs had gone back to Artemis and she was safe. But not for long, for the woods were full of wild animals. Other bears and foxes, wolves and wild boars roamed between the trees. Callisto, although a wild animal now herself, was afraid of the other animals. She could not approach any humans because they were afraid of her and would kill her, thinking she was a real bear, and she was no longer able to speak and so could not explain what had happened to her. Callisto lived a lonely, miserable existence for the next few years.

Then, one day, she saw a boy in the woods. At first she didn't recognise him, and thought he was just a boy out hunting, for he had a spear and knife with him, but then Callisto realised that this was Arcas, her son, now almost grown-up.

Here at last, she thought, was someone who could help her. Her own son, surely, would recognise her as his mother, even though she had the appearance of a bear. Callisto came out from the trees where she was hiding and ran towards the boy. She tried to speak, to explain, to tell him, but all he saw and heard was a wild brown bear running towards him.

Arcas lifted his hunting spear high above him. He balanced, ready to plunge it into the heart of the bear who would surely kill him if he didn't kill it first. The bear came closer, he could feel its breath on his face. He gripped the shaft of the spear, ready to thrust it...

High in the sky above them, the God Zeus watched. He saw what was about to happen, and knew he must stop the boy. Zeus leaned down and picked up the bear and the boy, lightly between his fingers. Then he placed them in the heavens amongst the stars where they would always be together; the Great and Little Bear, together in the sky for eternity.

The night sky is exciting, and there is so much to find out about it. The next time you hear the nursery rhyme 'Twinkle twinkle little star' you might ask yourself which star, and what is its story.

By the way, you might be interested to know that the star that twinkles most is Sirius. Sirius is the Dog Star, and is always just a bit below and to the left of Orion, exactly where you would expect a well-behaved dog to be! It twinkles so much because it's so bright, and because it's always low down in our sky so we always see it through the earth's atmosphere.

Maybe you could find out more about the spectacular stars in our sky.

Dear God, Thank you for the wonders of the sky. Help us never to take for granted the beautiful things we can see, but help us to appreciate our world and universe. Amen

Theme 3: Christmas

The fourth wise man... and the ruby

You have all heard the story of the first Christmas, and of how Jesus was born in Bethlehem and the shepherds and kings came to visit him. You have probably written your own version of the story. Perhaps you tried to write the story from the point of view of one of the angels, or one of the shepherds. Or perhaps you wrote about a character that isn't mentioned in the original Bible story, like an innkeeper's wife, or a child in Bethlehem.

Many writers have retold the Christmas story from different points of view, and one writer, called Henry Van Dyke, wrote his story of the fourth wise man over a hundred years ago. This is an adaptation of that story, and it's in three parts, as a serial.

In the days when Caesar Augustus ruled the Roman Empire, and Herod was king of Jerusalem, there lived a man called Artaban in the country of Persia, east of the Zagros Mountains. Artaban had three friends whose names were Melchior, Caspar and Balthazar.

All four men were students of astronomy; they studied the stars, and they knew a great deal about the night sky and the movement of the stars and planets, and what the different stars meant.

One night, when the four men were together under the star-gazing window of Artaban's attic, they saw the two great planets of Jupiter and Saturn move across the night sky.

'Look!' said Melchior. 'The planets are moving into the star cluster of Pisces, the fish.'

'It's the sign we've been waiting for,' said Caspar, excitedly.

'It means a new king, a great king, a king of kings is going to be born to the Jewish people,' said Balthazar,

'And a star will appear and lead us to him,' said Artaban.

The four wise men decided to wait until the new star appeared in the sky, for they knew it would come soon, then they would follow it and find the new-born king. They knew the star would lead them to the west, so they decided to meet each other in Babylon exactly twenty days after the appearance of the star.

'We'll meet at the Temple of the Seven Spheres,' said Melchior. 'Then we can cross the desert together. It'll be safer that way; the desert is a dangerous and lonely place for travellers.' And the four men went home to make preparations for the journey.

Artaban sold his house and all his possessions except for his horse, he would need that for the first part of the journey, and he bought three jewels as gifts for the new-born king. He bought a ruby as red as a holly-berry, a sapphire as blue as the sky, and a glistening shining pearl, as pale as the moon.

Then, Artaban watched the sky, and waited. Every night from dusk until dawn he gazed at the stars. And at last the new one appeared, just as he knew it would; a perfect, dazzling, shimmering, sparkling, glittering star, edging over the horizon and up into the night sky. It grew larger and more brilliant as Artaban watched, and he knew the time had come to set off on his journey.

Everything was ready, and Artaban was well on his way by the time the new star began to fade into daylight. He knew he had no time to lose. The journey to Babylon would be long and hard, and he had to arrive at the Temple of the Seven Spheres in time to meet the others. He was looking forward to seeing his friends again and to making the next part of the journey together.

After twenty days of travelling, Artaban saw the city of Babylon in the distance. Not much further to go. Nearly there. He would be just in time. But as Artaban took the road that led to the gates of the city, he saw a man lying in the dirt. The man was obviously very badly injured and looked as though he'd been set upon by robbers. Artaban stopped.

'Help me,' moaned the man.

Artaban didn't know what to do. If he stayed to help the injured man he might miss his friends and miss the chance to follow the star and find the new-born king, yet if he did nothing to help this man, he would surely die.

But even as he asked himself what he should do, Artaban knew the answer. He was a skilled doctor and couldn't leave this man to die. 'Anyway,' he told himself, ' to care for someone is an act of love, and that is what God teaches us to do. I must help him,' and Artaban climbed down from his horse and took medicines and bandages out of his bag.

It took a long time to clean the man's wounds, but Artaban knew he could not leave him until he was well enough to walk into the city for further help. Slowly, gradually, the man began to revive.

'It's very kind of you to help me,' he said, when he was feeling a little better. 'But I don't know why you've bothered. You're not even from the same country as me.'

'It doesn't matter which country a person's from if he needs help,' answered Artaban. 'And to help another human being is to serve God. So you see, I had to help you, even though now I might be late.'

'Late for what?' asked the man.

'I am meeting my friends in Babylon and we are travelling west towards Jerusalem in search of the baby who is to be born king of the Jews. We have seen his star in the sky and we are going to worship him.'

'I might be able to help you,' said the man. 'I have read in books that the king of kings will not be born in the great city of Jerusalem, but in the small town of Bethlehem. Leave me now, and go meet your friends, then go to Bethlehem and look there for the new-born baby. Bless you for helping me, and may your God go with you on your journey.'

So Artaban said goodbye to the injured man and hurried to the Temple of the Seven Spheres to meet Melchior, Caspar, and Balthazar. But it was already past midnight and his friends were nowhere to be seen.

'I'm too late,' whispered Artaban. 'They've gone without me.'

He looked around him, wondering what to do next, and saw a small piece of parchment wedged under a stone. It was a message from his friends.

"We can delay no longer. We have to begin the search while the star is still bright in the sky. Follow us and catch us up. We hope to see you soon. M.C.B."

Artaban looked out across the cold, dark, inhospitable desert, and felt disappointed and afraid. How would he ever catch up with his friends? Would he ever find the new-born king of kings?

He decided that the only thing to do was to sell one of his precious jewels to buy camels and provisions, then set off by himself across the desert. He knocked on the door of the jewel merchant.

'What do you want at this hour of the night?' grumbled the merchant.

'I want to sell this ruby,' said Artaban, holding the jewel in his hand like a drop of red blood. 'What will you give me for it?'

The fourth wise man... and the sapphire

The jewel merchant paid a good price for Artaban's ruby, and also bought his horse. With the money Artaban bought things he would need for the journey across the desert. He bought two camels, one for him to ride on and one to carry provisions. He bought a tent and blankets, food and water, more medicines in case he should need them, and some water carriers.

Then he set off. He travelled at night so that he could follow the star and not lose his way. It was bitterly cold in the desert at night, and Artaban was glad of the extra blankets he'd bought. During the day, he sheltered in his tent from the blistering heat, and tried to sleep. He met no-one on the journey and he could see no sign of his friends in the distance.

Once, a sand-storm blew up and kept Artaban in his tent for several days. It was impossible to go on through the storm, impossible even to tell night from day, or light from dark. But as soon as the storm had passed, Artaban continued with his journey. He lost track of the hours and of the days and had no idea how long he'd been travelling. His whole world had become filled with heat and cold, and with endless ridges and hills of sand. But beyond the sand, above the horizon, high in the night sky, the star always shone brightly, leading him on and showing him the way.

Eventually Artaban reached the western side of the desert, and he once again had grass and earth beneath his feet. He saw sheep and cattle on the hillsides – the first living creatures he'd seen for weeks. Artaban looked again at the star. It had stopped. All the time he had been travelling, the star had been slowly moving across the sky, leading him westwards. But now it had stopped. It was gleaming and glowing and brighter than ever. It seemed to be pointing down to earth. Artaban looked beneath the star and saw the town of Bethlehem, spread out before him like a map. He was here.

Artaban left his camels and goods at the edge of the town and walked towards the main street. It was deserted. There was no-one about. No-one to ask. No-one. And there was a strange feeling of danger and desolation in the air.

Artaban walked towards one of the inns, thinking that perhaps his friends had stayed there and he could ask where they were, but the inn was closed and the door was boarded up. The next inn was closed, too, and the third was all in darkness as though everyone had left.

Then Artaban heard a sound, a soft sound of a woman singing a lullaby. He followed the singing to a small house and found a young woman cradling a baby and rocking it to sleep.

'Ssh,' she said as he approached. 'Don't wake him.'

'Is he your baby?' asked Artaban.

'Yes,' said the woman, and she touched the baby's face gently with her finger. 'He is my first child, my son.'

'I am looking for a baby,' said Artaban. 'I am searching for a baby who is born king of the Jews. I have seen his star in the sky and I have come to worship him. My friends are looking for him too; we were supposed to travel here together but I missed them.'

'There were some strangers here,' said the woman. 'Three richly dressed men from the east came looking for a child. They said they'd followed a star here. They said the baby was a great king, but I don't think he could have been. He was born in a stable to a young couple who'd come here because of the census. Anyway, the strangers thought he was important because they brought valuable gifts. One of them even gave him gold, I think.'

'Are the strangers still here?' asked Artaban.

'No, they've gone,' said the woman. 'And the young couple with the baby have left, too. Someone told me they've gone to Egypt to escape from the soldiers. You see there's a rumour going around that King Herod is going to kill all the baby boys.' And the young woman again gently touched the face of her sleeping baby. 'Many people think it's true and they've already left,' she added. 'But I have nowhere else to go.'

Just then there was a noise and commotion outside the woman's house. Artaban looked out and saw soldiers with knives and swords running down the street. They were pushing into people's houses and killing any babies they found. The air was suddenly filled with screams of terror. Artaban looked at the young woman and saw fear in her eyes. She held her baby more tightly to her. 'Help me,' she said to Artaban.

He looked again at the soldiers and back to the woman. What should he do? If he did nothing the baby would certainly be killed. What could he do? But even as he asked himself, he knew the answer. He felt in his pocket and took out the purse containing the two remaining jewels. He held the sapphire in his hand. Then he went to the door of the house.

'Soldier! Here!' he called, and one of the soldiers came over to him.

'There's nothing for you in this house,' said Artaban. 'Look! I'll give you this jewel if you go and leave me in peace.' And Artaban held out the sapphire as blue as a baby's eyes.

The soldier snatched it, then called to the others, 'There's nothing here. Go to the next street.'

'Why have you done that for me?' asked the woman. 'You don't know me.'

'To help someone is an act of love, and that is what God teaches us to do,' said Artaban.

'Thank you. And may God bless you,' said the woman.

Artaban thought of his jewels. He had now used two of them to help other people, and had only one left to give to the king of kings. He wondered if he would ever see the king, or ever see his friends again.

The fourth wise man... and the pearl

Artaban left Bethlehem and made his way to Egypt, since that was where he thought the baby king and his parents had gone to escape from Herod's soldiers.

He asked at all the inns, but no-one had seen the strangers from the east, or the young couple with the baby. He enquired at many houses, but no-one knew where they were. He searched everywhere but no-one knew anything about them. By now the bright new star that had led Artaban this far on his journey had faded and could no longer be seen.

Artaban went to a Jewish rabbi to ask for help and advice. He told the story of his journey, then said, 'So what do you think I should do? Where should I go? How can I find the king of kings?'

'It is said that the king of the Jews will be a people's king,' said the rabbi. 'It is said that he will live not in a great palace with the wealthy, but in the simple homes of the poor. Perhaps it is amongst these people that you should search?'

Artaban thanked the rabbi for his advice, and then began to search every city, every town, every village in the land. He went to the poorest parts of every place and asked if the king of kings lived there, but the answer was always the same, 'No king lives here! We don't know the king of kings you are searching for'. Some people thought he was mad. Others laughed at him. A few were kind to him. But no matter how anyone treated Artaban, he was always kind, helpful and courteous to them.

Artaban used his skills as a doctor to help as many people as he could. There was always someone in every village and town who needed his help. He never asked the people to pay, but gave his skills and his time in return for a little food or somewhere to stay for the night.

And from time to time he would look at the milky-white glistening pearl, the last of his jewels, the last of his gifts for the king, and wonder if he would ever have the chance to give it to the king of kings.

Artaban travelled the world, searching for the king, caring for the sick, befriending people who had no friends, for over thirty years, until he was an old man. He'd never found Caspar, Melchior and Balthazar again, and he had almost given up hope of ever finding the king of kings.

'My days on this earth are nearly over,' he said one day. 'But I will make one last journey to Jerusalem, one last search for the king, in the city where I thought he would be born all those years ago.'

So Artaban travelled to Jerusalem to make one final search before giving up. When he arrived, the city was crowded with people pushing and jostling and talking. There was a strange feeling of foreboding in the air, as though something terrible was about to happen.

'What's going on?' asked Artaban of some men who were hurrying down the road.

'There's going to be a crucifixion,' said one of the men. 'A man called Jesus of Nazareth says he's the king of the Jews.'

'Could this be the man?' thought Artaban. 'Could this be the king I've been searching for all these years? It must be, and if it is, I must save him. I must go to the Roman Governor and give him my last jewel. I must ask him to set Jesus free in return for the pearl,' and Artaban turned to go to the Governor's palace.

But as he did so, he saw a young girl being dragged down the street by some men.

'Help me,' she cried to the people nearby. 'My father owes money to these men, and they are selling me as a slave to pay it back.' The girl looked straight at Artaban. 'Help me,' she pleaded again.

Artaban didn't know what to do. He had only one jewel left. Should he offer it to the Roman Governor and ask him to release the king of the Jews, or should he give it to these men so that the girl could go free? But even as he asked himself what he should do, Artaban knew the answer. He knew that to help another human being was to serve God. So Artaban pulled the old leather purse out of his pocket and held the shining pearl in his hand.

'Take this,' he said to the men. 'And let her go,'

One of the men grabbed the pearl and pushed the girl towards Artaban. And as he did so, the earth shook, the sky became dark and thunder rumbled. Dust filled the air as buildings toppled and fell. The crowds ran for their lives, but Artaban and the girl crouched beside a wall until the earthquake stopped. Above them the tiles on the roof became loose and began to fall. One of them hit Artaban on the side of his head and he fell to the ground.

The girl leaned over him and gently stroked his face. She knew he was dying. And then a voice spoke.

'My blessings be upon you, Artaban. You have lived a good life and helped many people. I want you to know that each time you have done something for one of my family, it is as if you have done it for me.'

'Thank you,' whispered Artaban. And he knew that he had used his jewels well, and that he had, at last, met the king of kings.

Artaban spent his whole life searching for the king. He never gave up because he had faith in what he was doing. He lived the sort of life that Jesus taught people to live. He helped everyone he could, regardless of their colour or their religion or their background. He didn't worry about trying to get rich. He wasn't selfish. And in the end he found the king he was looking for.

Artaban's story tells us that Christmas is about giving, not getting; it's about looking for the truth, and not letting greed and selfishness get in the way.

Thank you , Lord, for Christmas. Thank you for the Christmas story and for all the different versions of it. Thank you for the magic and excitement of Christmas. Help us to see beyond the tinsel and presents, and to understand the real message of Christmas – that we should love and care for everyone in our world family. Amen

January

Theme 1: Three millennia

The first millennium: spreading the news

Two thousand years ago a baby was born; a baby that would affect the whole world for thousands of years to come. Two thousand years ago a baby was born; a baby so important that all the calendars were reset to start at the beginning again. The Christian Era had begun.

Who was the baby? Yes, it was Jesus.

At first, only the people of Bethlehem and the local shepherds knew about the arrival of this special baby. Then the wise men came. Their visit is celebrated at Epiphany – January 6th – and Epiphany means 'showing'; Jesus was shown to outsiders, to foreigners, to the rest of the world, when he was shown to the Wise Men. The Wise Men probably told lots of people about Jesus, as they made their way back to their own country.

But the news of Jesus really started to spread after he had finished his work for God. The trouble was, even after Jesus had died, he still had many enemies, so life was difficult and dangerous for his friends.

After Jesus died, his friends, the disciples, knew that they had to continue his work. They knew they must tell people about Jesus's life and teach them to love one another, as Jesus had taught. But the disciples knew the work would be difficult. The Romans were in control of their country, and the Romans hated Jesus and would stop at nothing to kill his friends.

The disciples turned to Peter as their leader.

'What shall we do?' they asked Peter. 'How can we do Jesus's work when the Roman soldiers want to kill us?'

'We must have the courage to stand up for what we know is right,' said Peter. 'I let Jesus down just before he died. I told people who asked me if I knew Jesus that I didn't know him. I said it three times, and now I'm sorry that I wasn't brave enough to stand up for him. But I've learned my lesson. I'm sorry for letting him down and I won't do it again. I'm going to tell everyone about Jesus. If the Roman soldiers don't like it, they'll have to kill me.'

A few days later, Peter and John were on their way into the temple for afternoon prayers when they saw a lame man sitting at the gate, begging for money.

'Spare me a coin?' said the man.

Peter stopped and looked at the man.

'I have no money,' he said. 'But I will give you what I have. In the name of Jesus of Nazareth, get up and walk!'

By now, other people on their way into the temple had stopped to watch.

'You're wasting your time,' said one man to Peter. 'He can't walk. He's been unable to walk for at least forty years. He always sits there. Leave him alone, can't you?'

But Peter said again, 'In the name of Jesus, get up and walk,' and he held out his hand to help the man to his feet. The man stood, then took a few faltering steps. Then as he felt the strength returning to his feet and ankles and legs, he thanked Peter and walked purposefully into the temple to give thanks to God.

The bystanders were amazed.

'How did you do it?' they asked.

'It was not me but the work of God,' said Peter. 'You shouldn't be surprised. God can do anything. He even sent his son, Jesus, to live amongst us. You think Jesus is dead, but he's not. He is alive again. He will live forever in the hearts of the people who believe in him.'

Just then, the officer in charge of the temple guards and some of the priests came striding up to Peter.

'What do you think you're doing?' shouted the guard. 'We'll have none of that talk of Jesus being alive. Jesus is dead, and I'm arresting you for causing a disturbance.' Peter and John were taken away and thrown into jail.

The next day they were brought before the High Priest and told that they must never again speak to the crowds about Jesus.

'Jesus is dead,' said the priest. 'You will promise not to speak of him again.'

'I can't do that,' said Peter. 'I have to obey God, not you.'

'How dare you speak to me like that?' said the High Priest, who was not accustomed to having prisoners answer him back so boldly. 'If you defy me I shall have you killed!'

'You must do what you think right,' said Peter. 'Just as I must do what I think is right.'

The High Priest was furious, but he was also afraid of upsetting the crowd that had seen Peter heal the lame man.

'Get out of here,' he said, and Peter and John were set free.

They went straight back to the gate of the temple, where an even bigger crowd was waiting for them. Word had spread that Peter had healed a lame man, and now the gateway was filled with sick people who hoped he could cure them too.

'This can't be allowed to continue,' declared the High Priest when he heard what was happening. 'Arrest them again and imprison them. I shall deal with them tomorrow.'

But that night an angel opened the prison gate and told Peter and John to go back to the temple and tell the people about Jesus. In the morning, the High Priest called a meeting of the whole Jewish Council, to decide what to do with Peter and John. They sent for the prisoners. But the guards came back with the news, 'They're not there. The prison is locked and the guards have been on duty all night, but the prisoners are not there. They must have escaped.'

'What!' roared the High Priest.

Just then a man came in and said, 'Are you looking for the men you put in prison? They're in the temple again, teaching the people about Jesus.'

'This time I shall kill them,' thundered the High Priest. 'They will not defy me again.'

But one of the Council members, who was greatly respected by all the people, said, 'Just ignore them. Killing Peter and John will only make matters worse. Leave them alone. All this talk of Jesus will die out of its own accord, you'll see. It'll go away by itself.'

So, reluctantly, the High Priest agreed not to kill Peter and John. Instead he had them whipped and he ordered them never to speak of Jesus again. But Peter and the others continued to teach the people about Jesus, despite the danger they were putting themselves in.

'I thought you said that the talk of Jesus would die out,' said the High Priest to the Council member who had persuaded him not to kill Peter and John.

'It will. It will,' he said again. 'These followers of Jesus will soon disappear... unless... of course... Jesus really is the Son of God... in which case nothing you can do will stop the story of Jesus spreading through the whole world.'

The story of Jesus, as we know, did spread through the whole world. And about 200 years after Jesus died, news of him spread to India, Africa and Europe. But during the first part of the first millennium it was still very dangerous to be a follower of Jesus, and many Christians were put to death by the Romans. Peter himself was killed by the Roman Emperor Nero, around the year 64, but the danger didn't stop Peter standing up for what he believed was right.

The first part of today's prayer is from an old English prayer, and is specially for Saint Peter, because Jesus is said to have given the keys of the Kingdom of Heaven to Peter.

'Pray for me, and I for thee, That we may merrily meet in Heaven.'
Help us Lord to have the courage of Peter, and always to stand up for what we believe to be right. Amen

The second millennium: William conquers England

Do you think it matters if you make a promise you can't keep? Do you think it matters if you break a promise?

The whole of our history for the last thousand years might have turned out very differently if it hadn't been for someone saying they'd do something, and then going back on their word.

It's a true story. Here's what happened.

Edward, King of England, made a promise to his friend William, Duke of Normandy.

'You can be King of England after me,' he said. 'I promise you the throne of England after my death.'

William was delighted.

Several years after this promise was made, King Edward sent Harold to Normandy to meet William. Harold and William became good friends and Harold stayed with William for almost a year. Whilst he was staying in Normandy, Harold helped William to win a battle against the people of Brittany.

'Thank you for your help,' said William. 'I am going to award you with my country's highest honour, I am going to reward you for your bravery.'

Harold accepted the award, but knew he had to give something in return, for that was the custom in those days.

'I give you my allegiance,' said Harold. An allegiance was a promise to serve William and obey him in everything; a promise to help William become King of England when the time was right.

Then Harold returned to England and told King Edward all about his adventures in Normandy.

'But William cannot become King of England,' said Edward. 'I have changed my mind. *You* must be King after me.'

'But we promised!' said Harold.

About a year later, King Edward died. The people wanted Harold to be their King, and he accepted. But as soon as he became King Harold, he broke the promises that had been made to William Duke of Normandy.

When William heard that Harold was now King of England, he was furious.

'They promised the crown to *me*!' he thundered. 'Well, if they won't give me the throne, I shall take it! Build me some ships to take my army across the sea to England. Gather the knights-in-armour! Round up the soldiers! Get ready to invade!'

Boatbuilders all along the coast of Normandy began to build the eight hundred ships needed to carry William, his army and its equipment to England. Two thousand knights-in-armour were made ready. Two thousand horses were prepared for the journey over the sea; it was to be the first time that an invading army had taken its horses with it in ships. Four thousand foot soldiers were trained to fight with spears and bows and arrows.

At last everything was ready... except the wind. It was blowing in the wrong direction, and without the wind, the ships could not set sail. William strode up and down the seashore, fretting and fuming and storming and shouting, waiting for the wind to change and for the invasion to begin.

Meanwhile, over in England, Harold was preparing his army, too. His plan was to attack William's ships as they approached the south coast of England. He would never let them land on English soil. But things didn't go as Harold planned!

Up in the north of England, another invading army had arrived. King Hardrada of Norway had sailed across the sea to capture England. Harold marched his soldiers to the north, where they fought hard and forced Hardrada back; but many English soldiers lost their lives.

Whilst Harold and the English army were defending their land in the north, the wind changed direction. William and his eight hundred ships, packed tight with soldiers and horses, set sail from Normandy and soon landed on the south coast of England. There was nothing to stop them. No soldiers. No ships. No army. No resistance. Nothing. William thought it very odd that they hadn't been challenged. They unloaded all their soldiers, knights, horses and equipment. They set up camp and waited. They were ready for battle.

Harold and his weary army marched back to the south. On the way, Harold ordered field workers and peasants to come and join them because he knew he needed more soldiers, but these men had no training, no equipment, no discipline.

At last, on October 14th 1066, the two great leaders and their armies faced each other at a place called Hastings. William's army advanced and Harold's tired men formed a shield wall to resist the onslaught. But the men were exhausted. The shield wall didn't hold. William's soldiers broke through and the fighting began. It lasted all that day. Men and horses were killed. One whole group of Harold's men defied orders and set up a battle against the Normans on their own. They were all killed.

And then Harold fell. Some say he had an arrow in his eye. Others say he was struck by a sword. But whichever it was, he died.

The English army turned and fled, running into the countryside to escape the Norman soldiers and their deadly weapons. The Normans rode on in triumph to London, and William, The Conqueror, Duke of Normandy, became King of England.

And how do we know that all this happened a thousand years ago? Shortly after the battle of Hastings, Williams' half-brother ordered a huge embroidered hanging to be made. The embroidery is still in existence today and is one of the world's great masterpieces. It is 70 metres long and half a metre wide. It's stitched in coloured wools and made like a comic strip; each section telling the next part of the story. It now hangs in a special display case in the town of Bayeux in France, and is known as the Bayeux Tapestry. If you ever go on holiday to France and get the chance to see the Tapestry, go and look at it. You'll be able to see the whole story, unfolding before your eyes, and you'll know you are looking at something which is a thousand years old. Wow!

It's strange how events change the course of history, isn't it? Just think, if Edward and Harold hadn't made that promise, things might have turned out very differently for all of us. And if the wind had allowed William to set off when he wanted to, Harold and his army would have been ready for the invasion, and they might have won the battle.

Dear God, help us to think before we make promises, and to only make promises which we know we can keep. Help us, in the early years of this new millennium to settle our differences without fighting. Help people to put an end to war. Amen

The third millennium: hopes and dreams

I wonder what the next millennium, the next thousand years, has in store for humankind. Here, in these early years of the third millennium, we are standing on the brink of the future. There have been huge changes in the world in the last two thousand years, I wonder what changes will come about in the future. I wonder what life will be like in another hundred years? And I wonder what planet Earth will be like in another thousand years, as it enters the fourth millennium?

We cannot look into the future, but in today's fictional story, someone catches a glimpse of what the future could be like.

Zak sat in front of his computer screen. His father had just e-mailed a message to him.

'Hi Zak. Be ready in ten minutes and I'll take you out to the theme park.'

'Great, Dad! See you soon,' replied Zak.

He pulled on his temperature-controlled, all-in-one outdoor suit, told his computer he'd be back later, and left his living cell to go and meet his dad. They climbed on the next electric travelcar that came along and fed their plastic cards into the control panel. Their information flashed up on the screen: names, identification numbers, addresses, and the date – January 10th 2020. The screen asked where they were going and Zak's dad tapped in 'Theme Park'. 'OK. Go ahead,' the screen responded. The travelcar was pre-programmed to go directly to the destination the customer wanted. The cost of the journey would be taken directly from Zak's dad's money account, through the family computer.

They soon arrived at the theme park, climbed out of their travelcar and waited for the next two-seater buggy to come along. The buggies were warm and comfortable and took you all the way through the theme park, past all the exhibits, through the drive-in fast food bay, eventually arriving at the exercise adventure area where you could get out and play, or go on the virtual reality activities.

Zak loved the theme park. He and his dad had been so often they knew every single bit of it. He liked the time track best. On the time track, the buggies took you back through time, past the millennium celebrations when the third millennium began, past all the famous inventions of the 1900s with its computers, machines, aircraft and cars; past the 1800s and 1700s, past the 1600s and the Tudors and Stuarts, past the 1000s and William the Conqueror, past the first years of our present time and Jesus and the Romans; down, down, through the years; past the time of the dinosaurs and back, back, to the very beginning of life on our Earth.

Their buggy arrived and Zak and his dad climbed into it. It set off on its usual pre-planned route. But then suddenly, without any warning, the buggy spun round, as though out of control, and headed off down a route they'd never seen before.

'What's going on?' called out Zak's dad.

'Are we going to crash?' said Zak.

The buggy slowed down, and rounded a corner, then it stopped. A white-haired old man wearing old-fashioned clothes stepped out of a small wooden building.

'Welcome to the future,' he said. 'I'd like to show you something. Walk this way please.' The man led Zak and his dad round the side of the building and along a small gravel path. It led to some steps. They climbed up.

'Look!' said the man, and he waved his arm to indicate the view spread out below them. It was beautiful. There was a river of sparkling clear water meandering through rolling green meadows of wild flowers. You could smell the fragrance of the flowers being carried on the breeze. There were trees and hedgerows and the sound of birdsong.

'Look Dad! An otter!' said Zak excitedly. 'And a beaver. I've never seen a real beaver before, except on video.' He turned to the old man. 'Where are we?'

'Yes. Where is this place?' asked Zak's dad.

'Anywhere on earth you want it to be,' said the old man. 'But come. I want to show you something else,' and he led them back down the steps and along the gravel path to the other side of the wooden building, and along a short concrete driveway. At the end he opened a high metal gate. Once more they were looking down on a view spread before them.

There was a small forest of wizened and stunted trees, but part of it was smouldering and smoke was pouring into the heavy grey sky. A river was choked with rubbish and it was covered with a brown foam of chemical pollutants. Litter and plastic bottles blew around the ugly concrete and metal buildings of a nearby town. There was dirt and graffiti everywhere. The smell of the place was indescribable. There was a crying sound from time to time like an animal in pain. 'Ugh! It's horrible,' said Zak.

'Wherever is it?' asked his dad.

'It's wherever you want it to be,' answered the old man. He said nothing else for several minutes, then he suddenly turned to them and said, 'Do you know that the earth is 4,600 million years old?'

'Well, yes, something like that,' said Zak's dad.

'Hard to understand, isn't it, something as old as that,' said the man. 'But if we make one year stand for every thousand million years, we can begin to see the whole picture.'

'We can?' said Zak's dad.

'What's he mean, Dad?' whispered Zak.

'I'll tell you what I mean,' said the man. 'Think of the earth like a person who is 46 years old. We know nothing of the first seven years of this person's life, in fact we know hardly anything about him until he's 42 when things begin to happen. Dinosaurs only appeared last year when the planet was 45. People as we know them have only been around for about four hours. Machines were invented about a minute ago! And during that minute, humans have made a rubbish tip of Earth. They have used up the earth's precious resources, they have caused hundreds of plants and animals to become extinct, and they have increased their own numbers until the planet is overrun with them.'

'Why are you telling us all this?' asked Zak's dad.

'Because I am the future,' said the old man. 'I am the first view you saw, or I am this one. It's up to you to choose.'

'But what can we do?' said Zak. 'My dad and I can't decide what happens to the earth in the future!'

'If everyone says that, then there is no hope for the Earth or the future,' said the old man. 'But if everyone does their bit to care for our Earth, then my hopes and dreams for the future will come true. What are your hopes and dreams?' he asked.

But before Zak or his dad had a chance to answer, the buggy came trundling along the driveway and it was time to go.

On their way home in the travelcar, Zak and his dad talked about their strange trip to the theme park.

'How did the buggy take us on that route?' asked Zak. 'We've never been along there before. And what did the old man mean?'

'I don't know how or why we went there,' said his dad. 'But I do know that it's up to each of us to look after our Earth and keep it safe. And I know that my hopes and dreams for the Earth in future are the same as the old man's. How about you?'

I wonder what Zak and his dad's hopes and dreams were for the future of the Earth? What are yours?

It's easy for us all to say 'Well there's nothing I can do about caring for the Earth. I'm only one person. I'm too small.' But if everyone tries to look after their little bit of Earth, and if everyone watches what the leaders of our world are doing, to make sure they are looking after it, then perhaps we won't let our Earth become ill and damaged, but keep it well and healthy. After all, if we look after the Earth, it will look after us! We can't live without it.

Thank you Lord, for the glory of our Earth. Help us to care for our planet, to protect it, to keep it undamaged, so that it can continue to care for us, and feed us and clothe us. Help us to remember that whatever we do to the Earth now, will affect all the people who will live in the future. Amen

Theme 2: Messages

I am going to advance

Have you ever been asked to take a message to someone? I think most of you will have been asked by your teacher, or someone at home, to deliver a message at some time or another.

If you have been asked to deliver a message, you'll know how important it is to deliver the right message. For example, it's no use your teacher asking you to go to the secretary and to ask for three red exercise books, if you forget what you've gone for and ask for nineteen plastic rulers instead!

But sometimes it's quite difficult to remember exactly what you've been sent for, and you have to keep saying it over and over to yourself so that you don't forget. But even this can sometimes go wrong!

There was once an army General who was about to go into battle with his troops. Everything was ready; the soldiers were prepared, the horses were groomed, the flags were flying, the cannons were polished. All that remained was for the General to give the order to advance. To go forward. To CHARGE!

He was just about to do so, when a messenger boy came galloping up to him on horseback.

'Please sir,' gasped the messenger. 'I thought you ought to know, sir. It's the other army, sir. They've got lots more soldiers hidden over the hill, out of sight. Their army is loads bigger than ours, sir, they're bound to win the battle.'

'Loads bigger than ours, you say?' boomed the General. 'Then we need more soldiers. We need reinforcements. And we need those reinforcements NOW!'

The General did a quick calculation in his head, then said to the messenger, 'Go and ride as fast as you can to the army headquarters back at base camp. Give them this message from me. Say "I am going to advance – will you send me reinforcements?". Have you got that, boy?'

'Yes sir,' said the messenger, and he repeated 'I am going to advance – will you send me reinforcements?'

'That's it,' said the General. 'Now go! Fast as you can. There's no time to lose.'

The messenger set off again on his horse, this time in the direction of the army headquarters base camp. As he rode he said to himself over and over again 'I am going to advance – will you send me reinforcements? I am going to advance – will you send me reinforcements? I am going to advance – will you send me reinforcements?' so that he wouldn't forget the message.

But the messenger boy was tired. He'd already had a long day. He'd had other messages to remember, other errands to run, and so as he rode along, this message became somewhat scrambled.

'I am going to advance – will you send me reinforcements? I am going to a dance – will you send me reinforcements? I am going to advance – will you send me thirty-four-pence?'

When he arrived at the army headquarters back at base camp, he rushed up to the Commander-in-Chief and spluttered 'I have a message from the General. It's important. He says, "I am going to a dance – will you send me thirty-four-pence?" And the messenger boy, having delivered his message, turned round and ran back to his horse.

'I've never heard anything like it!' said the Commander-in-Chief. 'What on earth does it mean? Why is he going to a dance. Why does he need thirty four pence?'

'It must be a coded message, sir,' said the Commander-in-Chief's private secretary.

'Yes, of course,' said the Commander-in-Chief. 'That's it! A coded message. It must mean... er... it must mean that... er... it must mean that the whole army... has been invited to a fancy dress ball. And it must mean... er... that... er... they haven't any money to hire costumes for it. Yes! That's it! Well that problem is easily solved.' And the Commander-in-Chief immediately ordered three hundred fancy dress costumes to be sent out to the waiting soldiers. And then, just in case he hadn't got the message quite right, for he had a feeling it was not quite right, he sent three hundred purses containing thirty four pence each, as well.

Meanwhile, the very tired messenger boy had changed to a fresh horse, and was riding back to the General.

'I've delivered the message sir,' he called as he approached him.

'Are they sending reinforcements?' asked the General.

'I think so,' answered the boy, and just as he said this, a huge carriage arrived, pulled by four enormous horses and loaded up to the sky with big cardboard boxes.

'What's all this?' asked the General.

'It's for the dance,' said the driver. 'Three hundred fancy dress costumes, just like you wanted. Oh yes, and three hundred thirty-four pences as well. Where do you want me to put it all?'

'Fancy dress costumes!' bellowed the General. 'What do I want with fancy dress costumes?'

'They're for the soldiers,' said the driver. 'You know, for the fancy dress dance.'

'Fancy dress dance?' said a soldier, who just happened to be passing and heard the General and the carriage driver talking. 'Are we having a fancy dress dance? Hey great! I'll go and tell the others.'

And so it was, that half an hour later, when the enemy army came swooping down over the hill ready to fight with the General's army, they found three hundred soldiers all dressed in fancy dress costumes, practising their dances in the middle of a field.

'Where's that messenger boy?' shouted the General. But no-one could find him. (He was in fact, dressed as Little Bo Peep and was dancing with a pirate, a caveman and Red Riding Hood at the time, but of course the General couldn't recognise him.)

It was no problem for the enemy army to surround the General's soldiers and take them prisoner. And thus the General's army lost the battle without even having started to fight.

In years to come, everyone remembered the disastrous day when a messenger boy set out with the message "I am going to advance – will you send me reinforcements", and it arrived as "I am going to a dance – will you send me thirty-four pence". I wonder what happened to him?

I hope you never get into a muddle like that if you take a message anywhere. Of course, if you do forget what you're supposed to say, the best thing is to go back and ask. That way you'll be sure to get it right.

Thank you God, for the ability to think and remember. Help us to think clearly and to remember accurately. Help us to deliver messages properly so that we don't cause misunderstandings or difficulties. Amen

Excalibur

Have you ever been asked to take a message somewhere, and then not taken it? I hope you haven't! Sometimes you might be asked to deliver a message and you don't want to, or the message seems unimportant, or you think it won't matter if you don't, but if you've agreed to take a message for someone you trust, you have a responsibility to deliver it safely.

Today's story is one of the legends of King Arthur. It's the last of the legends and is about King Arthur giving a message to his friend, Sir Bedevere, about Excalibur, the magic sword.

King Arthur and the Knights of the Round Table fought and won many battles for England. They kept their promise to fight for what was right, and to help the poor and needy; and during King Arthur's reign, England became strong and wealthy. But King Arthur had many enemies, and his enemies also grew stronger.

One day, Sir Modred, who was King Arthur's own nephew and one of the Knights of the Round Table, betrayed King Arthur and started a terrible war in which a hundred thousand men were killed. All of King Arthur's men, except one, were dead.

'I wish I knew where Modred was,' cried King Arthur. 'I would kill him with my own hands for doing this to my Knights.' Just then he saw Sir Modred in front of him, leaning on his sword in the middle of the battlefield.

'Traitor!' cried King Arthur. 'This is all your doing!' and he thrust his spear under Sir Modred's armour and killed him... but not before Sir Modred struck him on the head with his sword.

King Arthur lay on the ground, dying. He knew nothing could save him now, not even his magic sword Excalibur. And now, as he was dying, he understood what the strange messages meant, which were written on the sides of Excalibur. They had always puzzled him, for one side of the sword said KEEP ME, and on the other side of the sword was written THROW ME AWAY.

King Arthur called his one remaining knight to him.

'Sir Bedevere?' he called. 'I want you to do one last thing for me.'

'I'll do anything you want,' answered Sir Bedevere. 'Anything.'

'I understand now what the messages mean on Excalibur. I have kept it during my lifetime but now it is time for Excalibur, and I, to leave this place. I want you to go to the lake and throw the sword away. Throw it into the middle of the lake and come back to tell me you have done it.'

'I will,' said Sir Bedevere, and he picked up the beautiful heavy sword.

Sir Bedevere took Excalibur to the lakeside and held it in his hands. The jewels on the hilt of the sword sparkled in the sunlight. The gold shone, and the metal blade shimmered and glistened.

'This sword is too beautiful to throw into the lake,' thought Sir Bedevere. 'I'll keep it. But I'll hide it and tell King Arthur it's in the water.'

So Sir Bedevere hid Excalibur under a tree and went back to the dying King.

'I've done it,' he said. 'I've thrown Excalibur into the lake.'

'What did you see?' asked King Arthur.

Sir Bedevere was surprised by the question. 'I saw the ripples on the lake as I threw the sword in,' he said.

'You are lying to me,' said King Arthur angrily. 'The message on the sword says THROW ME AWAY, you must do it. Go!'

Sir Bedevere went again to the lakeside and took Excalibur from under the tree. Again he held the magnificent sword in his hands. He could see the message written quite clearly on the side of the sword: THROW ME AWAY. He turned the sword over and saw KEEP ME written on the other side.

'I'll keep it,' he thought. 'I know he told me to throw it away, but he'll never know.' So once again Sir Bedevere hid Excalibur in the undergrowth by the side of the lake, and went back to King Arthur to tell him he had thrown the sword in the water.

'And what did you see?' asked King Arthur again.

'I saw the ripples where the sword went down,' he answered.

'You have betrayed me,' thundered King Arthur. 'You have not done what the message says. Is my sword worth more to you than my wishes? Go! Do not keep the sword but throw it into the lake.'

Sir Bedevere went again to the lakeside and held Excalibur in his hands and he felt ashamed that he had disobeyed the wishes of the King. He gazed at the wonderful sword and knew that the time was right to throw it away. He lifted Excalibur high into the air, and threw it as hard as he could towards the centre of the lake. It glittered as it twisted in the sunlight. But as Excalibur fell, an arm and hand reached up out of the lake and grasped hold of the sword's jewelled handle, brandished it three times, then vanished with it into the depths of the waters.

Sir Bedevere watched in amazement then returned to King Arthur.

'I have done what you wanted,' he said. 'I am sorry I disobeyed you before.'

'And what did you see this time?' asked the king.

'I saw a hand rise up out of the lake and take the sword into the water,' said Sir Bedevere.

'Then it is done,' said King Arthur. 'And I forgive you. Now carry me to the water's edge for I must go.' As Sir Bedevere carried King Arthur to the lakeside, a boat sailed towards them, and Sir Bedevere gently laid him on board. The boat carried the king to the Vale of Avalon, where it is said his wounds were healed.

As for Excalibur, no-one ever saw the magical sword again.

Sir Bedevere had a duty to do what the king had asked him to do, even though he wanted to keep the sword for himself. If someone you trust gives you a message, it's your responsibility to see that it's carried out.

Of course, if someone you *don't* trust tells you to do something, you have every right to say no.

Dear God, help us to act responsibly when people we trust ask us to do something. Help us never to say we'll do something, then later decide we won't bother. Please help us to be trustworthy. Amen

Tony Bullimore

There are many different ways of sending messages; some are simple and some are extremely complicated. Perhaps the simplest way of sending a message is tapping on something to let someone know you are there. Not long since, some miners were trapped underground and the only way they could let their rescuers know they were still alive was to tap on the walls of the mine. The rescuers were able to find them and dig them out.

But there are much more complicated message-senders as well which use electronic beams and satellite dishes. These are wonderful in emergencies – providing you happen to have one of them with you!

In today's true story, tapping and electronic beacons were both used to send messages.

Tony Bullimore is a yachtsman, and in January 1997 he took part in a single-handed round-the-world yacht race; 25,000 miles non-stop round-the-world on his own. What a challenge! But Tony Bullimore was an experienced sailor and he had all the best equipment on board his yacht, the Exide Challenger. He had every hope of winning.

Everything started well, and by the beginning of January he was in the Southern Ocean between Australia and the Antarctic; half-way round the world, only half way left to go!

Three days later the bad weather started. Tony knew the safety rules. He lashed everything down so that nothing would get swept overboard. He pulled in the sails so that he could control the boat better in the rough sea. Then he looked out into the worsening weather and saw a massive patch of grey up ahead. At first he thought it was mist and rain, but then he realised it was water. A huge wave, as high as seven houses and holding hundreds of gallons of water, followed by another wave, then another, was heading his way. Tony went down into the cabin and waited. As the water hit the Exide Challenger the boat tipped over. There was a snap snap as the twin masts both broke off. The boat righted itself again then tipped once more as the next wave engulfed it. This time the boat tipped right over. There was another snap as the boat's keel broke off. There was no way now that the Exide Challenger could right itself. It had capsized.

The cabin, now upside down with the ceiling where the floor used to be, was in total darkness. Water started pouring in through a broken cabin window. 'I'm going to drown,' thought Tony.

But the upside-down boat was floating. An air pocket had formed in the damaged cabin. And although Tony was trapped and cold and wet and scared, he had air to breath and he was alive. He tried to stay calm and to think clearly.

He reached in the darkness along the walls of the upside-down cabin for the electronic signaller which was for emergencies. All boats have to carry emergency equipment, 'And I think this counts as an emergency!' thought Tony. He tied a length of rope to the signaller, switched it on, and pushed it through the broken cabin window. It bobbed on its rope up to the surface of the water and sent its electronic beam into the sky.

The beam hit a satellite dish high above the earth and was sent back down to a receiving station in France. The electronic message told the receiver that it was the Exide Challenger in difficulty, and it gave the boat's exact location. The people in France sent a distress signal to Australia and the people there contacted Australian Sea-Rescue.

But Tony and the Exide Challenger were1500 miles from land. They were out of helicopter range. Larger aircraft could fly over where they were but couldn't land to give any help. The nearest ship was four days' journey away, even sailing at top speed.

'Tony's not going to make it,' the rescuers said. 'He's probably dead already. No-one could stay alive in those seas.' But they had a responsibility to save him if they could, and they sent out a rescue ship.

Tony lost track of time in his upside-down cold wet cabin, although he could tell the difference between day and night because the sea changed colour and became a paler shade of green in the daytime. He found a tin of beans and some bottles of drinking water in all the broken stuff on the ceiling of the cabin which was now the floor. Then he found some chocolate. None of it tasted pleasant, mixed with sea water, but it kept him alive a bit longer.

He wondered if anyone had received his electronic signal. He wondered if anyone was searching for him. He wondered if they'd be able to find him, so far from land. And sometimes he wondered what it would be like to die. But he tried to stay calm and to be positive.

After four days, the rescue ship reached the Exide Challenger.

'It's there,' they said. 'Up ahead. But it's upside-down. No-one can still be alive in there.'

'Send a signal to it anyway,' said the captain. 'Then we'll know for sure.'

A sonar signal was sent under water to the capsized yacht.

Inside the underwater cabin, Tony Bullimore thought he heard a faint sound.

'No. I must be hearing things,' he thought. But there it was again, the dull thud thud thud of the sonar signaller, waiting to pick up any sound that Tony could make.

He banged on the side of the cabin.

'He's in there!' said the astonished rescuers. 'He's still alive.'

'We're coming,' they called, as they launched the rescue dinghy. But Tony Bullimore had spent quite long enough in his underwater upturned cabin, and was on his way to them.

'I'm here. I'm coming!' he shouted and he swam through the broken cabin door, through the upturned engine room, out into the cold heaving sea, and up to the surface and the first daylight he'd seen in four days. There in front of him was the best sight he could ever hope to see... the rescue ship and men's faces peering down at him from the ship's rail. They were amazed to see him not only alive but swimming towards them.

Four days later the rescue ship arrived back in Australia. The quayside was lined with thousands of people who'd come to welcome Tony back. They cheered and sang, waved flags and let off balloons. Tony hadn't won the race, but he was safe, alive and well. The best prize he could have.

As soon as he got off the ship he was surrounded by press and television journalists.

'How does it feel to be safe?'

'Did you think you'd be rescued?'

'Is there anything you want to say?'

I want to say thank you,' said Tony. 'The biggest thank you in the world to all the people who worked hard to rescue me. Thank you. I owe you my life.'

Tony's rescue was successful because of the messages that were sent and received. Modern technology has given us many things. It has given us television and computers, calculators and electronic games. But it has also given us satellites and electronic signalling, and without those, Tony Bullimore wouldn't be alive today.

By the way, he was talking not so long since, about sailing round the world again. What would you do? Would you try it again?

Thank you, Lord, for the messages that can be sent by modern technology. Thank you for people like Tony Bullimore who take on the challenge of difficult journeys. Help us to be brave and not to give up when we are faced with difficulties in our lives. Amen

Theme 3: Rules

Making jelly

(Basic props needed for this assembly are: a packet of jelly, jug of cold water, measuring jug or bowl, spoon and plate.)

Do you like jelly? I do, and I thought I would make some in assembly today, and then I'll eat it later, when it's set, with my tea.

I've put the things I'll need on this table. There's a mixing bowl and a spoon, some water, and of course a packet of jelly. I'll just read the label and see what I have to do.

It says: 'Directions for use.

1. Place jelly in measuring jug.
2. Add boiling water up to 150ml mark.
3. Stir until dissolved.
4. Make up to 550ml with cold water.
5. Pour into serving dish and refrigerate until set.'

Well, that all sounds straightforward, so here we go!

1. 'Place jelly in measuring jug.' That's easy to do. There it is in the jug.
2. 'Add boiling water to 150ml.' Oh dear! I haven't a kettle here. Still, never mind, I won't bother with the boiling water, I don't suppose it'll matter. I'll just put cold water in instead and give it a good stir. It says 'stir until dissolved', but nothing much seems to be happening... I'll just stir it a bit more.

It's still not dissolved, so I won't bother waiting any longer, I'll go on to the next instruction.

3. 'Make up to 550ml with cold water.' That's easy enough. There we are. It's the same as one pint.

Now, what's next? Oh yes. 'Pour into serving dish and refrigerate until set.' Well I haven't a serving dish here, so it can stay in the jug. And there isn't a fridge here in the hall, but I don't suppose it'll matter. By the time we've sung a song together I'm sure it'll be ready.

I'll take a spoonful of jelly and serve it onto this plate. I wonder if anyone would like to come and taste it? No, I thought not! It hasn't worked, has it? I wonder why it's gone wrong, and I wonder why I'm making jelly for you in our assembly today? Any ideas?

Well done! I didn't follow the directions properly. In other words I didn't follow the rules. Directions and rules are almost the same thing. They're there to help us. They're there to make things work.

If I don't follow the rules of the road when I'm driving my car, I won't last very long as a driver. If I don't follow the rules when I'm cooking, I won't make very good things to eat. And if I don't follow the rules in our school and our community, I won't be a very good citizen.

Sometimes we might not like the rules and we might not want to follow them, like me with the jelly, but if we don't, then whatever we are trying to do won't turn out very well.

Dear God, help us to understand that rules are there to help us and guide us and keep us safe. Help us to abide by the rules in our school and community and to co-operate with other people. Help us to try to be fair in all our dealings with others. Amen

Joshua saves his dad

Rules are there to help us. They are a guide for how to do something, or how to behave. You wouldn't have much fun trying to play a game if there were no rules telling you how to play. And can you imagine what it would be like if there were no rules of any kind in your house or here at school? It would be totally chaotic if everyone just did what they wanted, when they wanted, without any regard for anyone else. Rules help us to live together, co-operatively. But rules can also save lives.

In today's true story, a boy saved his dad's life because he knew the rules.

Joshua is ten, and lives with his mum and dad and younger sister. Joshua's dad, Peter, is a joiner, and works for a building firm. Peter is also a diabetic, which means he has something wrong with the sugar levels in his blood. In order to control the sugar levels, Peter has to have injections of something called insulin every day, and he has to eat very regular meals. But even so, his blood sugar levels can still sometimes get very low, and when this happens he feels tired and dizzy. If his blood sugar levels get really low, Peter could collapse, and he'd have to be taken to hospital. But usually, the insulin and the regular meals keep everything under control.

One day, Joshua and his dad were out in the car together. They'd been to see someone that Peter was going to do some joinery work for, and they were on their way home. But the visit had taken longer than they'd planned, and now they were stuck in a traffic jam on a busy main road. Peter began to feel tired and a bit dizzy.

When he felt like this, he knew he had to have something sweet to eat or drink. He had a Mars bar and a can of Coke in his jacket pocket, but his jacket was in the boot and he couldn't get at it whilst the car was moving.

'I'll be OK,' he thought. 'We'll be home soon and I'll be able to have my dinner.'

But the traffic jam got worse. There were some road works up ahead which were slowing everything down. Peter could feel himself getting more and more tired, and more dizzy.

Joshua, sitting next to his dad, was chattering away about school and the football match he was going to play in the following week.

'It'll be great because we always beat the team that are coming. I bet we win about ten nil. Maybe I'll score another goal. I've scored four this season so far. Will you come and watch me play, Dad? It's after school.'

But Peter didn't answer, and when Joshua looked at his dad, he realised something was terribly wrong.

Peter was almost unconscious. He couldn't see or hear or concentrate properly. He certainly couldn't drive the car, but he was still sitting behind the wheel and the traffic was now moving again quite quickly.

'We'll crash if I don't do something,' thought Joshua. He spoke to his dad again. 'Dad! DAD! Wake up.' But Peter was unable to hear his son, and unable to wake up.

Joshua remembered his teacher at school telling them that if ever they were in any difficulty, the first rule was to stay calm. So he didn't panic. He didn't shout for help out of the window. He didn't cry. He stayed calm and thought about the rules for driving a car.

'Well I know ten-year-olds are not allowed to drive,' he said to himself. 'But this is an emergency! And I know what to do,' and with that he took hold of the steering wheel and guided the car onto the nearest grass verge. Then he pulled on the handbrake to slow the car down, and when it stopped he clicked the handbrake tight and turned off the engine.

Having brought the car safely to a stop, he then stayed calm and thought about the rules for helping his dad. 'Rule one. Get help from an adult,' he said to himself. 'Rule two. Get someone to ring for an ambulance.'

Joshua got out of the car, stood on the pavement, and flagged down the next car that passed.

'Can you help me please? My dad's diabetic and he's ill. We need an ambulance.' The car driver looked at Peter, slumped in the driver's seat, and knew that he must help.

'Here, let's go to this house and telephone for help,' he said, running down the garden path of the nearest house and knocking on the door. Luckily it was the house of a police superintendent, who knew exactly what to do.

He telephoned for an ambulance, and gave Peter a drink of coke whilst they waited. By the time the ambulance came, Peter was already feeling a bit better, but he was taken to hospital for a check-up anyway.

Afterwards, the local newspaper heard how Joshua had taken control of the situation, and they interviewed him and his dad.

'How did you feel when you were in the car and you realised your dad was ill?' the reporter asked.

'I was scared, but I knew I had to stay calm and get help,' said Joshua. 'I knew the rules for driving the car, and I knew the rules for helping my dad when he's ill, so it wasn't too bad because I knew what to do.'

'And how do you feel about what your son did?' the reporter asked Peter.

'I'm very proud of my son,' said Peter. 'He's a hero! He stayed calm and knew exactly what to do. He's brilliant!'

The story has a happy ending because Joshua knew the rules. He knew about staying calm; he knew how to drive the car because he'd learned by watching his dad do it; and he knew how to get help in an emergency. I wonder what would have happened if he hadn't known what to do, or if he'd panicked when he realised his dad was ill.

Dear God, help us to think clearly and to stay calm when we are in difficult situations. Help us to remember the rules of safety when we are out and about. Help us to keep to the rules in our homes and at school, so that our home and school families work successfully. Amen

Charlie's new bag

Some rules in life are very clear and are written down for everyone to see. For instance, the Highway Code tells people exactly how they should behave when they're on the road. There are rules in the swimming baths which tell you how to behave so that everyone stays safe. You will probably have rules in your school or in your classroom which tell everyone how to behave in school so that it is a pleasant and safe place to be.

If you play any kind of game, from team games like football and rounders, to board games like monopoly and snakes and ladders, there are rules to tell you how to play. And even if you play a game on your own, like some card games, or games on your computer, there are rules to play by so that the game is fair.

Rules are there to help us. But some rules are not actually written down. For example, I don't suppose there is a notice in your local shop saying DO NOT STEAL, yet you know that the rule is there. Rules that are not actually written down are often 'common sense' rules – in other words, rules that you know about if you just stop to think.

In today's story, the boy didn't think about 'common sense' rules at all.

Charlie was going on a school trip. His class had been learning about animals in captivity and endangered species, and his teacher had organised a visit to the zoo. Charlie's mum had bought him a new bag for the trip.

'You'll need it to put your sandwiches and drink and spare jumper in,' said his mum. 'I've bought a big one so you'll get everything in.'

'Thanks Mum,' said Charlie, and he took the new bag to his bedroom to pack the things he would need for the trip.

The bag was brilliant! It had a big central compartment with a zip right round the top, and smaller pockets with flaps and zips on each side. It had padded shoulder straps so that he could wear it like a back-pack, and it was purple with a bright orange drawstring with toggles on the end. He'd wanted a bag like that for ages.

In the morning Charlie's mum put his packed lunch with some fruit and a carton of juice in the bag, and insisted he take a spare jumper in case it got cold. Then off he went to join the others in the playgound to wait for the coach that was to take them on the visit.

'What's your favourite animal, Charlie?' someone asked, then said, 'Mine's lions!' before he had chance to reply.

'Mine's monkeys!' said someone else.

'I want to see the snakes,' said Charlie's friend Pete.

'Mine's...' said Charlie, but no-one was listening because the coach had arrived and everyone surged towards the door.

The zoo was wonderful! Every bit as interesting as their teacher had said it would be. The children spent the first part of the visit going to the different sections of the zoo in groups with their group leader. They saw elephants and harvest mice, ostriches and humming birds, huge snakes and tiny lizards. They saw the aquarium, the tropical house, the nocturnal house, and the monkey house. They saw the deer park, and they visited the farm.

At lunchtime they were asked which animals they'd like best, and which they'd like to see again in the afternoon. And this is where the problem began because every child had a different favourite. In the end the children were told they could go with their group leader to a section of the zoo, then they could look round on their own providing they stayed in that area.

Charlie had no problem in deciding where he wanted to go. He headed straight for the farm, even though the rest of the children wanted to go back to see lions or tigers or elephants or snakes.

Those animals were OK, he thought, but they were all inside pens and cages. You couldn't get at the animals or touch them or hold them, but on the farm there were lambs and goats and rabbits and even piglets that you could hold and stroke.

Charlie spent the rest of the afternoon in the farm area, and for most of the time there was only him, and the farm keeper, and a family with two very small children in there. If there'd been more people about, perhaps he wouldn't have done what he did. Perhaps if his friend Pete had been with him, he'd have told him it was a stupid idea. But no-one was with him, the keeper and the family weren't looking, and Charlie told himself it was all right because there wasn't actually a sign anywhere to say he shouldn't.

He'd only just done it when his group leader came looking for him.

'Come on Charlie. We've been looking for you everywhere. It's time to go, the coach is waiting.'

Charlie climbed onto the coach and put his bag down very carefully on the seat next to him. He held his jumper in his hand.

'Why don't you put that in you bag, then you won't lose it?' his teacher suggested.

'No, it's all right, Miss,' he said. Then to his horror she moved his bag up and sat down next to him.

'Well Charlie, have you had a good day?'

'Yes thanks, Miss,' he said, and turned away to look out of the window so that she wouldn't ask him any more questions.

When they arrived back at school, Charlie's mum was there to meet him.

'He's been very quiet on the way back,' explained the teacher.

'Tired I suppose,' said Charlie's mum. 'Shall I carry your bag for you?'

'No thanks Mum,' said Charlie.

'He's not wanted to be parted from that bag all the way back,' laughed the teacher.

When they got home, to Charlie's mum's surprise, he disappeared straight upstairs to his bedroom, and said he didn't want any tea. A little later his mum said to his dad, 'I think I'd better go upstairs and see if he's all right. I wonder if he's feeling ill. It's unusual for him to be so quiet.'

She went to his bedroom and knocked on the door.

'You can't come in,' shouted Charlie, but his mum went in anyway.

Charlie was sitting on his bed. The new bag was lying down next to him, and next to the bag was... a very small, very pink, very smelly, and very squeaky... baby piglet.

'Oh Charlie! Whatever have you done?' said his mum. But the look on Charlie's face told her that he knew exactly what he'd done, and knew that he shouldn't have done it, despite his excuses.

'Well it didn't say you couldn't bring them home,' he said. 'It didn't say you hadn't to. How was I supposed to know? It didn't say,' and Charlie burst into tears.

'It didn't need to say, did it Charlie?' said his mum. 'Your own common sense should have told you! Come on!'

'Where are we going?' asked Charlie.

'We're going to the zoo,' said his mum. 'You've got some explaining to do!' and she picked up the piglet and went downstairs.

Charlie was quite right in that there wasn't a notice at the farm saying you couldn't take the animals home. I don't suppose there was a notice on his new bag either to say he shouldn't put piglets in it! But these are unwritten rules called common sense, which are things you know if you think about it.

Help us, Lord, to think about what we do. Help us not to use the excuse that we didn't know, when we've done something wrong. Help us to be honest and to own up when we've done something wrong. Help us to think before we act. Amen

February

Theme 1: Friendship

Mr Watson and the garden party

How many of you have a friend? Everyone! It's good to have friends, isn't it? But have you already found out that it takes at least two to be friends? You can't be friends with someone if they don't want to be friends with you. And do you know that to have a friend, you need to be a friend?

Maybe you have already discovered for yourself that how you behave to someone else affects how they behave towards you. If you're pleasant and friendly to others they'll usually be like that to you. And of course, if you're downright horrible to others, they'll probably be equally unpleasant to you.

In today's story, someone didn't know about this, and he probably wondered why he had no friends. Luckily though, an 'accident' helped the situation.

Mr Watson moved in to number 12 Sandiford Lane on the Tuesday, and by the Friday of the same week he had fallen out with every one of the neighbours and made himself extremely unpopular.

'I just don't understand why he has to be so unpleasant to everyone,' said Mrs Smith from number three. 'He's so grumpy. I only said Good Morning to him yesterday and he bit my head off.'

'He's not a bit friendly, and he's very ungrateful,' said Mrs Brown from number ten. 'I took him a packet of tea and a pint of milk on Tuesday when he moved in, and he told me to take them away again because he didn't want them.'

'And you should have heard how he shouted at our Jenny when she went into his garden to get her ball back,' said Jenny's mum.

'He certainly doesn't like children,' said Andrew's dad. 'My boy fell off his bike outside Mr Watson's gate on Wednesday, and he never even asked if he was all right or offered to help him. He just told him to clear off!'

'He really is a most disagreeable and unfriendly man,' they all said.

On the Saturday after he'd moved in, Mr Watson got up early and went outside. Then he began to knock down the small wall which surrounded his garden. He'd just about finished demolishing it when a delivery van arrived and unloaded some huge panels of garden fencing. The delivery men helped Mr Watson to put up the new fence, and by the end of the afternoon it was finished.

'Well, that should keep everyone out all right,' laughed one of the men. 'It's the biggest garden fence I've ever seen!'

But Mr Watson didn't think it was funny.

'It's nothing to do with you!' he snapped. 'That fence is going to keep nosey parkers out. That fence is going to separate me from the rest of the world! I don't like people and they don't like me. That's how it is.'

'OK mate. Keep cool!' said the delivery men, and they grinned at each other as they left.

Mr Watson went back into his house, certain that the new fence would allow him to be his usual grumpy self, and that it would keep all the neighbours at a very safe distance. But things didn't quite work out as he had planned. Instead of the fence helping him to live the isolated life he wanted, it actually made people more curious about him.

'Why has he put up such a big fence?' people said. 'What is there in his garden that he doesn't want anyone to see?' Of course there was nothing in the garden for anyone to see. The children soon discovered that when they climbed to the top of the fence to look over and see.

'It's just full of flowers and grass and stuff,' they said.

'I need something else to keep people away,' said Mr Watson to himself. 'I know, I'll put up a sign saying DANGER, that'll keep them all away. So he cut some large pieces of card and wrote one big letter on each piece:
D A N G E R.

Then he wrote KEEP OUT on another piece of card, just for good measure, and went outside and fastened all the pieces of card to his new fence.

Unfortunately, there was a very strong wind that night, and Mr Watson's notice blew down. The pieces of card were found in a muddled and muddy heap at the base of the fence the next morning by a man out walking his dog.

'What's all this then?' said the man as he picked up the letters. 'Look at this, Bonnie. I wonder what all these letters say?' and he spread them out to see what they were. 'There's a G, and an A. There's an R, and a D, and an E, and an N. Oh, I see what it is. It's a notice saying GARDEN. I can't read what this other one says, it's too muddy. But if this is a garden, the other notice will probably say FREE ENTRY. COME IN, because people who have gardens usually like to share them.' And with that, the man with the dog wrote FREE ENTRY - COME IN on the back of the last piece of card, then he fastened all the cards again on Mr Watson's fence.

On Sunday morning, Mr Watson slept in. He was probably tired after all his hard work on the fence the day before. It was after eleven when he finally opened his bedroom curtains, and he could hardly believe what he saw.

There were people everywhere. Some were walking up and down his paths, others were looking at his flowers, some were sitting on his garden furniture. One family was having a picnic under his tree, a group of children were playing football on his lawn.

He threw open his bedroom window and bellowed, 'WHAT...' but he didn't get any further because all the people began to speak at once.

'Hello, you're here at last.'

'What a brilliant idea to invite everyone into your garden.'

'It's just like a party. In fact it is a party. It's a garden party!' and everyone started to laugh.

'Thank you for thinking of this. It's wonderful.'

'What a lovely way to settle into the neighbourhood and get to know all the people who live round about.'

'There's just one thing missing – how about serving tea and biscuits,' and everyone laughed again.

Mr Watson could not believe it. He, who hated people and had no friends, had *crowds* of people in his garden. He, who had never invited anyone to his home ever before, now apparently had dozens of guests, and he had no idea how or why they were there.

He quickly got dressed and went downstairs, intending to tell everyone to push off and leave him alone, but when he got outside he found he couldn't do it! He discovered that all these people liked being invited in; and more to the point, Mr Watson discovered that he liked having them there, so he went back into his kitchen and made drinks for everyone, opened his best biscuits and cut into his newly-baked fruit cake. Then he invited everyone to join him for elevenses, even though by then it was well after twelve.

Mr Watson had a wonderful time. He'd never enjoyed himself so much in all his life. Afterwards, when he was talking to one of his new friends about the garden party, he said that he didn't know people could be so nice.

'Ah well, that's because you were nice to them,' said the friend. 'When you first moved in, we all thought you were a bit cross and bad-tempered. In fact we didn't think we'd like you at all. But when you invited us all to your garden party, it showed us that you wanted to be friends after all. It was a really good idea to invite us all to the party. I'd never have thought of doing anything like that.'

'No, neither would I,' thought Mr Watson.

Mr Watson discovered for himself that if you are friendly to others, they'll usually be friendly to you. In order to *have* a friend, you need to *be* a friend. That doesn't mean you have to *give* people things to make them be friends with you, but it means you need to behave in a friendly way towards them.

If everyone treated other people in the way they would like to be treated themselves, I think the world would be a friendlier place.

Thank you God, for our friends. Help us to understand that making friends involves being friendly to others. Help us to treat everyone as we hope they will treat us. Amen

The broken plate

This morning I want to show you something. Here it is. *(Produce an old plate from a bag.)* What is it? It doesn't look much, but do you think it's useful? Do you think it's valuable? In what way do you think it could be useful or valuable? *(Discuss.)*

I'm going to show you a trick with this plate, but first I need to wrap it in this. *(Produce an old towel from the bag and wrap the plate well, then put it on a firm table.)*

Now, I need someone to help me. *(Choose an older child to come to the front, then produce a large hammer from the bag.)*

I'm going to ask A to hit the plate a couple of times with this hammer... and we'll see what happens! *(In my experience, the child usually needs a little persuasion to actually use the hammer! When the plate is broken, unwrap it from the towel, show the pieces to everyone, and put them down on the table.)*

Well done A! You did a good job there! Now, I have another small job for you to do before you go and sit down again. *(Produce some [child-friendly]glue from the bag.)*

Just stick it together again and make it as good as new! *(Give the child the glue, encourage them to start the task, then move away from the table a little and address the rest of the children whilst A carries on with the repair.)*

Whilst A gets on with that, I want to tell you a very short story.

Once upon a time there were two children called Tom and Sarah. Most of the time they were the best of friends, but every so often, just like all children, they fell out with each other.

One day they were playing table tennis in Tom's garage when they began to argue about who was winning. The argument became very heated, some dreadful things were said, and Sarah hit Tom. He retaliated by kicking her, she pulled his hair and he punched her. By this time they were both in tears and Tom's mother came out of the house to see what all the noise was about.

'She started it!' yelled Tom.

'It's your fault then, is it?' said Tom's mum. 'We'll see what your mother has to say about this,' and she marched Sarah round to her house.

When Sarah's mother saw the two children in tears and Tom's mum looking really annoyed, she became angry too, and in no time the two grown-ups were arguing.

Later that afternoon Tom's mum and dad came round to see Sarah's mum and dad and the argument started all over again and some really hurtful things were said. Afterwards, Tom's mum told him he was never to play with Sarah again, and Sarah's mum forbade her even to speak to him.

In the end, the two families never made up their differences. The children saw each other at school, but were never best friends again, and the adults, who had also been good friends and used to go out together sometimes in the evenings, didn't speak to each other any more.

And all because of a game of table tennis! Isn't it sad!

And what has all this got to do with a broken plate? Well, let's see how A is getting on with mending it. *(Check on progress, and discuss with A what the repair problems are.)*

You'll remember that the plate was very easy to break. Just like friendships; they're easy to break as well, just look at those people in the story and how easily they all fell out.

But you can see that it's very much harder to *mend* the plate. Just like friendships; they're really hard to mend when you've broken them. Sometimes they're impossible to repair and they stay broken forever.

It's better to try to look after friendships so that they don't get broken in the first place.

And as for the plate: well it's an old one of mine and I don't need it any more. I think it's past repair, so I think I'll throw it away. But thank you A, for trying to mend it. You did well.

Dear God, help us to remember how easy it is to break a friendship. Help us to care for our friends and to try not to do anything to break the friendship. Help us to understand that we all need friends, and to understand the importance of friendship. Amen

Saint Kevin and the king's goose

Friends are important, and best friends are even more important still. When you have a best friend you are usually very loyal to them; you look after them and try never to let them down. Sometimes people go to great lengths to look after their best friend.

In this story from Ireland, a king was prepared to give anything to help his best friend..

Saint Kevin had a problem. He wanted to build a monastery and a church, but he had no land and no money.

He lived all alone in a cave by the side of a lake in County Wicklow, in Ireland, and spent most of his time talking to God and helping any animals who needed help. Saint Kevin had a way with animals. He seemed to understand them, and they trusted him. Some people say he even had a blackbird once lay an egg in the palm of his hand, and he kept his hand quite still until the egg hatched and the fledgling could fly away.

Saint Kevin's nearest neighbour was the king, who lived in an enormous castle at the head of the lake. Of course, although Saint Kevin knew that his neighbour was the king, the king did not know that his next-door neighbour was Saint Kevin who lived in a cave and who wanted to build a monastery but had no money.

The king, in fact, didn't know very much at all, except that he was extremely worried. You see, the king's best friend was a beautiful white goose. She'd been his best friend for years and years, but now she was old and ill and unable to fly any more. The king was sure she would soon die, and he didn't know how he was going to cope without her. After all, best friends are very hard to come by. You can't just go out and get another best friend if you lose the first one, even if you are the king of County Wicklow. The king was distraught.

One day he was out walking along the edge of his lake, when he came across Saint Kevin. Of course, the king didn't know it was Saint Kevin, he thought it was just a young man.

'Good morning to you,' said the king, who was polite to everyone even though he was so important.

'Top o' the morning to you, your Royal Highness,' said Saint Kevin.

The king looked astonished.

'How do you know who I am?' he asked.

'Never mind that,' said Saint Kevin. 'How are you? And more to the point, how is that goose of yours?'

The king looked even more astounded that this young man should know so much about him.

'She's not at all well,' answered the king. 'I'm extremely worried about her. Why do you ask?'

'I ask because I may be able to help,' said Saint Kevin.

'How can you help a goose who is old and sick and not long for this world?' sighed the king.

'I can make her young again,' said Saint Kevin. 'What would you give me if I did that for you?'

'If you did that for me, I'd give you anything you asked for,' said the king.

'Anything?' said Saint Kevin.

'Anything!' answered the king.

'Would you give me all the land that she flies around, if I can make her fly again?' said Saint Kevin.

'Certainly,' said the king. 'It's a deal!'

So the king went to get his beautiful white goose, and he carried her back to Saint Kevin. The young man spoke softly to the goose, made the sign of the cross on her head, then gently pushed her into the air. The snow-white goose flew up, up into the sky for the first time in many a long day. She flew to the end of the lake, up over the woods, across the fields and over the hills, then on out of sight. She flew all around the edge of the kingdom then back to the king, who hugged her and stroked her and turned to the young man.

'That's remarkable,' said the king. 'You don't know what this means to me. I don't know how to thank you.'

'You can thank me by keeping your word,' said Saint Kevin. 'All the land she flew round is to be mine?'

'That was the deal,' said the king. 'And I always keep my word. The land is yours, even though it is my entire kingdom. Friendship is worth more than a kingdom.'

And that is how Saint Kevin came to have enough land and money to build his monastery and church. But he didn't forget the king. He allowed the king to continue to live in his palace, and they became the best of friends – well, second best friends, because the king's very best friend was the goose.

I wonder why the king had a goose for a best friend in the first place? I wonder why he didn't have a person as his best friend? Do you think it's harder for a king to make friends than it is for ordinary people? And I wonder what you would have done if you'd been the king?

Thank you, Lord, for our friends. Help us always to care for our friends, help us always to be loyal to them, and never let them down. Help us always to remember our old friends when new ones come along. And help us to share our friends and to remember that we don't own them. Amen

Theme 2: Feelings

The evacuee

Can you put yourself in someone else's shoes? It doesn't mean literally putting your friend's shoes on! It means can you see things from someone else's point of view. Can you understand how they feel? Let's try an experiment and see if you can understand how the boy in today's story felt when he was evacuated during the Second World War.

You may know that children who lived in big cities were evacuated to the countryside so that they would be safe during the bombing raids. Evacuation meant they had to leave their homes and their parents and go and live with strangers, miles away from their own home. Here's the story.

Billy lived in London with his mum and his baby sister. When the bombing started it was decided that all children over three would be sent to live with families in the countryside.

'I don't want to go,' said Billy. But he had no choice in the matter.

'Can you and Sally come too?' he asked his mum.

'No Billy,' she said. 'Sally will stay here with me. You have to go on your own. It's for your own good.'

So Billy was given one small cardboard suitcase to put his clothes in, he was dressed in his best jumper and trousers and coat, he was given a gas mask in a box and told to carry it all the time, and he was taken to the railway station by his mum.

When they arrived at the station it was crowded. There were hundreds of children waiting to be put on the trains that would take them to the countryside.

'What's his name?' said a large official-looking lady to Billy's mum.

'Billy Carter,' she said.

'Age?'

'He's ten,' said Billy's mum.

'He's not very big for ten, is he?' barked the lady, and Billy began to feel that he was somehow not quite good enough to be evacuated.

'Here, put this on,' she said, handing Billy a large cardboard label on a safety pin. She'd written his name and the number ten on the label as she'd been talking. Billy assumed the ten stood for his age, but the lady went on, 'Train ten. You'll need to queue over there. No need for mothers to hang about. I'm sure you all have things to do.'

Billy's mother steered him over to where the woman had indicated. Then she thrust a paper bag of sandwiches into his hands, and hugged him and said, 'I have to go now Billy. Take care. Be good. Write to me soon,' and she hurried away. Billy thought she was crying, but he'd never seen his mum cry before so he wasn't sure.

The train journey wasn't too bad. Billy sat with some children who went to his school, but most of them were with their brothers or sisters so they didn't take much notice of him. He watched the London streets out of the window as the train rattled out of the city. Soon the view changed and there were lots more gardens. Then he saw fields and farms.

The train rushed through several small stations but he couldn't read the names and had no idea where he was. After about an hour, a grown-up told them they could eat their sandwiches. It seemed that every child had a packed lunch of some sort. Billy wondered when and where he would have his tea. He liked his meals and was always hungry.

About an hour later, the train stopped and about thirty children were told to get out. Billy wondered where they were going. The train moved off again and he looked at them standing on the platform with an adult he didn't know trying to make them all walk in twos in a line.

Ten minutes later the train stopped again. This time all the children in Billy's carriage were told to leave the train. They lined up on the platform and were taken to a village hall. They stood in a long line against the wall, and a woman with a list of names called out each one and they had to answer like having the register taken at school.

Then a group of women from the village came into the hall.

'Here are the evacuees,' said the lady with the list. 'You can choose which ones you want.'

The first woman walked up to the line of children and looked at every one.

'I'll have this one,' she said, pointing to a big twelve-year-old girl. 'She can help me around the house.' The woman took the girl home.

The second woman walked along the line of children.

'I'll take these,' she said, as though she was buying a pound of potatoes, and she pointed to six-year-old twins.

The next woman chose a small girl called Jenny. 'Such a pretty name,' she said. The woman behind her chose two brothers to take home, and the next woman took a brother and two sisters. 'They look nice and strong,' she said.

By now, only a tiny three-year-old girl, and Billy were left. All the women had gone. The lady with the list picked up the little girl and gave her a cuddle. 'You can come with me, little one,' she said. 'But I don't know what we're going to do with you,' she said to Billy. 'All the people who volunteered to have evacuees have already taken them.' Billy looked down at the floor and felt ashamed that none of the women had chosen him. What was wrong with him? Why didn't anyone want him? He felt miserable and alone and the odd one out.

Suddenly the lady with the list stood up. 'You'd better follow me,' she said, and she marched out of the hall. Billy picked up his small cardboard suitcase and followed her.

She walked out of the hall and down the lane. She passed several tidy-looking houses then pushed open the gate of a rather dilapidated cottage. She knocked at the door.

After what seemed like a long time to Billy, the door was opened by a rough-looking old man.

'What do you want?' he asked gruffly.

'This is Billy,' said the lady with the list, pushing Billy into the old man's doorway. 'He'll have to stay with you. We've run out of houses. There's nowhere else for him to go,' and she turned and marched back down the garden path, still with the little girl in her arms.

'Oi! Wait a minute!' shouted the old man after her. 'You can't leave him here! I can't look after a child. I don't know anything about children. Come and take him back!' But the lady with the list was already half-way down the lane. She turned and called back, 'There is a war on you know. It's your duty to help.'

'I can't...' began the old man again. Then he looked at Billy and sighed, 'Well, I suppose now you're here you'd better come inside.'

The story stops there. I wonder what Billy felt like when he was left all alone with the old man? And I wonder what the next few days were like, and how long he stayed with the old man. How would you have felt if you'd had to leave your home and parents and friends and travel miles away all on your own? I suppose Billy went to school in the village. How do you think he felt starting at a new school? Have you ever gone to a new school? How did it feel on your first day?

If someone new comes to your class or your neighbourhood, try to help them to settle in so that they don't feel like the odd one out.

Dear God, help us to be aware of other people's feelings. Help us to be welcoming and kind to people who are new to our school or neighbourhood. Help us never to make people feel as though they are the odd one out. Amen

The odd one out

Have you ever been the odd one out? Can you remember how it felt? Perhaps all your friends were invited to someone's birthday party, and you weren't. Or maybe everyone was playing a game in the playground and you weren't asked to join in. There are times when we all feel left out, and it's not a pleasant feeling, is it?

Today in assembly I'd like to play a game. I'll need ten people to join in, but I only want you to volunteer to play if you think you'll be able to explain to everyone how you feel, during the game. Who'd like to help?

(It's necessary to have some ready-prepared cards of different colours and shapes. You can make whatever combinations you wish, but you need to end up with one odd colour, and one odd shape. I find the simplest cards to prepare are:

- *a red, a green, a blue and a yellow square*
- *a red, a green and a blue triangle*

- *a red and a green rectangle*
- *a red circle*

This uses ten children and is usually sufficient especially where space is limited.)

Here are the ten children who are going to play 'odd one out'. I'm going to give you each a coloured shape. Now I'd like you to find the other people whose colours match yours. In other words, put yourselves in colour groups.

Good!

Let's see what we have. We've a group of four red shapes. Another group of three green shapes. Then we've a small group of two blue shapes. And one yellow shape, all by itself.

How do you feel, yellow shape holder, to be all by yourself?

(Responses will vary and there are no right or wrong answers. Most children will reply that they would prefer to be with the others, but the more confident extroverts may say they prefer to be by themselves. That's fine. The children are simply saying how they feel, and the 'audience' can be told this.)

Let's play again, but we'll change the sets. This time find the people whose shape matches yours. In other words, put yourselves in shape groups.

Good!

Let's look again and see what we have. There are four squares, three triangles, two rectangles, and one circle all by itself. I wonder if the circle holder feels the same as the yellow shape holder; I'll find out.

(Discuss how this child feels to be alone. The response may or may not be the same as before. If it's the same, it's useful to ask the other children in the groups how they would have felt if they'd been left the odd one out. You could open the discussion to include other children in the 'audience'.)

Sometimes it's good to be alone. But at other times it's good to be part of a group and not to be the odd one out. In our school and our families, let's try to make sure that we respect people's wishes when they don't want to join in, but that we never make them feel left out, or unwanted, or disliked. Let's try never to make anyone feel that they are the odd one out.

Help us, Lord, to be aware of how other people feel. Help us never to pick on people or to be deliberately unkind to them. Help us never to make anyone feel that they are the odd one out. Help us to care for others. Amen

From tomorrow on

I wonder how many different feelings you've felt already this week? I hope lots of you have felt happy or pleased or cheerful. I think some of you might have felt cross or angry or annoyed or disappointed if something's gone wrong. I hope not too many of you have felt sad or worried about something. But all these feelings are quite normal for us to have; the important thing is how we deal with them.

Sometimes it's hard to deal with difficult feelings. The girl in today's story was living in terrible conditions and must have felt hungry, cold, lonely, tired and sad. She wrote a poem to help her to deal with her feelings of sadness.

The girl was thirteen and lived in Germany at the time of the Second World War. But she was Jewish and Jewish people were not welcome in that country at that time.

At first the girl lived in the house where she'd always lived with her mother and father, her brother and her two older sisters. But then the troubles began.

The Jewish children were told they couldn't go to school any more, and the Jewish adults were told they couldn't go to work. This meant that no-one could earn any money, but they weren't allowed to go in the shops anyway, so they had nowhere to spend it if they had any. Slowly the Jewish people began to starve.

Then they were made to wear a big yellow star on their clothes so that everyone could see they were Jewish. People made fun of them and pushed and kicked them and called them names. They were forced out of their houses and made to live in tiny areas called ghettos. They were not allowed to go out of the ghetto.

And then the transportations began. At first no-one understood what was happening when groups of Jewish people were rounded up by the Nazi soldiers and put on trains and trucks. But they quickly learned that they were being sent to concentration camps. 'You can work in the camps,' they were told.

The girl was put on a train with her brother and sisters, and sent to a concentration camp called Auschwitz camp. Her mother and father were sent to a different camp; the girl didn't know where. Her aunts and uncles and her grandparents were also sent away, but not with her parents.

When the train arrived at Auschwitz camp, soldiers were shouting and pushing people into lines. The girl's brother and sisters were sent one way and she was sent another. She cried out to be allowed to go with them but a soldier hit her on the head with his gun and she fell to the ground.

A woman standing behind the girl helped her up and then stood with her, and the soldiers must have thought they were together because he let them both go through the barrier together.

They were sent to a huge wooden hut. The hut was freezing cold, it was made of thin wood and had no glass in the windows. Inside the hut were hundreds of bunk beds, but there were no blankets or pillows on the beds, just a bit of dirty straw where the mattress should have been.

The girl climbed onto one of the beds and lay down. The woman who had been kind to her lay down on the bunk underneath. 'I'll look after you,' she said.

There was nothing for any of them to eat that night, and the next morning the soldiers came again. 'Hurry up. Get outside,' they shouted. The women from the hut all lined up outside and some of them were taken away. The girl didn't know where they'd gone, but she never saw any of them again.

Each morning it was the same; the soldiers came and took away some of the women. One morning they took away the woman who had been kind to the girl. Now she knew no-one in the hut. She was frightened and hungry. She was lonely and scared.

One day she found a bit of paper on the floor and a stub of pencil. It must have belonged to one of the soldiers. She picked it up and put it in her pocket. That night the girl sat on her bunk and wrote a poem.

"From tomorrow on I shall be sad,
From tomorrow on,
But not today.
Today I will be glad.
And every day,
No matter how bitter it may be,
I shall say
'From tomorrow on I shall be sad,
But not today'."

The girl read the poem to herself every day after that. And she tried so hard to do what the poem said. She tried to find something to be glad about every day, even though it was very difficult to do.

The girl died in the concentration camp at Auschwitz, but someone found her bit of paper with the poem on it, and saved it, so that she would be remembered, even though no-one knew her name.

The girl at Auschwitz lived in conditions that we can hardly imagine, yet she tried to be brave and to be cheerful and to be positive. She tried not to give in to feelings of sadness and misery.

Instead of a prayer today, we'll listen to her poem again.

"From tomorrow on I shall be sad,
From tomorrow on,
But not today.
Today I will be glad.
And every day,
No matter how bitter it may be,
I shall say
'From tomorrow on I shall be sad,
But not today'." Amen

Theme 3: Power

A remarkable victory

Do you sometimes think that it's only big, powerful people who succeed at things? Sometimes of course, they do. And sometimes big, powerful people try to get what they want by using their power and by bullying others. But it doesn't necessarily work. Small people can be just as strong, providing they think and use their brains. Today's story is a fable from China, and it's about an army that was so big it felt sure it would win.

Once upon a time there was a large and powerful army. The army was made up of many different companies, each with hundreds of foot soldiers, horses and horsemen. There was a Captain in charge of each company, and a General in charge of the whole army. Altogether, there were more than seventy-five thousand soldiers. The army was so strong that it rarely lost a battle.

One day the General decided that the army would attack a small state in Southern China.

'It won't be difficult,' he said to his men. 'The state is so small and insignificant, it will only have a tiny army. We can defeat it with no problem.'

So preparations for battle were made. Each of the seventy-five thousand soldiers was given his orders. Everyone knew what they had to do. Equipment and food rations were shared out. Everything was ready.

'Time to go!' decreed the General, and the army set off. Line after line of soldiers and horses, all led by the Captains and the General, marched off to war.

After several hours they arrived at a river which separated their land from the small state they were going to invade.

'Halt here,' called the General, and the entire army came to a stop. The General shaded his eyes and looked across the river towards the distant horizon. There was nothing to see except grass and a few trees, and one old tumbledown hut that looked as though it had been built by a woodsman in days gone by.

'What can you see?' asked the Captains.

'Nothing!' answered the General.

'Can you see their army?' asked the Captains.

'No. There's no sign of it,' said the General, looking puzzled.

'Are we going to advance?' asked the Captains.

'I suppose we'd better,' said the General. 'But I don't know how we're going to fight them if they're not there,' and he sounded quite disappointed.

Whilst the General and his Captains had been talking, the soldiers had been discussing things amongst themselves. Word had somehow spread about that the opposing army was bigger than they had first imagined.

'I've heard their army is three times as big as ours,' said one soldier.

'And I hear that they've got the greatest General in the world on their side,' said another.

'Maybe this battle isn't going to be as easy as our General says it is,' said a third soldier.

Soon, all the soldiers were feeling nervous, anxious and worried.

The General ordered all the men to line up and prepare to advance. Then he gave the word. CHARGE! The lines of horsemen, followed by the footsoldiers, began to move forward into the wide, fast-flowing river.

Just then, a man came out of the hut on the other side of the river. Someone on horseback at the front of the lines of advancing soldiers shouted, 'It's the General of the enemy army,' and someone else called, 'It's a trap! Retreat! It's a trap! Go back!'

And suddenly there was pandemonium. The horsemen at the front of the army turned round and began to go back across the river, the way they'd come, but the soldiers behind them, not understanding what was happening, continued to move forward. The General fell off his horse and was last seen clinging to a tree stump in the middle of the river. Some of the Captains were swept down-stream by the strong current, and most of the soldiers thought that the ones coming back across the river were enemy soldiers, so they began to fight with them, not knowing that they were their own men.

In no time at all, the large and powerful army was reduced to a handful of wet, shivering soldiers, who quickly decided that the safest thing to do was to return to base as quickly as possible.

Meanwhile, the man who had just emerged from the hut on the other side of the river, called to three more men who were still inside.

'You can come out now. They've gone. You don't have to fight them.'

'It wouldn't have been a very fair fight, Sir,' said one of the men. 'They must have had seventy-five thousand men on their side; we've only got an army of four!'

'And that's twice as many as we needed,' said the greatest General. 'We only needed two men: one that they thought was the greatest General in the world, and another to shout 'Retreat, it's a trap,' at exactly the right moment. You see you don't have to be the biggest to win. You don't have to be the most powerful to come out on top. You just have to use your brains and think! If you do that, you can win, no matter how small you are.'

What a victory! The message of the story of course, is that great big powerful bullies don't necessarily win, and that even if you're small you can still be successful if you use your brains and think!

Help us Lord, to think wisely. Help us not to bully those smaller and weaker than us. Help us not to be afraid of people who try to bully us. Help us to know that we can do most things if we try, even though they may seem difficult. Amen

The great council of rats

Sometimes, we are given responsibilities which put us in charge of something, or even of other people. Maybe you've been put in charge of something in your class, or maybe you've been put in charge of looking after a younger brother or sister or a new child in your class. If you've ever been given that sort of job, you'll know that being in charge of something or someone is a great responsibility; you'll know how important it is to do the job properly.

In today's story, God gave a great deal of power to a group of animals, but... well, let's see what you think!

A long, long time ago when the world was still new, God chose the rats to be his right-hand creatures.

'You are small and quick and intelligent,' he said. 'So you can be in charge of the animals. I shall trust you to organise the animal kingdom in a suitable way. I am sure you will be able to do it,' and with that God left them to it, whilst he got on with other important work.

'What an honour for us to be chosen to be leaders of the animals!' they said. 'Yet, on reflection, it is only right that we should be chosen, because after all, we are very special creatures,' and they squeaked amongst themselves for days about how special and clever they were.

Eventually they decided to begin work, for if they were to be in charge, they had to be seen to be working.

'We need a committee,' said one.

'Good idea!' said another. 'We need a group of us to make the decisions and tell everyone else what to do.'

So it was decided that a committee of twelve rats should be chosen to do the work of being in charge of the animal kingdom, and to represent all the rest of the rats. The choice of twelve was not particularly difficult, since exactly twelve rats were bigger, bolder, stronger and somewhat pushier than the rest.

'I'll be on the committee. I'm good at being in charge,' said each of the twelve rats.

'We'll call ourselves the Great Rat Council,' said the largest rat of all.

The day after the Great Council had been formed, it met together so that work on being in charge of the animal kingdom could begin.

'Well! Where shall we start?' asked one rat.

'I'm not really sure what we have to do,' said another.

'How do we go about being in charge?' asked a third.

'Has God left a job description for us?' said another.

'It's clear that none of you has the vaguest idea how to be in charge of the other animals, so I can see I shall have to do it all myself!' said the largest rat of all.

'Oh would you?' said the others, who were all secretly relieved that someone else was going to take over, since they had no idea what to do and were all basically quite lazy, therefore happy to let somebody else do all the work.

'First of all, I need to be named as the leader,' said the largest rat. 'From now on, you will call me Your-Worship-the-Leader, or Almighty-Superstar-Rat. You will obey all my commands and do exactly as I say. Now, down to business. The first job is to see that all the animals have enough food and water. That's a priority.'

The other rats of the Great Council nodded their agreement.

'Of course', went on The Leader, 'We rats will have the best of all the available food, and since I am leader, I shall have the best of the best.'

The other rats of the Great Council looked at each other and said nothing.

'And then there is the question of accommodation,' said Almighty-Superstar-Rat. 'We must ensure that every animal has a suitable place to live.'

Again the other rats of the Great Council nodded their agreement.

'And it goes without saying that we rats will take the best living quarters for ourselves, and of course, the best of the very best will be reserved for me. That is only right since I am The Leader of you all,' he continued.

Once more, the other rats of the Great Council looked uncomfortably at each other, but said nothing.

The following day, Almighty-Superstar-Rat rearranged the living quarters and the food distribution for all the animal kingdom. Most of the animals were unhappy with the new arrangements, but since Almighty-Superstar was working directly for God, they thought there was little they could do about it.

Soon, the whole animal world was altered. The rats became the most important of all, with all the others animals working as their servants. No animal was allowed to hunt, or move to a new home without the permission of the Great Council of Rats. Almighty-Superstar ordered that no rat must do any work of any kind, but that other animals must do anything the rats wanted. He ordered golden palaces to be built for the rats to live in, and golden carriages to be built so that no rat ever had to walk anywhere.

Then he made new laws about the animals' children. He decreed that every female rat must have at least one hundred children in her lifetime, but other species of animals were allowed to have only two.

And it was at that point that God saw what was happening.

'I trusted you to be in charge of the animals,' he said to the rats. 'And you have let me down.' He turned to the largest rat, 'And as for you, I am ashamed of you. You have bullied and pushed your way into power, just because you are the biggest. But you haven't realised that power brings responsibility. You have misused your power.'

God then turned to the other rats. 'And why were you so lazy that you let him take all the power. You had a responsibility too. I put you all in charge; not just him.' And then God turned to the other animals, 'And why didn't you tell me what was going on?' he asked. 'I can't begin to put things right if you don't tell me what's wrong in the first place!'

God then took the leadership job away from the rats and banished them to the darkest corners of the land. And there they have stayed ever since. They are found in every country of the world, but nowhere are they liked or respected, because they once misused the power they were given.

What do you think about the way the rats behaved when they were put in charge? What do you think of people who keep all the best of everything for themselves when they're in charge?

I hope that when you are put in charge of something that you remember you have a responsibility to do it properly.

Dear God, help us to remember that when we are put in charge of something, we have a responsibility towards whatever it is. Help us never to take advantage of a situation when we are in charge, but always to do our best, so that people can trust us. Amen

Two brothers

Have you noticed that people who behave as though they're strong and powerful are usually treated as though they're big and important; and people who behave in a quiet, timid, frightened sort of way, are often treated as though they're weak and of no importance? And have you noticed that the people who make the most noise and fuss and commotion, often have fewer sensible and important things to say than others who quietly think things through?

Today's story is from India, and it tells of two brothers – a strong one and a weak one – well, that's what everyone thought.

Naresh was the elder of the two. He was big and strong and noisy, and a bit of a bully. Everyone listened when Naresh spoke, and everyone did what he said.

Kumar was the younger of the two. He was small and quiet and always kind. No-one listened to Kumar, and no-one ever did what he said because he didn't dare tell anyone to do anything.

One day Kumar was at the market, standing in a queue waiting to buy fruit and vegetables for the evening meal, when he noticed a small mouse running up the trunk of a nearby tree. It was trying to reach some sacks of nuts which were dangling from the branches. The stall holder had hung them there to keep them out of the way. But the sacks were too far away from the trunk for the mouse to be able to reach them.

Kumar watched and waited for the mouse to give up and run away, but it didn't. It tried all ways to reach those nuts. It ran along the branch and tried to climb down the string holding the sacks, but it fell off and landed in the dust on the ground. It climbed up onto a pile of nearby boxes and tried to reach the nuts that way, but they were still out of reach. So the small mouse ran up the trunk again, took a mighty leap, jumped across the gap and landed on one of the sacks. It nibbled a hole in the sack and stole a nut before jumping to the ground and running off.

Kumar laughed. People in the queue turned to look at him.

'Did you see that?' he said. 'That mouse over there.'

The people in the queue looked over to the tree but could see nothing unusual.

'There was a small mouse,' went on Kumar. 'What an example! It has more determination than any of us. And if you saw how far it jumped! It almost flew onto the sack! It just proves that you don't have to be big and powerful to achieve the things you want to. All you need is determination. We can learn a lot by watching animals.'

'You're mad!' the people said to Kumar. 'Flying mice indeed!'

The next day, Naresh heard about the incident in the market place, and sent for Kumar.

'I understand you've been telling tales about flying mice!' said Naresh. 'Well, you can just stop your silly stories. Everyone knows you're my brother, and they'll think I'm mad, too. I can't have you bringing shame on me, so clear off. Go on! Leave.'

Kumar could see no point in staying where he wasn't wanted, so he packed his bag and went to live in the forest with the animals. 'I'll probably learn more from the animals than from the people of the village, anyway,' he said as he left.

A few days later, Naresh was in the market place, talking to some important people of the village, when he suddenly noticed a small mouse jumping from a tree trunk onto a sack of nuts which was hanging from the tree. The mouse stole a nut and ran away with it.

'Hey, look at that!' said Naresh. 'We could learn a thing or two from that little mouse. What an example! It has more determination than any of us. And did you see how far it jumped? It almost flew onto the sack! It just proves that you don't have to be big and powerful to achieve the things you want to. All you need is determination. We can learn a lot by watching animals.'

The people who were with Naresh all started talking at once.

'You are so clever,' they said. 'Only you could see a lesson for us all in the actions of a small mouse. What knowledge you have! How wise you are! And how generous of you to share your thoughts with us.' Everyone, of course, had completely forgotten that Kumar had also seen the small mouse and had also commented on the message it could teach. Naresh was hailed as the wisest man in the village. Everyone came to him with their problems and difficulties, and people paid him for his advice.

Years went by and Naresh became as important as a God. People from far and wide brought him gifts and offerings. Whatever he said, whether it was sensible or foolish, was treated as great wisdom. His words were golden. No-one remembered that he'd once had a younger brother, a boy who was quiet and shy and who loved animals. And Naresh, if he remembered Kumar, never spoke of him.

And then illness came to the village. It was probably brought by the visiting strangers, but in any event it was dreadful and devastating. The very old and very young were the first to become ill. The villagers turned to Naresh for help.

'What shall we do? What medicine shall we give? Tell us, Naresh. Advise us, before we all die of this illness.' But Naresh had no answers. Oh, he said he did. He suggested medicines and potions, but nothing worked. He told them to bury stones in the ground; he told them to dance by the light of the full moon; he even told them to swim across the river nineteen times then lie out on the grass to dry, and the people believed that doing these things would cure them. But of course they didn't. The illness became worse.

Deep in the forest, news was spreading fast.

'There's illness in the village,' said the monkey to the snake. 'Illness in the village,' said the snake to the rat. 'In the village, illness,' said the rat to the mongoose. 'Illness!' said the mongoose to the mouse.

'Illness in the village?' said Kumar. 'Which village? Where?'

'In the village where Naresh lives,' they said.

Kumar wasted no time, but gathered leaves and grasses and herbs from the forest. Living in the forest with the animals, he had learned which plants to use to treat illness and pain and injury.

He hurried to the village. He built a fire and set a pan of water to boil. He made a mixture for the fever, a medicine for the sickness, a potion for the pain. He gave his remedies to the people, and slowly, gradually, they recovered. And slowly, gradually, they remembered.

'We know you!' they said. 'You're Nareshe's little brother. How clever you are to come back just when we needed you. And how clever of you to know how to cure us of the illness. We asked the great Naresh to help us, but he couldn't. Yet you, his little brother, have done what he could not. How did you do it?'

Kumar smiled. 'I learned a long long time ago that you don't have to be big and powerful to achieve the things you want to. All you need is a bit of patience and determination.'

'Who taught you to be so wise?' the people asked. 'It must have been someone hugely powerful and important.'

'Yes. A little mouse taught me,' answered Kumar.

By the end of the story, the villagers had changed their mind about who was the stronger of the two brothers. It's not always the noisy important-sounding people who know the most. And you don't have to be big and brave and bold and fearless to succeed. You need patience and determination. With those two qualities, you can achieve almost anything you set your mind to.

I wonder what you'll decide to achieve?

Dear God, help us to understand that the strongest may not be the most clever, and that small can be powerful, too. Help us to know that success can be achieved with patience, perseverance and determination. Help us to have the determination to see things through. Amen

March

Theme 1: Care of animals

A marmoset goes on holiday

I wonder how many of you have pets at home, and I wonder what sort of pets you have? Some of you might have large animals, like a dog or even a horse. And I know some of you have smaller animals like rabbits or hamsters, and some of you have birds or fish as pets.

Those of you who have pets will know that if you have an animal, you have a responsibility to look after it. And animals are not easy to look after. They have to be given the right food to eat, they have to have somewhere suitable to live, they have to have exercise and they have to be kept clean. All this takes a lot of time and effort, and sometimes, I'm sure, you would rather be doing something else than taking your dog for a walk or cleaning out the guinea pigs! But imagine what it would be like if you had a tiny baby marmoset to look after, which needed feeding every single hour of the day and night.

In today's true story, two children looked after a marmoset, even when they went on holiday.

Eleven year old Ben and his eight year old sister Hannah, were quite used to looking after unusual animals because their dad, Michael, was the animal keeper at Roundhay Park's Tropical World in Leeds.

One day, one of the marmosets at Tropical World gave birth to two tiny babies. Michael was delighted. The marmosets were pygmy marmosets and were very rare. They were also an endangered species, so to have two more baby marmosets born at the Tropical House was really good news.

But, within a few days of the babies being born, the mother marmoset became ill with an infection. Ben and Hannah's dad knew that it would be difficult to keep her alive. He also knew that if she died it would be even more difficult to keep the babies alive because they would have to be hand-reared without their mother. He watched carefully over the marmoset family but it soon became apparent that one of the babies had caught the infection as well. Within a few hours the mother and one of the twins had both died..

The baby that was left was very tiny. Michael picked it up and looked at it. It was small enough to fit into the palm of his hand. He knew that this baby was likely to die too, unless it was looked after very carefully. Michael knew that the baby marmoset would need feeding every single hour for the next few days. It would need to be kept warm and it would need lots of love. But how could he give it the care it needed, especially as he and his family were about to go on holiday to Whitby for a few days? It would be impossible. Maybe he should cancel his holiday... But maybe the baby would die anyway...

Michael decided to take the baby home with him.

'We have to try and look after him,' he said to the family. 'But I don't know what we're going to do when we go on holiday.

'No problem,' said Ben. 'We'll take him with us.'

'How can we go on holiday with a baby marmoset?' said Ben and Hannah's mum.

'Well other people go on holiday with tiny babies,' said Hannah. 'So I don't see why we can't!'

So the baby went along as part of the family.

They put him in a hold-all with blankets and a hot water bottle and they packed a tiny feeding bottle, a syringe and some baby food. The four of them took it in turns to keep a 24 hour watch on the baby marmoset. He was fed on the hour, every hour, wherever they happened to be, because the hold-all simply went everywhere with the family. They took it with them for a walk on the beach. They took it with them when they walked up the 199 steps to Whitby Abbey. They even took it with them to the museum. The baby must be the only marmoset who has travelled all over Whitby on holiday!

When the holiday was over and the family went home, the marmoset went too, and moved into a cardboard box instead of living in a hold-all. Michael thought that Ben and Hannah would be tired of looking after the marmoset by the time the holiday was over, but no! They were determined to continue looking after him until he was old enough to go and live in the Tropical House with his dad.

Soon the baby was strong enough to be fed more food but less often, and then he was big enough to start eating solid foods by himself instead of being hand-fed through a syringe. By now the marmoset was no longer a baby, but almost big enough to go and live in the Tropical House.

'I'm glad he's big and strong enough to go and live with the other animals,' said Hannah. 'But I wish he had a name. He's nearly grown-up now, we can't call him 'baby' any longer.'

'It's funny you should say that,' said her dad. 'Look!' and there in the local newspaper was an article all about the baby marmoset and how Ben and Hannah had helped to look after him, even on holiday.

'The paper is running a competition to choose a name for him,' said Michael. 'I wonder what it'll be?'

I wonder what name *you* would have chosen for the baby marmoset? Do you think you could have looked after the marmoset like Ben and Hannah did? It must have been very difficult to feed the marmoset every single hour, and not forget. And I suppose there were times when the two children would rather have been doing something else, but I suppose they knew that the baby marmoset's life depended on the care they gave it.

The name they gave him, by the way, was Mogwai. You could go and say hello if you're ever visiting Tropical World in Leeds.

Dear God, thank you for all the animals in our world. Help us to care for the animals we have at home and at school. Help us never to hurt any living thing.

And help us to do what we can to ensure that endangered animals do not die out and become extinct. Amen

Petsearch

If you have a pet you'll know how upsetting it is if it goes missing or gets lost. Pets become part of your family and it's very worrying if they go astray and you don't know where they are. Nine years ago two people who cared about animals started Petsearch to try and reunite lost animals with their owners.

Here's how it happened.

Harry Greaves went out to buy his morning paper as usual, and as he approached the shop he saw a sad-looking Old English sheepdog sitting outside.

'He's looking a bit sorry for himself,' said Harry to the newsagent.

'He's been sitting there since five o'clock this morning,' said the newsagent. 'He must be lost.'

As Harry left the shop with his paper, the dog looked up at him with big dark sorrowful eyes. Harry bent down to stroke him. The dog was wearing a collar but no identity tag.

'Poor old boy,' said Harry. 'I wonder where you live.'

Harry decided he couldn't leave the dog all alone outside the newspaper shop, so he took him home, until he could find out who he belonged to. On the way home, Harry noticed the dog was limping badly.

'He needs to see a vet,' said Harry's wife. 'He might have broken something.'

So Paula and Harry put the dog in the car and took him to see the vet. They explained how Harry had found him outside the shop that morning.

The vet examined the dog. He looked in his ears and mouth and eyes, he felt under his fur, he listened to his heartbeat and breathing, and felt his legs.

'Well, there's nothing broken,' he said. 'He's actually in quite good shape for his age. He's been well looked after, but he's an old dog now. Someone must be really missing him.'

Paula and Harry took the dog home again and Harry rang the police, the RSPCA, the local dogs' home, the local animal sanctuaries, and the rest of the vets in the area, but no-one had any record of a missing sheepdog.

Paula mixed up a bowl of meat and biscuit for the dog, but he wouldn't eat it, he just curled up in a corner, obviously pining for his real owner.

The next day Harry rang the local radio station and the local newspapers to see if they could track down the dog's owner, but there was no response. Days turned into weeks and the sheepdog grew thinner and more and more unhappy.

'He's pining away,' said Paula. 'And there's nothing we can do.'

Harry and Paula had almost given up hope of ever finding the dog's owner, when suddenly, one morning, the phone rang.

'Hello?' said a worried-sounding woman's voice. 'I'm looking for my dog. He's called Lucky, and the RSPCA tell me that you might have him.'

'Thank Goodness!' said Paula. 'Come round straight away. He's missing you such a lot.'

A few hours later Lucky's owner arrived, together with another Old English sheepdog. 'You just don't know how relieved I am to see them like that,' she said, as they all watched the two dogs running around the garden. 'Those two have been together since they were puppies,' she went on. 'Sally has missed Lucky as much as he's obviously missed her. These last weeks have been dreadful. I honestly thought I'd never see Lucky again. Thank you so much for taking him in and looking after him for me.'

It turned out that Lucky had strayed from home one day, wandered several miles away, and then been unable to find his way back. Paula and Harry had concentrated their search near to where *they* lived, not knowing that Lucky lived miles away, and that's why it had taken so long to find his owner.

'Well, all's well that ends well,' said Harry, when Lucky, Sally and their owner had gone.

'Yes...' said Paula, hesitantly. 'But it hasn't ended. I've had an idea! There must be lots of animals out there, every day, who get lost, and whose owners have as much difficulty as Lucky's in finding them again. Suppose we set up a register to keep track of all the missing animals and all the owners who have lost them, all over the country. Wouldn't that be good?'

'It would,' said Harry.

'Then let's do it!' said Paula. 'We'll call it Petsearch.'

So Harry and Paula set up a register where owners could report their missing animal and give details of the date, place and time it was lost, together with a description. Anyone who found an animal could ring in to see if it had been reported missing. Paula advertised the service in the newspapers and on posters in shops, libraries and police stations. Soon the telephone was ringing non-stop.

'Hello? Petsearch? I've just lost my budgie. He flew out of the window when I was cleaning him out.'

'Hello, my cat has gone missing. He's called Milky and he's ten and I'm ever so upset. Do you think anyone will find him?'

'Is that Petsearch? I've lost my tortoise.'

'Um, is this the right number? I've just found a green budgie in my apple tree.'

'Hello! Has anyone lost a tortoise? I've just found one in my cabbage patch.'

'Paula Greaves? A white cat turned up on my doorstep this morning, he's here in my kitchen having a saucer of milk. Has anyone reported him missing?'

And so it went on. Petsearch grew and grew until it there are now 220 branches all over the country. They even have a website on the Internet and owners from as far away as America report their missing pets in the hope that someone, somewhere will find them.

The most important part of Petsearch's work is still reuniting owners with their missing animals, but they now do other work as well and many branches have their own pet ambulances.

Petsearch is paid for by donations, but Paula and Harry give their time for nothing. They are pleased to be able to do something to help animals.

All over the country, and even the world, there are people, like Paula and Harry, who work hard to care for and look after animals.

(Donations can be sent to Petsearch, 851 Old Lode Lane, Solihull, West Midlands, B92 8JE. Further information [SAE please] from the same address, or 0121 7434133 or www.ukpetsearch.freeuk.com or ukpetsearch@freeuk.com)

Thank you God, for all the people who work hard to look after animals. Help us to look after our pets and never to hurt them. Amen

The small brown dog

I know that all of you here who have pets, look after them well and care for them properly. But not everyone does. Some people neglect their animals – that means they just don't bother looking after them as they should. Others are deliberately cruel, though it's hard to understand how people can do that to animals who trust them.

In today's story, an old woman didn't care for her animals as she should. I'll be interested to know, at the end of the story, if you think she should have got into trouble about it.

The small brown dog jumped up onto the chair by the window and looked out onto the dirty back-yard. He barked a greeting at someone walking by, but as soon as the old woman who owned the dog heard his bark, she took the sweeping brush handle to him, as she usually did.

'Quiet!' she shouted, as she hit him with the brush. 'And get down from there. How many times have I told you!'

The small brown dog cowered under the table, and licked himself where the woman had hit him. He was pitifully thin; the shape of his ribs showed through his thin matted fur, and he had sores all over his body. He didn't know how long he'd been living at the old woman's house but it seemed a long time. He couldn't remember much about the past although he had a vague memory of being with his mother as a puppy and playing on some grassland. His next memory was of wandering the streets and being hungry. He was always hungry. Then, somehow, he'd ended up at the old woman's house, and he'd been there ever since.

The inside of the house was dirty and smelly. She never cleaned. She had about six dogs altogether, although the number varied; sometimes a dog would go and another one would come, but the small brown dog didn't know why.

The dogs were fed on scraps when the woman had some, and it wasn't unusual for them to fight over the food. They were put out into the yard every morning, but she never took them out for a walk. The small brown dog could barely remember what the world looked like on the other side of the big battered brown fence that enclosed the yard.

One day the old woman went out and somehow didn't close the latch on the yard gate properly. The small brown dog pushed his nose into the gap and waggled his head. The gap widened. He pushed again and slid his head and shoulders into the space. He looked up and down the street then walked through the gate and trotted down the pavement.

The man from next door was watching him, and as the small brown dog trotted past his house, he called to him.

'Come on, old boy,' he said gently. 'You come here to me and I'll give you something to eat.'

The small brown dog hesitated. He'd learned long ago not to trust people, but he could smell the man's dinner cooking inside his house, and he was very hungry.

He followed the man into his kitchen. The man took the lid from a pan on the stove and spooned out some meat and gravy. He stirred it round the dish to cool it, then gave it to the dog. He ate it greedily, unbelievingly, cautiously, afraid it would be suddenly taken away from him. The man understood.

'She doesn't look after you, does she?' he said. 'I wish you could live here with me. I'd look after you, and feed you, and get you back into good condition again.' The small brown dog looked at the man as if to say, I wish that too.

Just then there was a shout from the door.

'I know you've got my dog in there. You've stolen it. You can't keep it, it's mine, give it back.'

The man was unsure what to do. He didn't want to give the dog back to the woman, for her to ill-treat again. But he knew it was her dog. If he refused to give it back she could call the police and he'd be in trouble for stealing.

'If I give it back to you, you have to promise to care for it properly.'

'I don't have to promise you anything,' said the woman. 'I'll do what I like with it. It's none of your business. Keep your nose out!'

'But look at the state of the poor thing,' said the man. 'It's cruel to let an animal get into that condition.'

'Give it back,' said the woman. 'It's nothing to do with you,' and she grabbed hold of the small brown dog by the scruff of its neck, and dragged it away.

Back at her own house she tied the dog to a chair. 'You'll not go out again and shame me in front of the neighbours,' she shouted, and she kicked it under the table. 'It's nothing to do with anyone else what I do with you.'

But that's just where the woman was wrong.

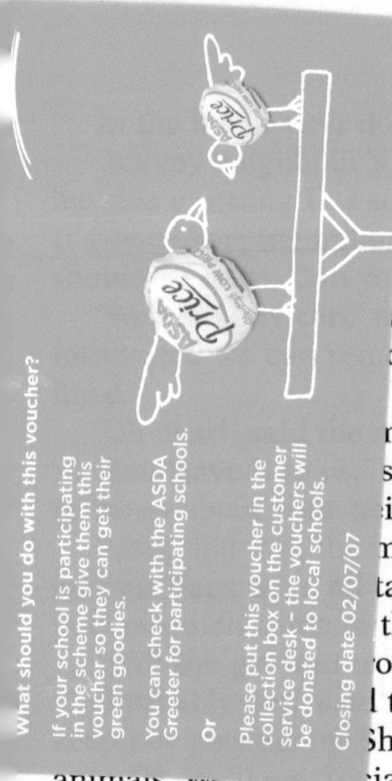

or, the man was telephoning the RSPCA.
dogs,' he said. 'I've been worried about them for ages,
en for myself what a dreadful state one of them's in.
ls like that and not looking after them. Something
u help?'
aid the woman from the RSPCA. 'If an animal is being
ove it to safety. The owner can be taken to court and

nan. 'I don't want any trouble.'
said the woman. 'You've done the right thing in letting
ighbour's dogs.'
man saw an RSPCA van outside the old woman's house
taken away in it. Then a police car came, and a
the man's house to ask for a statement.
ouble?' asked the man.
l the police. 'Though it's unlikely she'll be allowed to
She can hardly look after herself, never mind look after
animals. We'll get Social Services to give her some help; she needs it.'

'And what about the dogs? Will they... they won't be put down, will they?'

'Not straight away,' said the policewoman. 'The RSPCA always try to find new homes for animals like that. Why, do you know anyone who wants a dog?'

'I might know someone who could give a good home to a small brown one,' said the man.

It was lucky for the dogs that the man was concerned enough to ring the RSPCA, otherwise they'd have probably died.

What do you think should have happened to the old woman? Do you think she should have been taken to court for cruelty? Or do you think she should have been let off with a warning? Do you think she should be allowed to keep a pet again?

It's good that there are organisations like the RSPCA, and the PDSA, who care for animals, but they don't alter the fact that if we have an animal as a pet, it's our duty and responsibility to care for it.

Thank you God, for our pets. Help us to know that it is our duty to look after our pets properly all the time, and not just when we feel like it. Help us to know that it is our responsibility to care for our pets, and not to expect other people to do it. Amen

Theme 2: Environment

Graffiti

What is graffiti? Yes, it's drawing or writing scratched or scribbled on a wall. People have been doing graffiti since ancient times. I suppose the cave paintings of stone age man are a sort of graffiti, and it certainly used to be done in ancient Rome, because graffiti has been found on the ruined walls of the ancient city of Pompeii. So graffiti is drawing or scratching on desks, writing on walls, and drawing slogans or words with marker pens or aerosols, especially in public places; and it's been around a very long time.

Some people think graffiti is vandalism. Some people think it's art. What do you think?

I know what I think! I know that it costs thousands of pounds each year to remove unsightly graffiti; money that could be better spent on other things. I know that areas that are covered in graffiti look poor and uncared for. I know how distressing and upsetting it is to find graffiti on our school walls or in our neighbourhood!

Today's story is about graffiti. It's based on something that really happened, although the details have been changed.

Darren and his friends lived on a big sprawling housing estate on the edge of a large city in the north of England. There wasn't much to do on the estate; there was no park and no youth club and if they played football in the street the neighbours used to tell them off. So mostly they hung around by the old chapel. It wasn't used these days, and it was becoming derelict.

The vandalism started by accident really. A group of them were kicking Darren's football against the chapel wall, when it went through the glass in one of the windows.

'I've got to get it back,' said Darren. 'It's my best football.'

They tried the door but it was locked. They dragged someone's dustbin over to the broken window and climbed up to try and get in that way, but it was too high and the jagged edges of the glass made it impossible to climb through. Then Jake called from around the back of the chapel.

'The door round here's locked but the wood round the hinges is rotten. A good push and we could break it in!'

The others ran round to Jake. They pushed their shoulders against the door and it gave way with a splintering of wood. They went inside. There was nothing in the old chapel. Any furniture had been taken out long ago. It was cold and damp and dark.

'Great place for a den,' Jake said, and the others agreed, despite the musty smell of the place.

After that, the group met most evenings in the chapel. They fooled around and laughed and told jokes, and then one evening Jake produced a can of spray paint.

'It's me dad's,' he said. 'Metallic blue. Look!' and he sprayed a great arc of paint across the damp wall of the chapel. He offered to let Darren have a go, and he sprayed 'kids rule OK' over the wall. Then the paint ran out.

The next evening several more of the gang brought aerosols or marker pens and they wrote and drew all over the inside of the chapel. It wasn't long before the graffiti spread to the outside walls, and soon the old chapel was covered with it.

The whole area looked a dump!

'Good, isn't it?' said Jake.

'Yea! Great!' said the others, agreeing with him yet knowing that it all looked a mess, and knowing they'd soon be in trouble. Somehow the fun had gone out of it all.

Trouble arrived the next day, but not quite as they imagined it would.

They were leaning against the chapel wall, under the broken window, when a car drew up and a tall thin young man got out. They waited for the telling off, and were surprised when it didn't come.

'Hi guys!' said the man. 'My name's Greg and I've bought the old chapel. I see you're into graffiti in a big way! That's good, I'm going to need some graffiti artists.'

Greg went on to explain that he was an actor and he'd bought the chapel to live in and to turn into a theatre. He wanted to set up a theatre group and use the chapel as its base. Would they be interested in helping?

Would they!

He wanted to get repairs done to the chapel and have it all cleaned up. He was going to turn the main section into the theatre and turn the small balcony into a flat for himself. The cellars would be used as storage areas and workshops for scenery and props.

'But I don't want it to look like a chapel from the outside,' went on Greg. 'And this is where you guys come in. I want a huge mural painting on the side wall, the one next to the road. You can design it and paint it if you want.'

'You mean you *want* us to paint on the walls?' said Jake in astonishment.

'Sure!' said Greg. 'I can see you've got some talent for it!'

So the work began. Builders moved on site to repair the chapel. Greg moved into his flat. A local joinery firm made a small stage, and the local supermarket donated a hundred fold-up chairs. Some mums and dads lent a hand to paint the inside of the theatre. The youngsters on the estate drew pictures of what they thought the mural should look like. Greg said they should choose the design, and in the end they decided on a group of children, looking remarkably like Jake and Darren and their friends, leaning on and climbing over an old gate.

'But we're not artists,' said Darren. 'How are we going to draw it on the wall outside. The people need to be lifesize.'

'Draw round each other on wallpaper on the floor,' said Greg. 'Then transfer the drawings to the wall. Surely graffiti artists like you can manage to do a full size wall mural?'

The children did as Greg suggested and discovered it worked. Soon, they'd cleaned off their old graffiti from the outside wall, had painted a plain background to work on, and had started to draw themselves on the gate. This was much more difficult than just squirting paint around, but it was much more fun.

Within three months of Greg first meeting the gang, the chapel was repaired, the mural completed and the theatre group up and running. Now when you walked down the street you could still see graffiti, but this was purposeful graffiti-art, not degrading graffiti-vandalism. And now when you walked down the street, the neighbourhood looked cared for, as though people took pride in it.

'Our theatre group needs a name,' said Jake. 'What are we going to call it?'

'Well, how did it all start?' asked Greg.

'With my can of me dad's paint, I suppose,' said Jake.

'What colour was it?' asked Greg.

'Metallic blue.'

'There you are then,' said Greg. 'The Metallic Blue Theatre Group.'

So if a theatre group called 'Metallic Blue' ever comes to your school or community centre, you'll know how it started off.

I'm glad the children on the estate found a better way of using their graffiti. And I'm glad they found a better way of using their time. They got a lot more fun out of the theatre group that out of aimlessly hanging around, didn't they? And their neighbourhood certainly looked better.

Help us Lord, to care for the environment we live in. Help us not to spoil buildings or gardens or trees. Help us to take pride in our school and our neighbourhood, and make them pleasant places for everyone to enjoy. Amen

Rainforests and burgers

Did you know that thousands of years ago Britain used to be covered with huge forests? Gradually, clearings were made in the forest, people settled in the clearings, and that's how the first villages began. Over the years, the villages spread into towns and cities, and more and more woodland was cleared to make way for farms and factories, houses and motorways. Nowadays, there are few large forests left and the bears wolves and boars that roamed in them have all gone.

Similar forest clearance is going on in the countries along the equator. South America, Africa, Asia and Australasia are all destroying huge areas of rainforest. The destruction is massive. The land is being damaged and the trees burned. The animals and people who live in the rainforest are being driven out. Dangerous changes are being made to the gases in the earth's atmosphere, by the fires and by the loss of trees. These changes are affecting every living thing on our earth.

If the destruction of the rainforest continues at its present rate, it will damage our earth forever. And why is the rainforest being torn down? Listen to this story!

Tom, Anna and their dad were going out for the day.

'Can we go to the burger bar, Dad?' they said.

'Do you want to eat rainforest and chips?' said Mr Jameson.

'No,' said Tom, looking puzzled. 'I want beefburger and chips.'

'You can't eat rainforest!' said Anna, scathingly. She was eleven, and felt she knew a lot more than her brother Tom, who was only eight.

'But that's just it!' said their dad. 'In some burger bars, that's exactly what you're eating.'

'What do you mean?' asked the children.

'Well, when fast food, like burgers, was first invented in America about 40 years ago, most of the beef came from cattle reared in South America. But the farmers had to clear great areas of rainforest to make grazing land for the cattle. The trouble is, when the trees went, a great deal of the goodness in the soil went too. With poor soil, the grass soon stops growing and the land becomes wasted. It's no good for cattle any more, so the farmers move on. They clear another chunk of rainforest to make new grazing land, and the whole thing starts all over again. Hundreds of square miles of rainforest have been lost in this way.'

'But I know that some of the beef for beefburgers comes from Europe,' said Anna. 'We talked about it at school. They don't cut down rainforests to make cattle farms in Europe, because there aren't any rainforests in Europe!'

'That's right,' said her dad. 'But have you thought about what the cattle is fed on?'

'Cattle food!' said Tom.

'Clever!' said Anna.

'Don't start arguing, you two, this is serious,' said their dad.

'Cattle are fed on food that makes them grow quickly. Food like soya bean. And where does soya bean grow? Places like South America, where the rainforest has to be destroyed to make space to grow the soya.'

'So can't we go to the burger bar ever again?' said Tom. 'Am I going to be burgerless for the rest of my life?' and he sounded so disappointed that his dad burst out laughing.

'No, I'm not saying you can't ever eat burgers again. What I am saying is just think about it. You should do a bit of research before you use a particular burger bar. You could find out where their beef comes from. You could find out where the food comes from that the beef is fed on. Then you could buy your burgers from the shops that are the most environmentally friendly.

'You could, of course, choose something different from beefburgers. Have you tried veggieburgers, or beanburgers? Or what about good old fish and chips? Or what about baked potatoes with a filling? Fast food doesn't have to be burgers and chips, you know!'

'Hey! Yea! I saw a kiosk selling baked potatoes in town the other day. It looked really good. They had *hundreds* of different fillings,' said Tom.

'Well, not hundreds, but ever so many,' said Anna. 'You don't cut rainforests down to grow potatoes, do you Dad? And they're not packaged in loads of plastic, so that's better for poor old Earth.'

'Not to mention being better for poor old you!' said their dad, as they went to find the baked potato kiosk.

The children in the story did some research as their dad had suggested, and they found out that some burger companies are much more environmentally aware than others. Anna and Tom made a point in future, of asking their parents to take them to shops and cafes and restaurants that are trying to look after our Earth.

'After all,' said Anna. 'Our poor old Earth isn't getting any younger. And if we don't look after it, who will?' It's a good point isn't it!

Dear God, help us each to take some responsibility for looking after our planet Earth. Help us to look to the future, and do nothing that will damage our environment. Help us to be aware of how shops and restaurants and manufacturers look after the Earth, and help us to campaign to change anything which is causing harm to the Earth. Amen

The otter who came back

Have you ever seen an otter? Perhaps you've seen otters in captivity at an otter sanctuary or an animal reserve. If you've seen an otter in the wild, you're very lucky indeed, for there are still not many otters living wild in Britain.

About forty years ago people were afraid that the otter would die out in Britain; that it would become extinct. More and more otters were being killed by harmful chemicals in our rivers, and people were hunting them as well. Now, there are laws to protect the otter, and people have realised they must do something to clean up the rivers. These animals are too precious to be allowed to die out just because of man's thoughtlessness and carelessness.

The otter in today's story in a way represents all the otters throughout Britain that have come back to live in our rivers.

Neil worked at the otter sanctuary by the river. It had been set up about a year ago as a place where otters could be bred in captivity and then released into the wild. There were hardly any wild otters living in the river now, pollution and hunting had seen to that, but the programme of breeding and release should soon get the otters living there again. In the meantime, the river had been cleaned up, and local firms were no longer allowed to tip their chemical waste into it. Things were looking better for the otters.

One Spring morning, Neil went to the main gate to collect the mail from the postman, and noticed an old cardboard box on the ground.

'Not like you to have rubbish around!' commented the postman, as he handed over the letters.

'No!' said Neil. 'Someone must have dumped it. I'll move it.' But as Neil bent to pick up the box, he saw there was something inside it. Crouched in the bottom of the box was something sleek and dark and brown, with piercing dark frightened eyes, and small ears almost hidden in the dense fur of its head. An otter.

'It's hurt!' said Neil. 'Look!' The otter's flank was cut and bleeding, and there was barbed wire caught round its hind leg and thick tail.

Neil carefully picked up the box and carried it into the sanctuary. The otter was clearly shocked and very scared. Neil set the box down and sat beside it. He talked to the otter; soothing nonsense that didn't mean anything, but in a calm quiet voice so the otter would know he meant it no harm. After a long time, Neil put his hand into the box. He looked at the otter's sharp yellow teeth that could bite right through a man's hand with one snap. But the otter didn't bite; it let Neil touch its thick heavy fur.

Neil lifted the otter out of the box, and the vet came and examined her. He cleaned her up and put stitches in the wounds. Later, the otter looked at Neil with her dark bright eyes which said 'Why have you done this to me?'

'I'm trying to help you. I'm not the one who hurt you,' said Neil. But the otter's eyes said, 'You're a man. You did.'

Gradually the otter's strength returned. Her wounds began to heal. She learned to trust Neil, and they played together every day. She showed him how she could swim; twisting her body and her long thick tail, paddling her forelegs, and shaking her thick brown waterproof coat completely dry as she emerged from the pool. He threw sticks for her, and she ran yelping excitedly to catch them and to bring them back to him.

Then, one morning, Neil came to her pen as usual... but she was gone. Two mistakes together, the door to her pen had not been bolted, and the enclosure gate had been left ajar.

'She won't live,' said Neil to the others. 'She's still too weak to fend for herself. She's too dependent on me. She'll die.' And he blamed himself for getting too close to her, for becoming her friend, for not checking the pen door, for everything.

That night he left the enclosure gate ajar again, on purpose this time, and he left her pen door open. He put food and water inside, but held out little hope that his plan would work. It didn't. The next day the food lay untouched, she hadn't returned.

Neil searched the river bank and looked and called. Nothing. That night he locked the enclosure gate. He bolted her pen door. No point in leaving them open. She'd gone. She wasn't coming back. But something made him leave a large cardboard box just outside the enclosure gate. Just in case.

In the morning when he unlocked the gate he didn't even bother to look at the box. Waste of time. But something about it made him stop. There was no sound. But he listened. There was no movement. But he watched.

Neil walked towards the box. Inside he saw sleek shining fur. And two piercing black eyes. She was back. And there, in the box, partly hidden under her thick long tail, were two newborn pups. Tiny, blind, silky-coated otters, just a few hours old.

Neil carried the box into the enclosure. The otter looked at him with eyes that said, 'Where's my breakfast. I'm hungry.'

The otter had come back. But not for ever. For Neil knew that the otter and her pups were wild animals and not pets. He knew that he must not allow them to become too dependent on humans and that they must one day be released back into the river. But not yet. Not just yet.

There are several otter trusts and sanctuaries now throughout Britain, where people work hard to protect otters and to help their numbers increase.

All over the world there are other animals in danger of dying out, in danger of becoming extinct, unless we humans do something to protect them. Animals in danger include the Panda in China, the African Elephant, the Indian Tiger, the Large Grey Wolf in Europe, the Osprey bird in Scotland, and the tiny dormouse in Britain. It's a long list, and sadly that's only the beginning of it. As men and women use up more and more of the Earth's surface, these animals are being pushed out. The trouble is, it's their earth too!

Animals can't speak for themselves, so we must protect them. Animals that are not endangered today, might be tomorrow; it's our job to see that living things do not become extinct because of man's greed or pollution.

Dear Father God, help us to care for our Earth, so that humans and animals can share it. Help us to do nothing to harm anything which lives. Help us to learn to enjoy the beauty of the earth without destroying it. Amen

Theme 3: Easter

The servant girl... in the city

Christians all around the world know the story of Jesus. It's an amazing story of a baby born 2000 years ago in a stable; a baby who was visited by shepherds and kings; a baby who had to escape with his parents from a jealous and angry king and become a refugee in another country; a baby who grew up to be a great teacher and leader. It's the story of a man who was killed by his enemies, but who rose from the dead.

The beginning of the story is remarkable, but the ending is even more so, because the ending was just the beginning! Christians believe that Jesus showed people a new and better way to live, that his death made up for all the wrong that people do, and that he rose again to prove that good will always win over evil.

The Easter story that I'm going to tell you this week is about the events that took place during the last week of Jesus's life. It's told from the point of view of a servant girl, who happened to work in Jerusalem at the time. Her name was Abigail.

The story is in three parts, as a serial.

There was a great commotion going on in the street outside the house where the servant girl worked. She hurried outdoors to see what was happening. Jerusalem was already crowded with people who had come to the city to celebrate the feast of the Passover, but now the street seemed busier than ever.

'What's going on?' Abigail called to a woman hurrying by.

'It's Jesus of Nazareth,' shouted the woman over the noise and bustle of the crowd. 'He's coming. He's coming here just as the prophets said he would. He's coming to be our king. Look!' And she pointed to the end of the street where the crowd was surging round the corner.

Abigail ran out of the house. She was swept along by the crowd who were pushing and jostling to get a good position to see the king. Suddenly a huge cheer went up and the crowd went wild with joy and excitement. People pulled down branches from the trees lining the road and waved them in the air like flags.

'He's here! Welcome King Jesus! Hurrah! Hosanna! Long live the King!' Abigail pushed her way to the front of the crowd. She could see Jesus riding on a donkey. She felt a little disappointed that this king was not riding in a golden carriage, but the crowd didn't seem to mind. Everyone was shouting in victory and celebration.

'Make way! Make way! Hosanna to the people's king!' And as the man on the donkey rode by, more and more people joined in the procession until the streets of Jerusalem were full.

Abigail, being pushed along at the front of the procession, saw some of the leaders of the city of Jerusalem stride towards Jesus. They looked angry and displeased with the way the crowd was welcoming Jesus. Abigail could see that the city leaders did not like Jesus, and she wondered why.

The men spoke to Jesus. 'There's too much noise and disruption,' they said. 'These people are disturbing the peace. Tell them all to be quiet!'

Jesus replied, 'If the people keep quiet, then I tell you, the stones in the road will start shouting!' and he rode on towards the temple.

Abigail ran on ahead. She had a friend who sold cloth in the market that was held in the temple courtyard. She would run and tell her that Jesus was going to come by. There would be more cheering and rejoicing – what an exciting day this was turning out to be.

Abigail hurried into the busy market and pushed her way through the jumble of stalls to find Anna. The market was even busier than usual, with stalls of every kind. People were selling eggs and meat and fruit and cheese. There were stalls of cloth of every kind and colour. There were ducks and geese and hens and goats for sale. And there were the tables of the money lenders, piled high with gold and silver coins.

'They'll make a good profit this weekend,' said Abigail to her friend.

Then, before she had time to tell Anna why she had come, Jesus strode into the courtyard. But the smile on his face was gone. Jesus looked angry and upset.

'Stop!' he shouted. 'This is God's house. Stop using it as a market place!' But no-one took any notice and the noise and bustle and buying and selling went on just as before.

Suddenly Jesus's anger erupted. He grabbed hold of the nearest stall and flung it on its side. Cheeses and fruit rolled onto the dusty floor.

'Hey! What do you think you're doing,' shouted the angry stall-holder. But Jesus didn't stop to answer. He turned to the next stall and the next, angrily tipping them all over and throwing the food and the goods onto the ground. Anna's rolls of cloth were thrown to the ground and they spilled bright colour onto the courtyard floor as they unravelled. Abigail pressed herself against the courtyard wall, afraid of the fury, the noise, the turmoil. Jesus tipped over the tables of the money lenders and opened the doors of the animal pens. Within seconds the temple courtyard was in chaos. People everywhere, animals frightened, food spoiled, goods trampled into the ground, debris all around; and stallholders angry.

'Who does he think he is?'

'Why doesn't someone do something. He wants locking up!'

Just then the High Priests and temple guards came striding into the courtyard.

'How dare you behave like this in our temple!'

'And how dare you treat God's house in this way,' answered Jesus. 'The temple should be a quiet place of prayer, and you have turned it into a den of thieves,' and Jesus strode away from the priests and back to the gate to talk to the crowds who were still waiting there for him. The Priests said nothing. They knew Jesus was right, and that they should not have allowed the temple courtyard to become a market place.

Abigail, Anna, and the others began to clear up the mess. The priests and leaders in Jerusalem talked amongst themselves about how they could get rid of Jesus. They didn't want him in their city. He was too dangerous. He had too many people on his side.

A few days later, they had their answer. One of Jesus's twelve disciples, the one called Judas Iscariot, went to the High Priests and said, 'I know you want to capture Jesus and kill him. What will you give me if I say I will help you?'

The priests could hardly believe their luck. 'We'll pay you thirty pieces of silver,' they said.

The servant girl... in the garden

Later that week, Abigail heard that Jesus and his friends were planning to eat the special Passover meal together. She and some other servant girls were asked to prepare the food.

Abigail watched the disciples arrive at the house where the meal was to be served. They all came; Peter, James, John, Matthew, Mark, Luke, Judas Iscariot, and the others. Twelve of them in all. Abigail watched Jesus wrap a towel round his waist, and begin to wash the feet of the disciples.

'What are you doing?' they asked him. 'Why are you doing the job of a servant?'

'If you want to follow in my footsteps, you must learn to serve each other,' said Jesus. Then he added, 'And I wash you so that you are clean, though one of you here is not.' And Judas realised that Jesus knew he was going to betray him.

A few minutes later, Judas passed Abigail on the stairs. He was going to see the priests, to tell them how they could capture Jesus; to earn his thirty pieces of silver. Jesus saw him go but said nothing.

The meal began and Jesus shared the bread and wine amongst his friends. As he broke the bread he said that his body would soon be broken, and as he poured the wine he said that his blood would soon be spilled. The disciples listened to him, but they didn't understand what he was saying.

After the meal, Abigail saw them all leave the house together, and she followed them. She'd heard them saying that they were going to the Garden of Gethsemane, just outside Jerusalem, because Jesus wanted to go somewhere quiet where he could think and pray.

On the way to the garden, Jesus and his friends talked.

'Soon, you will all leave me,' said Jesus. 'But we will meet again, I promise you.'

'I won't leave you,' said Peter. 'I'll always stand by you.'

'No you won't,' said Jesus. 'Even you, Peter, will say you never knew me. By tomorrow morning you'll have said it three times.'

Abigail hid by the entrance to the garden, and saw Jesus go in with his friends.

'Wait here for me please,' he said to them. 'I want to go further into the garden to pray.' He took Peter, James and John with him and the others sat down on the grass to wait. Everything was dark, peaceful, still. Abigail could well understand why Jesus had come to this quiet place to pray.

For a long time there was silence. The disciples had fallen asleep, and Abigail could just see Jesus and the other three deep in the garden. Jesus was kneeling on the ground, but the other three looked as though they were asleep.

Suddenly, in the distance, Abigail saw lanterns flashing. She heard the sound of soldiers marching. They were coming this way. All at once she felt afraid, not for herself, but for Jesus. Should she try to warn him? Should she shout to the disciples? But what notice would they take of her, just a servant girl? She hid further behind the tree and pulled the low branches round herself so as not to be seen.

The soldiers marched into the garden led by Judas Iscariot. Abigail recognised him as the man who had passed her on the stairs on the day of the

Passover meal. What was he doing here with the Roman soldiers? The peace and quiet of the garden was destroyed as soldiers shouted orders, torches blazed, swords and spears clattered. Abigail saw Judas lead the soldiers to Jesus. He spoke to him, and immediately the soldiers seized Jesus and dragged him away. The rest of the disciples ran away to hide.

The soldiers took Jesus to the house of Caiaphas, the chief priest, and pushed him inside. A small crowd had followed the soldiers as they marched through the streets with Jesus, hoping to see what would happen next to this man who, only four days ago, had ridden into Jerusalem in triumph as a king. Now it looked as though he was going to be killed.

Abigail looked at the faces of the people to see if there was anyone she knew. No-one. But there was one man with his cloak pulled closely around his shoulders, half hiding his face. Something about him looked familiar to Abigail She stared at him. Then she recognised him. It was Peter. She'd seen him at the Passover meal, then again walking with Jesus to the garden. He seemed nice. He was the one who'd said he would always stand by Jesus,

Abigail walked across the street to him.

'Hello,' she said. 'Don't I know you? Aren't you one of Jesus's friends?'

Peter looked at her, startled. He glanced around at the soldiers who were guarding the house of Caiaphas, and then he looked back at the girl.

'No!' he said. 'I don't know what you're talking about!' and he began to walk away. Just then another girl joined Abigail.

'You're right,' she said. 'He does know Jesus. I've seen him with him.'

'No,' shouted Peter, feeling a growing fear and panic. 'I don't know anyone by that name!'

'You must do,' shouted someone else. 'Jesus is from Galilee and you speak with the same accent.'

'No!' shouted Peter again. 'I've never heard of him!' and he ran away down the street, brushing past Abigail as he went. She saw that he had tears in his eyes, and she knew that he had betrayed Jesus, just as Jesus said he would.

The servant girl... on the hill

The next morning, Abigail joined the crowd that followed Jesus as he was taken from the house of Caiaphas to the palace of Pontius Pilate, the Roman Governor.

Pilate came out onto the balcony above where the crowd was standing.

'What do you want me to do with this prisoner?' he asked the people.

'Kill him,' someone shouted.

'But he has done nothing wrong,' answered Pilate.

'He claims to be the king of the Jews, and it is against the Roman law to claim to be a king,' called one of the soldiers. 'Kill him!'

'I could set him free,' said Pilate. 'I am allowed by law to set free a prisoner at the time of the Passover. I can free him, for he has done nothing wrong.'

'No! No! Kill him. Kill him,' cried the same crowd who had hailed Jesus as a king only the week before.

Then Pilate turned to the priests.

'I am having nothing more to do with this man,' he said. 'You deal with him,' and Abigail knew that Pilate was afraid of going against the wishes of the people.

Soldiers led Jesus away to a hill called Calvary. The crowd followed, some of them laughing and jeering. The soldiers dressed Jesus in a long purple cloak and put a crown of thorns on his head. They wrote out a notice which said, 'Jesus of Nazareth, King of the Jews', and they pinned it to the cross.

'What a fine king you are!' they mocked. 'We'll all bow down and worship you,' and they laughed and sniggered and jeered. Jesus said nothing, but endured their taunts with dignity.

After a time, the soldiers grew tired of their cruel teasing and they nailed Jesus to the cross and left him there to die. The crowd started to drift away now the soldiers had gone. Soon, the only people left were a few of the disciples, and a small group of women. Jesus called out to one of the women who was crying, and Abigail realised she was Mary, Jesus's mother. A little later, Jesus died. His friends took him down from the cross, carefully wrapped his body in fine cloth, and laid him in a cave in a garden set into the hillside. They rolled a huge stone across the entrance to the cave so that no-one could disturb the body. And then they left. Abigail felt immensely sad at the way things had turned out.

However, two days later, she was astonished to hear that Jesus was alive!

Anna, her friend whom she'd last seen in the temple market place, the day Jesus had overturned all the tables, came to see her.

'He's alive,' she said. 'The news is all round Jerusalem.'

'That's impossible,' said Abigail. 'I saw him die. I was there. He can't be alive.'

'He is,' said Anna. 'Mary Magdalene saw him. She went to the garden this morning, and when she got there the cave was open and the tomb was empty. Then she saw a man walking towards her. She thought it was the gardener at first, then she realised it was Jesus. He spoke to her. He told her to tell the others that he's alive.'

'Where is he now?' asked Abigail.

'No-one knows,' said Anna, as she went off to tell some other friends the news.

Abigail thought that would be the last time she heard any news of Jesus, but several days later she saw for herself that he was alive.

She had gone to see some relatives who lived by the Sea of Galilee, and she was walking along the edge of the lake when she noticed some fishermen out in a small boat. She recognised Peter as the man she'd tried to talk to outside the house of Caiaphas the night that Jesus was arrested, and she remembered that another man had said he had a Galilean accent.

'He must live near here,' she said to herself. 'I suppose after Jesus died there was no reason for him to stay in Jerusalem,' for Abigail didn't really believe the story Anna had told, of Jesus being alive again.

Abigail shielded her eyes from the sun and looked at the other fishermen on the boat. There were seven of them altogether, and Abigail thought she recognised them all as friends of Jesus. The fishermen didn't look as though they'd had a very good catch. The baskets on board were empty, and the nets were hanging limply over the side of the boat.

Then suddenly, a man called to the fishermen from the shore.

'Have you caught anything?'

'No,' they called back. 'We've been fishing all night, but we haven't caught a single fish.'

'Throw your nets over the other side of the boat,' said the man.

The fishermen did as he suggested, although they didn't think it would do any good. They'd fished everywhere in the lake and so far had caught nothing. But as soon as the nets touched the water at the other side of the boat, they teemed and bulged with fish. The nets were so heavy with fish that the men could not pull them in. One of the fishermen looked out across the water to the stranger who'd called to them.

'It's Jesus!' he said in astonishment. The others looked up in amazement.

Peter jumped into the water and swam ashore, and the others rowed back as quickly as they could, pulling the nets full of fish behind the boat.

Abigail saw that Jesus had built a small fire on the sand and had a basket of bread nearby.

'Bring some of your fish here and we'll have breakfast together,' he said to his friends.

And Abigail quietly crept away because she did not want to disturb them.

For the rest of her life, she thought about the strange and wonderful things she had seen and heard since the arrival of Jesus into Jerusalem; and she wondered about the man they called Jesus.

It's a remarkable story. It must have been even more remarkable to have been there at the time, like Abigail.

Although the Easter story has some sad and distressing parts to it, it is a story with a happy ending, a story of rejoicing, a story which gives all Christians hope for the future.

Thank you, Lord, for sending your Son, Jesus Christ, to live with us on Earth, for showing us by his example how to love and care for one another, and for proving by his death that good will always triumph over evil.
Thank you for the joy of Eastertime. Amen

April

Theme 1: Choices

Noah's choices

Have you ever had to make a choice that's been really difficult? Maybe you have eight friends but your mum has told you that you can only have six people to your birthday tea. How on earth do you choose who to invite? Or perhaps you've at last been told you can have the pet you've wanted for ages. You go to the pet shop and there are three rabbits or kittens or whatever. How do you choose which one to take home when they all look so nice? I wonder how Noah chose which animals to take with him on the ark. He had to take two of each kind, but how did he choose which two?

Today's story is about Noah making those choices.

The ark was almost finished when the clouds gathered and the sky began to grow dark. Noah knew it was time to gather the animals. God had told him to put a male and female of every animal on the ark, so that each kind would be safe during the flood, and afterwards life could begin again.

Noah called for his wife, his three sons and three daughters-in-law.

'Shem, Ham and Japheth,' he said. 'I want you to finish building the ark. The rain will come soon and we haven't much time.'

'Wives, I need you to get everything ready inside the ark. Food for us and the animals, bedding, pots and pans, water carriers; everything we shall need to keep us alive whilst the flood covers the earth. While you do that, I shall go and gather together all the animals.'

Noah went into his house and collected an assortment of boxes, baskets, cages and nets. Then he set off into the countryside.

'Where shall I start?' he thought.

Just then a small blue butterfly fluttered past. Noah took out his net and was just about to catch the butterfly, when another one with black and red wings fluttered by. Noah put down the net and scratched his head.

'Which one shall I take?' he thought. 'What did God tell me to do? Should I catch two butterflies of every kind and every colour to put in the ark, or did God mean just any two butterflies?'

Noah was in such a dilemma that he decided to leave the question of the butterflies until later and concentrate on something else instead. He noticed a rabbit hopping by underneath a tree, and stealthily crept towards it. The rabbit stopped to nibble some grass and Noah quickly brought down the net on top of it. The rabbit was trapped. It looked at Noah with bright frightened eyes. 'I'm not going to hurt you,' said Noah. 'I'm actually going to save you.' But the rabbit looked so afraid, and Noah felt so sorry for it that he let it go again.

'This is all much more difficult than I thought,' he said. 'I'll start with the birds instead, perhaps that'll be easier.' Sitting in the tree above him were seven chattering magpies. Their black and white feathers glistened in the rain. They all looked beautiful, and they all looked exactly the same.

'How can I choose which to take?' said Noah. 'It's impossible to decide.' And as he stood there pondering, the seven magpies took to their wings and flew away.

'The hens will be easier,' thought Noah. 'I'll start with them.' He went back to the farmyard where the cockerel and hens were pecking at the corn which Noah's wife had fed them. He easily caught hold of the cockerel and gently put him in a box. Then he picked up a small brown hen and was just putting her in the box when he noticed a larger russet-brown hen. 'That one will be better,' he thought, but as he put the small hen back in the yard and picked up the larger hen, he noticed another; bigger and more brightly coloured than either of her sisters. 'That one will be better still,' thought Noah, and he picked her up and put her in the box. Then he saw a large white hen and changed his mind again. He let the russet one go and put the white one in the box, and then scratched his head and said, 'But maybe I should have kept the little brown one I chose in the first place. Oh dear! This is much too difficult. I'll decide later,' and he let the hen and the cockerel out of the box.

In the corner of the barn was a mother cat with her litter of kittens. 'I'll choose two of those,' thought Noah. 'Shall I have the tabby and the tortoiseshell or the ginger and the black and white? I suppose I could take the ginger and the tabby, or... maybe... I'll keep them all! How can I possibly choose just two?'

And so it went on. Noah went from animal to animal but found it impossible to choose which two to take with him in the ark.

'You have asked me to do something which is too hard,' he said to God. 'Tell me what to do!' but there was no answer from God.

Noah went back to his family in the ark.

'Well?' said his wife. 'Have you got the animals? Your sons have finished the ark. Your daughters-in-law and I have prepared everything inside. We're ready to go. Where are the animals?'

'They're not here,' answered Noah. 'I can't choose. It's too difficult.'

'But you have to,' said his wife. 'God has told you to.'

'I know,' said Noah. 'I've tried but I can't.'

'You should just go and get any two of each animal,' said Shem.

'No, you should bring back the first two of each animal you see,' said Ham.

'No, don't do that. You should choose the biggest and strongest of each animal,' said Japheth.

'STOP!' shouted Noah. 'You're all giving me different advice. It's not helping me at all.'

'Then you must go out again and choose the animals you want to bring to the ark,' said Noah's wife.

'But that's just it!' cried Noah. 'I don't know which animals to choose.'

'Perhaps God will tell you what to do,' said one of the daughters-in-law.

'I've asked him and he didn't reply,' answered Noah miserably.

'I think he did reply,' said another daughter-in-law. 'Look!'

Noah and his wife and their three sons and daughters-in-law all looked out of the window of the ark. There, walking tidily in twos towards the ark was a long line of animals; one pair of every animal that Noah had ever seen, from the tiniest beetle to the tallest giraffe. And above the line of animals, flying in formation, were pairs of every kind of bird.

The animals walked quietly into the ark and settled into their places.

'I didn't have to choose, after all,' said Noah. 'God did it for me. I knew I could trust him to show me the way.'

Noah stood by the door and waited for the last of the animals to enter, then he closed the door tight and locked it and waited for the rain.

Making choices is not easy, as Noah found out. Luckily for him, he didn't have to choose; God solved the problem for him.

We often have choices to make in our lives, and, like Noah, sometimes the choices are made for us. But at other times we have to make them ourselves. If the choice is difficult, we just have to do the best we can. If you have a difficult choice to make, it's a good idea to think about it, and perhaps ask someone else's advice, and then choose whatever you think is right.

Dear God, please help us to think clearly when we have difficult choices to make. Help us to remember to consider the feelings of other people when we have to make choices. Help us always to choose to do what is right. Amen

Recipes

Do you like cooking? I do. I have lots of recipe books at home and one of my favourite things is looking through and choosing what to make. When I've chosen a recipe, say for a cake, I sometimes choose different ingredients from what the book says, and I might make a lemon cake instead of a chocolate one, or almond biscuits instead of currant ones. Choosing what to cook is half the fun of doing it.

I've brought one of my recipe books into assembly today and I thought we could play a game! I'll read out some ingredients and you can tell me what the recipe is going to make when the ingredients are all mixed.

Here's the first recipe. To make this, you need milk, sugar and custard powder. What is it? Yes it's easy - it's custard.

Here's the next recipe. You need melted chocolate, cornflakes. Oh, and some paper cases. That's right - chocolate crispies.

Here's another recipe. A bit harder this time: some flour, an egg, some milk, a pinch of salt. You'll also need a frying pan, and maybe some lemon and sugar, or perhaps some treacle, or even some maple syrup to put on them when they're cooked.

Well done – these ingredients make pancakes.

Let's try another. What about margarine, sugar, eggs, flour, cocoa? And you might need some icing sugar to go on top. Yes – chocolate cake.

And I wonder if you'll know this one: butter, sugar, eggs, flour, currants, raisins and sultanas, some cherries, a few almonds, and maybe some sherry or brandy? You'll need marzipan and icing for the top of it as well. Yes – it's Christmas cake.

The next recipe is a trick recipe because it doesn't make anything to eat. I wonder if anyone will be able to tell me what it is a recipe for? If you mix together a handful of friends, a loving family, a comfy home, some cheerfulness, a lot of contentment and a few smiles. What do you have? Yes, well done, it's a recipe for happiness.

This recipe makes a particular sort of person. What sort of person do you think it is: a lot of friendliness, some cheerfulness, some helpfulness, a bit of generosity, some thoughtfulness and some caring? Yes, I would agree with you; that recipe would make a very kind person.

Here's the last recipe. What sort of person would this recipe make: a lot of meanness, some nastiness, a lot of unfriendliness, a bit of spite, a bit of greed, a lot of selfishness? Yes, I think so too; that's a recipe for a bully.

And what have the people recipes got to do with the recipes for cooking? Well, they all involve choices. When you do some cooking, you choose what to make. When you're with other people, you choose how you're going to behave. You choose what sort of person you're going to be.

I wonder if you could write down the recipe for you? I'd be very interested to read all your recipes to see what you put!

Today's prayer is called the housewife's breakfast prayer and is from an old cookery book.

Oh Lord, help me to be not like porridge, thick and slow and heavy to stir; but like cornflakes, light and quick and ready to serve. Amen

The dare

How many of you have friends? Everyone I expect.

It's good to have friends, but it's important that you don't get led into trouble by wanting to impress them or by wanting to be the same as them. For example, if your friend has the latest designer label or the latest computer gear, you might want it too. But remember, you are who you are due to your personality, not your clothes or what's in your home. Sometimes it's good to be like the others, but it's important to think for yourself and make your own choices about things.

In today's story, a girl was dared to do something she knew was wrong.

She was worried her friends wouldn't stay friends if she didn't do it.

There were five children in the group, three boys and two girls. They usually played together after school and at weekends, mostly at football or on their bikes or just hanging around together in the street.

This particular Saturday morning, Helen and Pete had been told they couldn't take their bikes out, and so they'd called for the others and all gone out with a football. They'd only been playing five minutes when old Mrs Conner at number seven came out and complained about the noise and the ball going in her garden.

'I'm sick of it,' she shouted. 'It's every Saturday. Clear off and go and play somewhere else.'

They took the ball in and wandered down to the local shops.

'Shall we get some sweets?' said Daniel.

'Who's got some money?' asked Rashid. 'I've spent all mine.'

'I haven't any,' said Tess.

'I haven't anything, either,' said Pete. 'My dad stopped my pocket money this week 'cos I was in trouble at school.'

'I've got 5p,' said Helen.

'Well that's it then!' said Rashid. 'We're not going to get much with 5p. Let's go.'

'But go where?' said Pete. 'There's nothing to do, nowhere to go. It's boring.'

'We could nick some sweets,' suggested Daniel.

The others stared at him. 'It's dead easy,' he went on. 'I've done it loads of times. You don't get caught.'

This was the first the others had heard of Daniel stealing sweets. They didn't know whether to believe him or not.

'I bet you never have!' said Tess.

'I have, too, so there!' said Daniel. 'Why don't you try it. It's easy. Go on.'

'I think we should go,' said Rashid, who didn't like the way things were turning out. 'Let's go and find somewhere to play football.'

'You can go if you want,' said Daniel. 'I'm staying here till Tess gets some sweets.'

'I never said I would,' began Tess. 'There's no way! I'm not a thief.'

'No, you're just a wimp,' said Daniel. 'Go on, I dare you to!'

'No,' said Tess.

'We won't be your friends any more if you don't, will we?' and Daniel turned to the others. They said nothing but all looked uncomfortable. Daniel had always been the leader of the group and they didn't want to fall out with him.

'Go on then,' he said to Tess. 'Take Helen's 5p and ask for something on the kid's counter but stand up by the till. When they go to get it for you, grab a chocolate bar and shove it in your pocket. Then pay the 5p. Easy Peasy. You can't fail.'

Tess stood still and looked miserable. Daniel moved the other children a little way away until she was standing by herself.

'I dare you,' he went on. 'You're a wimp if you don't. Wimpy! Wimpy! We won't be friends if you don't get us some chocolate. Go on wimp!'

Just then a few people went into the sweet shop together. It was only a small shop and Tess knew it would seem full with that number of people. She quickly darted into the shop.

Daniel looked astonished. 'I never thought she would,' he said. 'I didn't mean it. I've never nicked anything, I just said I did. She'll get caught. Quick. Run for it,' and the four children took to their heels and ran.

Inside the shop, Tess grabbed a chocolate bar and ran outside. She looked round for the others – they'd be so proud of her. She could hardly believe that she'd actually done it. She was as brave as Daniel now; he'd be her friend forever. But where was he? There was no sign of him.

As she looked around, Mr Patel came rushing out of the shop.

'Hey! You!' he shouted. Tess turned and ran as she'd never run before. Mr Patel went back into the shop, where old Mrs Conner happened to be buying her newspaper. 'It's Tess Matthews,' Mrs Conner told him. 'Mind you I'm surprised she's done that. She's not a bad girl usually. I'll give you her address and you can contact her parents.'

Have you ever done something your friends have told you to do, even though you know you shouldn't? It's hard to say no, isn't it, when they're egging you on. But you don't *have* to do as they say. The choice is yours. If there's something you don't want to do; say no. You're not a coward; it takes courage to say no and stand up for what you know is right. And remember, *real* friends won't give you dares like that.

Dear God, help us to know that it's our choice how we behave. We don't have to do what our friends tell us. We don't have to do something if we know it's wrong. Help us to have the courage to say no when it's right to do so. Amen

Theme 2: Different perspectives

Two sides to every story

Have you ever been in an argument with a friend and had to go to a teacher, or one of your parents, or another adult to help sort it out? I think that's happened to most of you at some time or another. But have you noticed that when each of you tells your side of the story, the stories are often different? Yet you were both there, so how can they be different?

This happens because you are each giving an account of what happened, from your point of view. Everyone sees everything from their own point of view, so everyone's version is that little bit different.

Let me show you what I mean. But I'll need two of you to help me. *(Choose two children who are fairly articulate and whose voices will be able to be heard by the rest of the children. Invite them to the front and ask them to sit on two chairs facing each other.)*

Now, let me ask the rest of you about this room we are in. Tell me about it. Tell me what is in here. Describe it to me. *(Invite responses.)*

That's good. So we are all agreed on where we are and on exactly what this hall/room is like. There can be no dispute about it.

I am now going to ask A to describe what s/he can see. *(Ask first child to tell everyone what they can see from where they are sitting.)*

And now I'm going to ask B to describe the hall/room. *(Ask second child to describe what they can see.)*

Well, A and B are here in the hall with the rest of us. But they have described two quite different pictures. *(Point out some of the differences in the children's descriptions, e.g. one might have been able to see the piano, windows, curtains, certain pictures, particular doors etc.)*

Why are the descriptions different? Is one of the children telling lies? Is one of them not being accurate about what they're telling us? *(Invite responses.)*

Both their descriptions are accurate and true. But the descriptions are very different because each of the children is describing the hall/room from their own point of view.

Whenever we tell anyone anything, we tell it from our own point of view. And that's how it should be. But at the same time, we have to take care to give people accurate information, and to tell the truth. And often, it's good to try and put ourselves in the other person's shoes; that means to try to understand things from their point of view. If everyone in the world did this, there'd be fewer arguments and less falling out! In our school this week, let's see if we can all try at least once to understand someone else's point of view. Then let's see if it makes a difference to how we all get along with each other.

Dear God, help us to be tolerant of each other. Help us to know that we don't have to be best friends with everyone, but we do need to get along with the people in our families and communities. When we disagree with someone, help us to see their point of view, so that even if we still don't agree with them, we can try to understand their reasons. Amen

Three shoemakers in Baghdad

Everyone sees things from their own point of view. So if two people are telling how something was, and they were both in the same place at the same time, they won't tell it exactly the same. This doesn't mean that one is right and the other wrong; it simply means that each is telling it from their own point of view. And everyone's point of view is different.

Take this story, for example.

Once upon a time in old Baghdad there lived a shoemaker. Now the shoemakers you might have come across in stories before are probably very poor. Story-book shoemakers are usually impoverished. They live in tiny houses and have great difficulty in earning a living. But not this shoemaker!

He was really a businessman more than a shoemaker. He had shoe shops in every area of Baghdad and had people working for him to actually make the shoes. And what shoes they were!

His workmen made shoes for the rich and famous of Baghdad at that time. Of course they were not shoes as we wear today. Oh no! They were far more interesting and flamboyant than that. They made sandals of the softest leather in gold or bronze, they made boots with coloured jewels up the sides, they made slippers of satin and velvet, clogs with silver soles, and even shoes with the longest pointed toes you could ever imagine that curled over and tied with tinsel threads to one's ankles. They were the most amazing shoes.

One day the shoemaker sent for his two best workmen, Abdhul and Mustafa.

'I want you to go out on a fact-finding mission,' he told them. 'You see, I have lots of shoe shops here in Baghdad, but it's high time I expanded. It's time I looked at the places around Baghdad, to see if there are any business opportunities there. I want you to travel to all the local towns and villages, to see how they are for shoes and shoe shops, and report back to me. Then I can decide whether to open any new shops.'

So the two men set off. They travelled together as far as the north gate of the city, then Abdhul set off towards the east and Mustafa travelled west. They planned to work their way round the outskirts of the city, in two halves of a giant circle, visiting all the outlying towns and villages, then meet again at the south gate of Baghdad from where they would return to the shoemaker and report their findings.

All went well. They each visited several towns and villages and made notes about the state of the shoes of the people living there. Then Abdhul arrived at a small town called Al Bahr, directly south of Baghdad. He wasn't sure whether he or Mustafa was supposed to be reporting on this town, but since he was here he thought he'd better do it.

Abdhul looked round and saw there were no shoe shops of any kind. Then he noticed that not one of the people was wearing shoes. Everyone, from the children to the old people, was bare-footed.

'What a brilliant place for us to open a new shop,' he said to himself. 'No-one has shoes so there's a real business opportunity here! We could sell shoes to everyone. What a find!' and he hurried away towards Baghdad and the south gate of the city where he was to meet Mustafa.

Abdhul had only just left the little town of Al Bahr, when Mustafa arrived.

Mustafa was also unsure whether he or Abdhul was supposed to be reporting on this town, but since he was here he thought he'd better do it. He didn't know, of course, that Abdhul had already visited the town and was now on his way back to Baghdad.

Mustafa looked around and saw that there were no shoe shops of any kind. Then he noticed that not one of the people was wearing shoes. Everyone, from the children to the old people, was bare-footed.

'What a terrible place for us to open a new shop!' he said to himself. 'No-one even wears shoes, so it's no use coming here with a shoe shop! It's a waste of time even to think about it,' and he hurried away towards Baghdad and the south gate of the city where he was to meet Abdhul.

They met each other without any problem and went to find the shoemaker so that they could report their findings.

'And the last place I visited was the best,' said Abdhul. 'We must open new shops there. There's so much opportunity.'

'That's funny.' said Mustafa. 'Because the last place I visited was useless as far as shoe shops are concerned. We most certainly couldn't open a new shop there. We wouldn't sell any shoes at all!'

'Where was it?' asked Abdhul.

'A place called Al Bahr,' said Mustafa.

'But I went there. It's the *best* place for a new shop!' said Abdhul.

'It's the *worst* place for a new shop!' shouted Mustafa.

'No! I'm right, you're wrong,' insisted Abdhul.

'I'm right. *You're* wrong,' said Mustafa. And the argument raged, until the shoemaker said 'STOP!'

'You're both right and neither of you is wrong. You've been to the same place, looked at the same people, and assessed the same situation. But! You've both looked at it from your own viewpoint, and that's right. The thing you're doing wrong is arguing about it, instead of trying to see it from the other point of view.

'It could be the best place for a new shop. It could be the worst place for a new shop. We'll all three sit down together and work out what to do next!'

So that's what they did! I wonder what they decided to do?

I wonder how many of you have ever been in a similar situation, where two of you are telling something but the versions are different and an argument starts. It might not mean that either of you is right or wrong; it might just mean that you are seeing the event from you own point of view.

Next time it happens, try to see it from the other person's point of view as well, and see if that helps you to sort things out.

Help us, Lord, to see the other point of view. Help us to know that everyone sees everything from a slightly different viewpoint. Help us to be tolerant of the other person's point of view. Amen

Twenty eighty

Everyone sees things from their own point of view, and that's right. But sometimes we decide in advance what someone or something is going to be like, and that's not such a good thing to do, because we may well be wrong. For example, have you ever had someone new join your class, or come to live in your street? Did you decide certain things about them even before you got to know them? We all do this from time to time, but it's very unfair to judge someone before you even know them.

Let's hear today's story, which is a true story by the way.

Jeff Anderson is a television producer. He makes TV programmes mainly about wildlife, but he's also very interested in people and the way they behave. He's very observant and he notices how people behave with each other, and how they behave when they're on their own.

One day Jeff was in town doing some shopping when he noticed an old woman struggling through the door of one of the shops. She was carrying several shopping bags and was having difficulty in opening the heavy door. No-one stopped to help her. Jeff was just about to go across the road and offer to help, when the door suddenly opened and she went inside.

Just then a pretty young woman came up to the door. She was also going into the shop but she no sooner had her hand on the door handle, when three people came to help. And that small incident set Jeff thinking.

'I wonder why no-one helped the old woman?' he thought. 'And I wonder why three people helped the younger one? Perhaps there just wasn't anyone about when the old woman went through the door. Or perhaps people behave differently towards older people than they do towards younger people.'

Jeff decided to do an experiment. He contacted a young actress he knew, called Joanne, and he asked if she would help him.

'I want you to go into town,' he said. 'I want you to go into the shops and cafes, the supermarkets and restaurants and see how people behave towards you. Will you do that?'

'Yes,' said Joanne. 'But I don't see what for.'

'Well, the next day I want you to do it all again,' said Jeff. 'But when you do it the second time I want you to be dressed up as an old woman. I want to see if people treat you differently. I don't want you to behave differently, I want you to be exactly the same on both days, except for your clothes and make-up. Will you do it?'

'Yes,' said Joanne. 'But if I'm just being me on both days, it won't make any difference what I'm wearing. People will treat me just the same. Won't they?'

'We'll have to see,' said Jeff.

The next day Joanne came to the TV studios as arranged. The make-up department did her hair and face, and she came out of the studios looking like the attractive twenty-year-old she was. Off she went into town and had a wonderful day.

She did some shopping and had her lunch in the new coffee shop. She went into the supermarket and did some more shopping then went for a coffee. Everywhere she went people were friendly and helpful.

'It'll be brilliant doing this again tomorrow,' she thought.

The next day Joanne went to the studios for her 'old' make-up and clothes. They gave her wrinkles on her face and grey hair. They dressed her in a dark grey jumper and skirt and old-fashioned shoes. They gave her a walking stick and she practised stooping over and leaning on the stick. She came out of the studios looking like a rather poor eighty-year-old lady.

Joanne did some shopping and had her lunch in the new coffee shop. She went into the supermarket and did some more shopping then went for a coffee. But what a difference from the day before.

People were impatient with her. They said she was slow when she was looking for money in her purse to pay at the till. People pushed in front of her in the queues, but most people simply ignored her. It was as though she was too old to be of any use to anyone any more.

Joanne was surprised and disappointed at the way she was treated by most people. Everyone was so different from how they'd been the day before, when she was young.

'Why are people like that?' she asked Jeff at the end of the day. 'Why does everyone treat me so differently from yesterday? I'm still the same me inside.'

'But they couldn't see that,' said Jeff. 'People could only see the outside of you and they all jumped to conclusions about what you were like. People have preconceived ideas; that means they think they know what someone is going to be like before they actually find out about them. People think they can know all about someone else just by looking at the outside of them.'

'But it's not fair, is it?' said Joanne. 'People shouldn't judge others until they've found out what they're really like.'

'You're right,' said Jeff. 'And maybe we can help people to understand this. Maybe we could make a TV programme about your experiences as a twenty-year-old and as an eighty-year-old. We could show everyone the different ways you were treated, and maybe it'll help someone to think more fairly.'

And that is exactly what they did.

I don't know how many people watched the programme when it was shown, and I don't know how much difference it made to the way people think about others. But if it helped just a few people to be careful about having preconceived ideas, it will have done its job.

Dear God, please help us to treat other people fairly. Help us not to jump to conclusions about what people are like before we get to know them. Help us not to have preconceived ideas about what people are like. Help us to get to know people on the inside and not just judge them on their outside appearance. Amen

Theme 3: Fables

The sparrows' gifts

As you know, there are lots of different kinds of stories. There are mystery stories, adventure stories, fairy stories and detective stories; there is historical fiction and science fiction; there are true stories, tall stories, folk stories, and traditional stories, like myths, legends and fables. I think you know already what myths and legends are, but what about fables? Do you know what fables are?

A fable is a story with a moral - a rule of behaviour - hidden inside it. A fable is a very clever story because you can listen to it and enjoy it just as it is, or you can treat it like a puzzle and try and guess the hidden meaning. Fables nearly always have animals or birds or insects in them, who speak and behave like human beings.

Let's try one, and see if you can find the hidden message. This fable is a very old one and it comes from Japan.

There was once an old woman who found an injured sparrow in her garden. It would have been easy for the woman at best to ignore it or at worst to kill it, but she was a kind old soul and didn't like to think of any creature being in pain or discomfort, so she gently picked it up and took it into her house. She found a small box, lined it with scraps of cotton and paper, and carefully laid the sparrow inside. She gave it water to drink and a few seeds and grains of rice to eat from her precious store. Little by little the sparrow recovered.

After several days the sparrow was well enough to fly, and it tested its wings round the old woman's house.

'I think it's time you went home,' she said, and she opened the window to let the sparrow out. It hopped onto the window ledge, then turned and looked at the old woman, and to her astonishment it spoke.

'Thank you for caring for me. I will repay you one day soon,' then the sparrow flew out of the window and up up into the sky.

The woman watched it until it disappeared from sight, then smiled to herself.

'Silly old woman,' she said. 'Fancy thinking that the sparrow spoke. Too much time on your own, that's your trouble,' and she got out her duster and began to tidy the room.

A few days later she was out in the garden hanging out some washing, when a flock of sparrows flew overhead. The birds circled the cherry blossom tree, then, chittering and chattering, landed on the grass at the old woman's feet. She was astonished to see that every sparrow carried a tiny box of brightly coloured paper tied with golden thread, in its beak.

'We've brought you a gift,' said the largest sparrow, and the old woman recognised him as the sparrow she had cared for. 'You may choose one of our boxes.'

'That's very kind of you,' said the old woman, and she knelt on the grass and looked at the boxes. They were all exquisitely beautiful, but one in particular caught her attention. It was by far the tiniest box and was made of midnight blue tissue paper with flecks of silver in it.

'This one is the prettiest. I'd like this one please.' She loosened the fine golden thread and undid the box. Inside was a single perfect shining pearl. 'It's the most beautiful thing I've ever seen,' she whispered. 'Thank you.'

Then the sparrows chirruped and sang and hopped and danced until the old woman laughed with joy at the sight.

'The rest of the gifts are for you, too,' sang the largest sparrow, and straightaway all the birds pulled the golden threads loose and tipped the contents of the beautiful boxes onto the grass. There was a ruby, a glittering diamond, a tiny piece of gold; a sliver of silver, a scrap of silk, a tiny piece of velvet; a grain of rice, a pomegranate seed, and an orange pip.

'Thank you, thank you,' laughed the woman, as she gathered up the treasures and the boxes.

'You're welcome...welcome... welcome...' twittered the sparrows as they flew high into the sky up and away.

The old woman took the gifts into her house and put them on the table. Later, she was surprised to see that the gifts had grown. The tiny scraps of fabric had become lengths of cloth, the jewels and seeds and grains and pips lay in piles on the table.

'I'm rich,' she laughed. 'I need never worry about money again.' But just as she said this, there was a knock at the door. Her neighbour had come to borrow a saucepan, but her eyes grew greedy and wide when she saw the table of treasures.

'Where did you get all that?' she asked. And the old woman told her everything that had happened.

'I want some!' shouted the neighbour, and she rushed home to get a net. She ran about the garden until she caught a sparrow, then she stunned it and carried it inside. For the next week she nursed it back to health, then opened the window to set it free.

'Thank you for caring for me. I will repay you one day soon,' said the sparrow as he flew out of the window and up up into the sky.

A few days later, the neighbour was standing in the garden, watching and waiting for the sparrows to come with their gifts. Suddenly, a flock of small brown birds flew overhead and circled the almond blossom tree. Then, chittering and chattering, they landed on the grass at the feet of the neighbour. She was delighted to see that each sparrow carried a small paper box in its beak.

'We've brought you a gift,' said the largest sparrow. 'You may choose one of our boxes.'

The neighbour knelt on the ground and scrabbled amongst the boxes.

'They're very small, aren't they!' she grumbled. She picked them up and turned them over with her fat probing fingers.

'I want this one. It's the biggest,' she said, grabbing a golden parcel and ripping off the silver string. But as she opened the box, stinging insects and biting beetles came running out all around her.

'The rest of the gifts are for you, too,' said the largest sparrow, and straightaway all the birds pulled the silken threads loose and tipped the contents of their boxes onto the grass. Immediately the woman was surrounded by buzzing, flying, crawling insects. Flies and bees and wasps flew round her head. Scorpions and centipedes ran onto her hands and feet. Slugs and snails and spiders crawled over her face. She jumped to her feet and ran into the house, shouting at the sparrows as she went.

'It's not fair. Why can't I have all the good things my neighbour was given?'

'You know the answer to that,' said the sparrows. 'You ended up with nothing because you were too greedy!'

Have you found the hidden message in the story? Yes, you've got it. The story is warning us about being too grasping and greedy. It's telling us that it's better to be helpful to others out of kindness, and not for any reward or payment we might get.

The first woman in the story helped the sparrow without knowing that it would give her the gifts. The greedy woman not only looked after the sparrow for what she thought it would give her, but she even injured it in the first place so that she could pretend to care for it. She didn't realise until too late that this sort of behaviour never usually works.

Help us Lord, not to be greedy. Teach us to help other people out of love and kindness, and not for what we might get out of it. Teach us to be caring and considerate to others and not to be selfish. Amen

The flight of the beasts

Have you ever done something just because a friend has told you to? And have you realised afterwards that maybe it wasn't such a good idea? I think at some time or another we have all followed someone else instead of thinking for ourselves.

In today's fable, an enormous group of animals very nearly found themselves in serious trouble. This story is from a large collection of fables from India, called the Jataka Tales.

Listen to the fable and see if you can find the hidden message.

Once upon a time there was a hare who lived amongst the roots of a coconut palm. One day as he was lying under his tree, snoozing, after eating his lunch, he began to daydream.

'What if the end of the world happened now?' he thought. 'What would become of me? What if the sky fell in and squashed me? What if the clouds all fell out of the sky and covered me up? What if the sun and the stars and the earth all collided in space?' The more the hare thought about these things, the more upset and panicky he became. He sat up and looked around him to check that all was well, but exactly at that moment, a coconut fell out of the tree and landed with a thud on the ground behind him.

'Oh no!' shouted the hare as he leapt to his feet. 'It's really happening. It's the end of the world. The sky is falling in! Save me! Save me!' and he ran faster than he had ever run before, out of the palm grove and over the fields, to try and escape from the dreadful crash that he knew would happen when the sky fell down to the ground.

Another hare saw him scampering by as though all the demons in the world were after him.

'Whatever's the matter, brother hare?' he called.

'Run!' shouted the hare without stopping. 'It's the end of the world. The sky is falling in!'

'Oh dear, that's dreadful!' said the second hare, and without bothering to check the facts he joined the hare in his headlong dash to escape from the terrible disaster.

As they raced over the fields, other hares stopped to look, rabbits popped out of their burrows to see what was going on, and deer looked up from grazing to watch.

'What's going on?' they all asked.

'Come on! Run!' shouted the hare. 'It's the end of the world. The sky is falling in!'

'That's terrible!' said the rabbits and hares and deer, and without waiting to check the facts, they too joined in the scramble to reach safety.

As the animals raced round the foot of the mountain, they passed the boars and the buffaloes.

'What on earth's going on?' they called to the animals racing by.

'It's the end of the world,' shouted the deer. 'The sky is falling in! Come on! Run!'

'How dreadful!' said the boars and buffaloes, and without waiting to check the facts, they took to their heels with the others.

As the gasping animals rounded the mountain and fled across the plain, they were seen by the rhinoceroses and the tigers and the elephants.

'What's going on?' they called.

'It's the end of the world!' shouted the buffaloes. 'The sky is falling in! Come on! Run, if you want to save your skins!'

'The sky's falling in! That's awful!' said the rhinos and tigers and elephants, and without waiting to check the facts, they too made a run for it and followed the hundreds of other animals tearing along the ground.

Ahead of them lay the tall dark cliffs and the long drop down to the sea.

Ahead of them lay the jagged rocks and the pounding angry waves.

Ahead of them lay certain death... and the lion who stood on the cliff.

The lion knew the sky was not falling in. He knew it was not the end of the world. He knew the animals had not checked their facts before rushing to join with the others. He knew he somehow had to stop the animals or they would hurtle over the cliff and be killed. He stood in their path and roared. The animals came to a slithering stop and landed in a tangled heap at the edge of the cliff.

'What are you doing?' asked the lion quietly.

'The world. It's coming to an end. The sky is falling in. It's the end of everything. We'll be crushed. We'll die.' The animals all spoke at once.

'How do you know this?' asked the lion.

'He told me. No they told us. No it was him. No, them,' said the animals all at the same time and all pointing to each other.

'Let's start with you,' said the lion to the elephants. 'Why did you start stampeding?'

'Well, the tigers told us the sky was falling in,' said the elephants.

'And how did you know, tigers?' said the lion.

'The rhinoceros told us,' said the tigers.

'And how did you know?' said the lion to the rhinoceros.

'The buffaloes told us,' they said.

'And you, buffaloes, how did you know that the world was coming to an end?' asked the lion.

'The boars told us, and the deer told them. We heard them,' said the buffaloes.

'And who told you?' said the lion to the deer.

'The rabbits and hares told us,' said the deer.

'And who told you?' asked the lion.

'He did!' said the rabbits and hares, all pointing to the second hare.

'It wasn't me! It was him!' said the second hare, pointing to the hare he had seen running out of the coconut palm grove. 'He told me!'

'I heard it,' whimpered the hare. 'I heard the sky beginning to fall. It's true. I did,' and he began to cry.

'Show me,' said the lion. 'Show me the place where you heard the sky falling.'

'I daren't go back there,' said the hare.

'Yes you can,' said the lion. 'I'll go with you.' So the hare and the lion, followed by all the other animals, went back to the coconut grove, and the hare showed the lion where he had been sitting. There on the ground was a coconut.

The lion shook the palm tree and dozens more coconuts thudded to the ground.

'Was that the noise you heard?' asked the lion.

'Yes,' said the hare. 'I'm sorry. I've been silly, haven't I?'

'It was an easy mistake to make,' said the lion. 'You let your imagination run away with you and you got into a panic, but you are not nearly as silly as the rest of these animals who followed you without bothering to think about whether they were doing the right thing,' and the lion turned to the other animals.

'Call yourselves tigers and elephants and buffalo,' he roared. 'You behaved like a set of silly sheep, all following on without thinking, without checking the facts for yourselves. Just think, next time I might not be at the edge of the cliff to save you, and then what will you do?' but the animals were already creeping back to their own homes, determined that there wouldn't be a next time, because next time they would think for themselves.

Did you find the message? Yes, the story is telling you to think for yourself. It's an easy message to find in the story, but not so easy to find in real life. Only the other day I had to tell someone off for doing something they shouldn't have been doing. When I asked them why they had been behaving in that way, they said that someone told them to! I was very disappointed that they hadn't thought for themselves, but had just done what someone else told them to, without thinking. The trouble is, we all do that from time to time. But we can't blame other people for our own actions. We're each responsible for what we do. We can't use the 'he told me to do it' excuse. We all have to think for ourselves.

Dear God, please help us to think for ourselves. Help us to know that we are each responsible for our own behaviour and actions. Help us not to blame other people for our faults and mistakes. Help us to think before we act. Amen

The eagle and the beetle

One of the most famous writers of fables was a man called Aesop. He lived in Greece about two thousand five hundred years ago. You've probably met some of his stories already. Have you heard the one about the boy who cried wolf? He lied so many times about a wolf stealing his sheep, that when a wolf really did come and attack the sheep, no-one believed the boy. The moral of that story is... don't tell lies.

Or maybe you've heard the fable about the dog and the bone? The dog stole a bone, but as he was crossing a bridge, he looked into the water and thought that the bone in the reflection was bigger than the one he had. He was so greedy that he tried to grab the bone in the water, but of course dropped the bone as he did so. The moral of that story?... Don't be greedy!

But have you heard the story about the eagle and the beetle? Listen for the moral and see if you can tell me at the end of the fable what it is.

Once upon a time a golden eagle and a tiny black beetle were the best of friends. They used to have breakfast together every morning and discuss their plans for the day. Each looked forward to their daily conversations, until something happened to change everything and to cause the two friends to fall out.

It was a Tuesday, and the tiny black beetle was on his way to the hilltop when he and eagle shared their toast and marmalade every morning. As he arrived for breakfast he noticed that eagle had not set the table.

'I don't fancy toast and marmalade this morning,' said eagle. 'I feel like something more substantial. I feel like something meatier. I feel like... rabbit!' and as she said this the golden eagle spied a small rabbit running down the hill. She lifted her beautiful wings wide, and swooped down over the terrified rabbit, with her talons stretched out and her beak ready to strike. The rabbit ran as fast as it could, screaming for help, but the only living thing it could see was the beetle.

'Help me, beetle. Please help me,' cried the rabbit piteously.

The beetle felt duty bound to help the rabbit, and called to the eagle in his strongest voice, 'Don't hurt the rabbit, eagle. Let it go. Do it for me!' but the eagle took no notice and grabbed the rabbit in its talons.

'Eagle!' called the beetle bravely. 'Leave the rabbit alone I tell you, or you'll have me to answer to!'

'You?' shouted the eagle haughtily. 'And what exactly do you think you are going to do about it? You're only a pathetic little miniscule beetle when you're all there. You're as nothing compared to me!' and she killed the rabbit and began to eat it for breakfast.

The beetle was horrified; horrified that his friend had killed the rabbit, and horrified that she had spoken to him in the way she had.

'You'll pay for this, eagle,' said the beetle.

'Oh yes? Well I feel really scared!' answered the eagle, sarcastically. But she had reckoned without the beetle's perseverance and will power; without his resoluteness and courage. He might have been small, but what he lacked in size he made up for in determination!

The beetle scuttled away and planned his next move. He decided that the best way to show the eagle how much he disapproved of what she'd done, was to destroy her eggs so that she could not teach any young eagles to kill as she had done.

The beetle made his way to the eagle's nest high on the hill. He waited in the short springy grass. He waited and waited. At last the eagle laid two beautiful eggs in the nest of sticks and leaves. The beetle crept closer. When the eagle was not looking, the beetle pushed one of the eggs out of the nest so that it fell to the rocky ground below and was smashed. Then he did the same with the second egg. The eagle was distraught, but laid two more eggs in the nest. The beetle pushed them out and broke them just as he had done with the first clutch of eggs. The eagle laid two more eggs, and the beetle destroyed them. She laid another, and the beetle rolled that one out of the nest.

The beetle destroyed so many eggs, that the eagle was in despair. She went to see the great god Jupiter, to ask his advice.

'Don't worry about it,' said Jupiter. 'In future you can lay your eggs in my lap. They will be quite safe there. The beetle will never dare climb onto me and push the eggs away.'

But Jupiter did not know how determined the small beetle was. He didn't know that the tiny beetle believed he could outwit the great golden eagle, and the great god Jupiter, and that believing it made it possible. He didn't realise that the little beetle knew that great determination can overcome almost anything.

Jupiter sat on his marble throne with the silken cushions. The eagle flew onto his lap and laid her eggs there. Three eggs. Safely positioned in the folds of Jupiter's robe.

'They'll be quite safe with me. You can go now,' said Jupiter, and he settled down amongst his cushions, knowing that he had to sit very still.

Meanwhile, the beetle was rolling tiny balls of earth at Jupiter's feet. As Jupiter slept, the beetle carried the balls of dirt onto Jupiter's marble throne, and rolled them into his lap. Soon Jupiter's lap was covered with dozens of specks of dirt. Then the beetle crept away to watch.

A little later, the great god Jupiter woke from his sleep. He yawned and stretched and opened his eyes. When he saw the dirt in his lap he stood up quickly and brushed it off, but he had forgotten the eagle's eggs hidden in the folds of his robe. As he brushed off the specks of dirt, the eggs fell to the floor and broke. He didn't notice a tiny beetle scurrying away with a satisfied smile on his face.

And since that day, so it is said, the eagle has laid its eggs high high in the craggy mountain cliffs, so that no-one, not even a small black beetle, can reach the nest and destroy the eggs.

And what do you think is the moral – the hidden message – of that story? Well done! It's that almost anything can be achieved with determination. The beetle was much smaller than the eagle or the great god Jupiter, but even though he was small, he succeeded in doing what he set out to do.

I just hope that when you are determined to achieve something, it's not as destructive as the beetle's achievement!

*Help us Lord, to know that we can achieve almost anything with courage and determination. Help us to persevere with things we find difficult and not to give up too easily when things are hard. Amen*1

May

Theme 1: Doing your best

The sponsored spell

Have you ever felt like cheating? I think everyone has felt tempted to cheat at one time or another. Maybe you thought you'd get out of trouble if you told a very small white lie; or maybe you thought you could win a game if you cheated just a little bit? But the trouble with cheating is that it makes you feel uncomfortable inside. Even if you wriggle out of trouble, or win the game, you somehow don't feel right about it if you've cheated.

Hannah, in this story, desperately wanted to do well in her school's sponsored spell. I'll leave it to you to decide whether it's a true story or not!

Hannah was in year six, and her school was having a sponsored spell to raise money for the local children's hospital. Everyone was excited about it, and everyone was determined to do well so that the school would raise lots of money.

The very youngest children in the Nursery were doing a colour recognition test, instead of a spelling test, but everyone else was doing spellings. The reception children had ten words each to learn; year one and two had twenty words to learn; year three and four had thirty words to do; year five had forty, and Hannah's year had fifty words to learn.

All Hannah's friends were working hard at getting sponsors and learning words. Hannah was enjoying getting the sponsors, and had asked her parents and her granddad; she'd spoken to her aunt and uncle on the 'phone and asked them; her mum said she could go and ask the neighbours, and she'd even written to her mum's friend in Canada to ask if she would sponsor her. Yes, it was good fun getting the sponsors and adding their names to the form. But learning the words… well that was a different matter. That was hard work. Hannah wasn't very good at spelling.

'You'll have to get on with it, and get them learned,' her mum said.

'I know,' said Hannah. 'There's plenty of time.'

But time has a nasty habit of running away if you don't catch it whilst it's there, and before Hannah knew it, the day of the sponsored spell had arrived. On their way in to school, all Hannah's friends were testing each other.

'Can you spell rectangle?'

'R E C T A N G L E!'

'Can you do quadruped?'

'Q U A D R U P E D!'

'I bet you can't spell avalanche.'

'A V A L A N C H E!' but Hannah didn't join in. She didn't know many of the spellings and she felt miserable. What on earth was she going to do? Everyone else would do better than her and all the people on her sponsor form would know how badly she'd done. She felt she would die of shame.

Hannah looked down at her crumpled spelling list. Mrs Matthews, the year six teacher was telling everyone to put all their books and papers away.

'Nothing on the desks now, except your pencils,' she said as she gave out the spelling test papers. 'And remember, don't look at anyone else's answers, and don't let anyone else look at yours. We don't want any cheating!'

There was a sudden noisy rustle as all year six tidied everything from the tabletops. Hannah looked round. No one was watching her, they were all too busy putting their things away to notice what she was doing. She put her tattered spelling list on her knee, just under the table. No one would know it was there. She could look at it during the test, and then she'd get all the spellings right. It wasn't really cheating. Not really. After all, it was her own spelling list she'd be copying. It wasn't as though she'd be copying from someone else.

The spelling test began.

'Mountain,' said Mrs Matthews clearly. They all wrote down the word. Hannah sat back a little in her chair and checked the spelling list on her knee. She copied the word down.

'Journey,' said Mrs Matthews. Again Hannah looked at her list.

'Because.' read out Mrs Matthews. Hannah looked at her list again. Then she glanced round. No one was watching. No one had seen. This was easier than she thought.

'Achievement,' went on Mrs Matthews. And Hannah continued to copy all the spellings from the list on her knee until the test was finished.

'Phew! That was hard,' said many of the children on their way out of the classroom for break. Just as Hannah was leaving the classroom, Mrs Matthews called her back.

'How do you feel about the spelling test, Hannah?' she asked.

'Er... it wasn't too bad,' said Hannah, feeling herself going rather red.

'And how will you feel when you collect money from your family and friends, knowing that you've cheated?'

'How did you know?' said Hannah, beginning to feel quite sick.

'You ought to know by now that teachers have eyes everywhere,' said Mrs Matthews.

Hannah started to cry. 'Now everyone will know I can't spell, and that I cheat,' wailed Hannah.

'No-one will know,' said Mrs Matthews. 'You can do the test again with me at lunchtime. This time just do your best. It doesn't matter how many you get right as long as you do the best you can. You might not end up getting the most spellings and collecting the most money, but that doesn't matter. It's taking part that matters. And doing your best that matters. No one can ever ask you to do more than your best - if you do your best you are being true to yourself. That's what matters.'

Hannah did the spelling test again at lunchtime. She scored 30 out of 50 and she collected £25 sponsor money for the appeal. It wasn't the most, and it wasn't the least. But Hannah knew she had earned the £25 honestly, and she knew she could be proud of her achievement and efforts because she had done her best.

Do you think it could be a true story? I'm glad Hannah was honest in the end. The trouble with cheating is that it's very difficult to live with your conscience afterwards. It's far better to be honest and trustworthy and just to do your best in everything you do. And remember, if you always do your best, no one can expect any more of you.

Dear God, help us always to do our best in everything we do. Help us not to be tempted to cheat, but always to be honest, even if it means not winning, or not doing as well as other people. Help us to know that when we do our best we are being true to ourselves, and that no one can ever ask us to do more than our best. Amen

The severed head

Doing your best often involves listening carefully to what you're asked to do. You can't do your best if you don't listen to what you have to do in the first place. This is especially true when you're doing tests, like the SATS tests that some of you are involved in at the moment.

Not long ago, I was in a school where some children were doing a test. A child who was very clever did very badly because she didn't read the instructions carefully; but another child, who was not nearly so clever, did very well because he paid attention to what the teacher told him to do, and he read the questions slowly and carefully, so that he knew exactly what was expected of him.

I have a folk-story for you today. It's to do with listening and doing your best.

Montmorency was walking through the forest one day on his way to work, whistling a tune and swinging his lunch-bag in time to the music. He was one of the king's woodcutters; it was his job to clear the dead wood from the forest and chop it into logs for the king's bedroom fire. (There was no central heating in those days, and the king liked to be warm.) Montmorency enjoyed his work. He liked being outdoors especially in the summer time; he liked the forest and its sounds and smells; he liked...

Suddenly, Montmorency stopped. On the path in front of him was a small tree stump; he remembered cutting down the tree only a few days before. But there on the tree stump was something strange... something horrible... something terrible... it couldn't be... no, it wouldn't be... but it was... Ugh... it was someone's HEAD! It was someone's chopped-off, severed HEAD!

Montmorency stared. How ghastly! What was it doing here? Where was the rest of the body? Who'd murdered it; for murder it must have been.

'What shall I do? Whatever shall I do?' thought Montmorency, but as he stood there feeling panic rise inside him, he heard a voice.

'Don't tell the king. Don't say a word.'

Montmorency froze, as thought someone had poured icy water down his back. It couldn't be... it just couldn't be the chopped-off head that had spoken. Unattached heads didn't speak. They just... well they just... Montmorency didn't know because he'd never seen one before.

The voice spoke again, and this time Montmorency saw the head's lips move.

'Don't tell the king. Don't say a word.'

'Oooh. This is scary,' whimpered Montmorency. 'This is weird. This is very uncool. Chopped-off heads don't chatter. Severed heads don't speak. Decapitated people don't discuss problems! I'm off!' And Montmorency turned and ran through the forest as though he had a pack of demons at his heels. He ran faster than the fallow deer who lived in the forest, faster than the swifts who flew overhead, faster than he ever believed he could, on and on, until BANG!

'Whoa!' said the king's guard, whose sentry-post Montmorency had crashed into. 'What's chasing you?'

Montmorency picked himself up from the floor and spluttered, 'Back there! It's the head! It's stuck on a stump. And it TALKS!'

'Don't be silly,' said the guard. 'Severed heads don't talk,' and he called to the other guards to come and listen to this strange tale of the head-on-the-stump that talks. The guards all laughed at Montmorency, but the more they laughed at him, the more determined he was that they should believe him.

'Take me to see the king!' shouted Montmorency. 'He'll believe me.'

So Montmorency was taken to the king's palace, and he told the king all about his walk through the forest and the decapitated head that spoke.

'I don't believe a word of it,' said the king. 'Is it some kind of trick to make me pay you more wages or something?'

'No. No. It's true,' insisted Montmorency. 'Come and see for yourself if you don't believe me. I'll show you the talking head.'

'You needn't think I'm going traipsing about in that cold wet forest looking for a head that can't even be bothered to stay attached to its own body!' said the king.

'No. If you're so insistent that it's there, and you want to prove it to me, then take my guards to the head and get it to talk to them. If it talks, they can come back and tell me and I'll give you a reward for your troubles. But if it doesn't, and you've been lying to me and wasting my time, then they can chop off your head and stick on the stump instead!'

Montmorency took the guards back into the forest and led them along the path to the tree-stump and the severed head.

'There! See?' said Montmorency. 'I told you!'

'Well, we grant you there's a head,' said the guards. 'But it could be any old head. It's not a *talking* head.'

'Just you wait and see,' said Montmorency, and he turned to the chopped-off head.

'Hello again, Head. It's me! It's Montmorency! Do you remember, I was here before?'

The head said nothing.

'I've brought the king's guards to see you. They want to hear you talk. Go on. Say something.'

The head remained silent.

'Speak!' pleaded Montmorency. 'Just say to them what you said to me. Go on!'

But the head said not a word.

'Oh please!' cried Montmorency. 'Just any old word will do! You don't have to say much. I mean, you don't have to hold an intelligent conversation or anything. Just a word. Or two. Please?'

The head didn't speak, but just stared ahead.

'Oh you're not being fair,' shouted Montmorency. 'You know you can talk. But if you don't prove it to the king's guards they'll chop off *my* head. Just SPEAK!'

But the head said nothing.

'You're wasting our time,' grumbled the guards. 'You've been having us on, and we don't like that. Neither does the king. No one messes around with the king's guards. Come on lads! Off with his head!' and without any more ado, poor old Montmorency had his head chopped off. It rolled on the path and bumped into the tree stump.

'Oh dear!' sighed the other severed head. 'I really didn't want that to happen. But I did tell him! I did say "Don't tell the king! Don't say a word!" But he didn't listen. And now look what's happened!'

The guards looked at each other in horror. What should they do? Should they tell the king? He would want to know what had happened in the forest. 'Remember,' went on the head, 'don't tell the king!'

The guards took to their heels and ran, as fast as the wind through the forest. They didn't stop until they came to the palace, where the king was waiting for them.

'Well?' he asked.

The story ends there. I wonder if they told the king. What do you think they should have done?

Poor old Montmorency came to a sticky end because he didn't stay calm and he didn't listen to what he had to do. You can't do your best if you don't listen to the instructions on the first place. If you listen carefully, and stay calm you'll be able to do the best you can, and no one can expect you to do more than that.

Dear God, help us to listen carefully when adults we trust give us instructions. Help us to do our best in everything we do. Help us to stay calm when we are faced with challenges. Amen

The acrobat

Everyone always tells you to do your best. Your parents and teachers have probably told you lots of times that as long as you do your best they will be pleased with your efforts. But there are times when you feel as though your best just isn't good enough. The acrobat in today's story did his best but people became very angry with him. Only one person understood.

Things could not have been worse for Banyo the acrobat.

He'd worked and lived in the circus all his life and had been happy there until now. But the circus had a new owner, things had changed, and now Banyo had had an accident and couldn't work for the time being.

'You'll have to go,' the owner said. 'I can't afford to keep people on if they can't work.'

'But what will I do and where will I go?' asked Banyo.

'That's your problem,' said Mr Malokovitch.

So without any further ado, Banyo was thrown out of the circus that had been his home since he was born. He made his way to the nearest town to try to find work and somewhere to live, but no one wanted to help an out-of-work acrobat with a sprained ankle and a bad back.

'Clear off! There's nothing for you here. Be off with you!' was what he heard over and over again.

By the evening of that dreadful day Banyo found himself outside a church on the edge of the town. He sat on the wide steps wondering what to do next, and as he sat there a long line of monks came walking past on their way into the church. They were singing the most beautiful songs as they walked.

Banyo stood up to let them pass, and the last monk in the line spoke to him.

'Why don't you come in and join in the singing?' he asked.

'I can't sing,' said Banyo.

'Well come in anyway,' said the monk. 'You look as if you could do with somewhere to sit. Perhaps you'd like to join us for a meal after the service?'

So Banyo went back to the monastery to share the monks' evening meal. He told them all about the circus and his accident and how he'd had to leave. He told them he had no money, no job and nowhere to live.

'That's no problem,' said the Abbot. 'You can stay here with us until you are strong and healthy again.'

'But what work will I do?' asked Banyo.

'You are not well enough to work just now,' said the Abbot. 'You don't need to work. We will look after you until you are better.'

'But you don't even know me,' said Banyo. 'Why should you bother to help me?'

'We try to help anyone who needs it,' said the Abbot simply.

Banyo stayed at the monastery for several weeks. The monks looked after him well and treated him as one of their family. And as he grew stronger Banyo began to find jobs to do to help repay the monks for their kindness. He washed the dishes and prepared the vegetables for dinner. He tidied out an old shed and weeded the kitchen garden. One day he was painting the door between the monastery garden and the street, when he heard a shout.

'Banyo! Banyo! It's you! It is, isn't it! Where have you been all these weeks? We've hunted high and low for you. Did you think your friends would forget you?'

Banyo spun round. He recognised the voice of the circus ringmaster.

'Reynaldo! What are you doing here?'

'Looking for you, of course. We've been looking for you ever since that meany Malokovitch threw you out. We all refused to work for him after he treated you like that. We want you to come back Banyo. The boss says you can, even if you're not strong enough to work yet. He says he'll look after you and he says he's sorry.'

'I'd like to come back,' said Banyo. 'The circus is my home, but first I have some things to do. Will you wait for me?'

'No problem,' said Reynaldo. 'Give me the paintbrush and I'll finish that door while you're sorting things out.'

Banyo went to find the Abbot.

'I've come to say thank you,' he said. 'My friends have been looking for me and I want to go back to the circus. But I know I owe you a great deal. If you hadn't helped me when I needed help, I don't know what would have happened to me. Thank you.'

'It's God you need to thank, not me,' said the Abbot. 'Why don't you go into the church and say thank you to God?'

Banyo went quietly into the church, but once there he had no idea how to begin to say thank you. He thought of the monks and how they spoke to God. They sang hymns and psalms, but he couldn't do that, he didn't know the tunes. They prayed to God, but he didn't know how to do that either.

Banyo stood at the door of the church and wondered what he could do. There was only one thing he knew how to do. There was only one thing he was good at. So that was what he must do to say thank you to God for caring for him. He would give the very best performance he could.

Banyo stood at the door of the church and looked down the long red carpet leading to the altar. He took a deep breath… and a small run… then a jump… he turned five perfect cartwheels, a double somersault, a back flip, four more cartwheels and a triple somersault which brought him right up to the edge of the high altar.

'OY! What do you think you're doing?' shouted a voice behind him.

Banyo spun round and saw one of the monks angrily coming towards him.

Other monks were hurrying in through the doors.

'How dare you!' they shouted.

'You can't behave like that in a church,' they yelled. 'It's so rude and disrespectful.'

'Get out,' they cried. 'Take your disgraceful behaviour back to where you came from,' and the monks hurried off to tell the Abbot about the dreadful way Banyo had behaved in the church.

'You've got to punish him,' they said. 'He mustn't be allowed to get away with it.'

'Punish him?' said the Abbot quietly. 'I will most certainly not punish him. He was saying thank you to God for the care he has had here.'

'But he wasn't saying thank you,' said the monks. 'He was doing cartwheels right down the middle of our church.'

'Exactly!' said the Abbot. 'He was doing what he does best. He was giving his best to God. Everyone is good at something and Banyo is good at acrobatics, so he was doing acrobatics for God.'

'We never thought of that,' said the monks, and they looked out of the monastery window to see Banyo turning cartwheels all the way down the road, with Reynaldo running along behind him trying to keep up.

I wonder what *you* would have thought if you'd seen Banyo doing cartwheels down the middle of the church? Do you think the monks were right to be angry with him?

Help us Lord, to do our best in everything we do. Help us to recognise other people's best efforts, even when they don't seem as good as ours. Help us to remember that everyone is good at something. Amen

Theme 2: Campaigners for change

Martin Luther King

Throughout history there have been many campaigners for change; people who have devoted their lives to trying to make the world a better place for everyone. A campaigner for change is someone who has a belief that is so strong, it becomes a way of life they have to follow. A campaigner for change is someone who sees something wrong or unfair in the world, and they devote their lives to changing it and trying to put it right.

Martin Luther King saw things that were wrong and unfair in America, in the way that black people were treated. He spent his life trying to improve things for black Americans.

Martin Luther King was born in Georgia, in the southern United States, in

1929. He quickly discovered that life for him, a black boy, was very different from that of his white neighbours. In America at that time, black people were not allowed to mix with white people. There were laws that segregated them. Black children couldn't go to the same schools as white children. Black people were not allowed to go to the same shops or cafes as white people. They couldn't go to cinemas or theatres where the white people went. They couldn't even sit with white people on buses or trains.

Martin was a bright boy, and he worked hard at school, determined even from a young age that he was going to do something to make life better for black people. When he left school, he went to a college in Boston, Massachusetts, where he trained to be a minister, like his father. He found that, there in the North, there was more freedom for black people. After spending six years at college, Martin went back home to Georgia.

One day, Martin saw a black woman arrested for sitting on a bus! She was sitting on a seat reserved for white passengers, and when the bus driver asked her to move, she refused. The police were called, she was arrested, and put in prison.

Some of the leaders of the black community wanted to help her, so they called a meeting to decide what to do. Some of them wanted to attack the white prison guards, some of them wanted to set fire to the bus depot, but Martin Luther King said No!

'We need to find a way to allow our black people the same rights on public transport that white people have. But we must do it peacefully. We must do it without resorting to violence.'

'How can we do that?' the others asked.

'We'll stop using the buses!' said Dr King. 'Most of the passengers on the buses are black. If we all stop travelling by bus, the bus company will go out of business. They won't want to do that, so they'll give us what we want. We'll tell them we'll start travelling on the buses again when they let us sit anywhere we want. They'll have to give in.'

'It's a good idea,' everyone said. 'We'll do it!'

For the whole of the following week, everyone worked together to avoid travelling on the buses. Black people walked to work, even if it took them two or three hours. They shared cars and even bicycles. They shared taxis, and taxi drivers charged their passengers only the price of a bus fare. But the bus company wouldn't give in.

'What shall we do now?' the people asked Dr King.

'Keep on avoiding the buses!' he answered. So the people kept up their boycott for the whole of the next month. But still the bus company wouldn't give in.

'What do we do now?' they asked.

'We keep on avoiding the buses for as long as it takes,' said Dr King. So his people kept up the boycott for the whole of the next year.

'All right!' said the authorities. 'You win! You can have the same rights on the buses as the white people, and you can sit anywhere you want.'

After this, Martin Luther King became well known all over America for his fight to improve things for black people. He went on television, he wrote articles in magazines and newspapers. And he gave a speech that was to become famous all over the world.

'I have a dream,' he said. 'I have a dream that my four children will be judged not by the colour of their skin, but by the content of their character.'

But although he wanted his black countrymen to fight for equality with the whites, he didn't want violence.

'No weapons. No fighting,' he said. 'We will fight by peaceful means.'

'How can we fight peacefully?' his people asked.

'We will go where we want, even if it's forbidden,' said Dr King. 'The police can arrest us if they want, but we won't fight back. They can put us in prison, but we won't fight back. Even if they beat us, we won't fight back. Even if they kill one of us, the rest won't fight back. We will shame our enemies into giving us equal rights.'

So the peaceful battle, the campaign for change, began again. For the rest of his life, Martin Luther King led his people in the struggle to make things fair and equal. They fought against unfairness and inequality. But always he taught his people to protest peacefully. No weapons. No fighting. Slowly, gradually, things altered. Black people were allowed to go into shops previously just for whites. Black people were allowed into cafes, restaurants, cinemas and theatres. Black and white children were allowed to go to school together. In 1964, Martin Luther King was awarded the Nobel Peace Prize for his work for people's rights.

Martin Luther King made many friends during his campaign for change. But he also made enemies; people who thought he was a troublemaker, people who wanted him out of the way. From time to time Dr King was attacked, beaten, stoned, and even stabbed. On one occasion someone threw a bomb at his house, luckily no one was hurt. Then, on 4th April 1968, as he was getting ready to go on a March with some black workers in Memphis, Tennessee, Martin Luther King was shot dead by a white man. He died for his dream; his dream that there should be equal rights for all people.

Martin Luther King and other civil rights campaigners fought hard to change the laws that made black people live completely separately from their white neighbours. Martin Luther King knew that those laws were unfair and unjust.

There are now new laws in America which ban segregation; but 'The bright daylight of peace and brotherhood' which Martin Luther King dreamed of, are still a long way off. There is still work to do!

Let's make sure we do our part of the work, here in Britain, by judging people by their character, and not by the colour of their skin.

In our prayer today, we'll think of the words of Martin Luther King. 'I have a dream; that my children will be judged not by the colour of their skin, but by the content of their character. I have a dream of a bright daylight of peace and brotherhood.' Amen

Mohandas Gandhi

What do you think is the best way to change things if they're unfair? Do you think it's best to fight and be violent? Or do you think there are better, more peaceful ways to make changes?

In India, a man called Mohandas Gandhi spent all his life fighting against the unfair laws that treated Indian people differently from others. But he believed very strongly that change should be brought about by peaceful means, not by fighting or by violence. He taught his followers not to accept unfair rules and laws, but to protest peacefully, and to use passive resistance – that means to calmly and quietly refuse to accept the things that are wrong.

Here's his story.

Gandhi was born in India in 1869. He was a quiet, shy boy who didn't like games. He made friends with another boy whose job it was to clean the toilets, but Gandhi was beaten for having this boy as a friend. There were laws that said that people who did cleaning jobs couldn't mix with other people.

'That's not fair!' thought Gandhi, and he resolved to do something about it when he was older.

When Gandhi was 19 he went to London to study law, and then when he'd passed his exams, he moved to South Africa. He quickly saw how unfairly the Indians in South Africa were treated. For example, there were laws that said the Indians couldn't travel where they wanted, unless they got written permission from the authorities. Yet non-Indians could travel where they liked.

'These laws are unfair; we must change them!' said Gandhi.

'But how?' said his friends.

'The government says we can't travel to another part of the country,' said Gandhi. 'But supposing we get everyone together, and we *all* travel. They'd have to arrest all of us, and that won't be possible.'

The following week, Gandhi led three thousand of his fellow Indians over the border into another part of the country.

'Remember!' he said. 'No violence. No fighting. This is a peaceful protest. Don't retaliate. 'If they arrest us, we'll go to prison. If they beat us, we'll accept the beating.'

The border police tried to arrest the protesters, but there were too many of them. The government changed the law and allowed the Indians to travel freely where they wanted.

'But you'll all have to carry papers to say you're foreigners,' they said. 'It's a new law.'

'Does everyone else have to carry these papers?' asked Gandhi.

'No,' said the government spokesman.

'Then we won't carry them, either,' said Gandhi.

'You have to. It's the law,' the man replied.

Gandhi encouraged his fellow Indians to refuse to carry the papers.

'If they punish us for it, we'll accept the punishment,' he said. 'But we won't carry the papers.'

Again, the Indians joined together in peaceful protest. Many of them were imprisoned, including Gandhi, but they didn't give up and they didn't fight back. Once more, the government gave in and allowed the Indians the same rights as the rest of the people in the country.

For the next 21 years, Gandhi lived in South Africa, working all the time to change the unfair laws. But he always used the same method – peaceful protest. Whenever a law was unfair, Gandhi asked his followers simply to refuse to co-operate with it, and then quietly accept whatever punishment they were given. Gradually, slowly, the laws were changed. Gandhi earned great respect from everyone because he didn't try to get riches or praise for himself, he was simply determined to do what he thought was right. He was given a nickname – Mahatma, which means Great Soul.

In 1915 Gandhi went back to live in India. He remembered the boy who'd been his friend all those years before, and thought about the way people who had cleaning jobs were treated. So Gandhi led protests against the rule that said cleaners couldn't mix with other people. Again, the government had to give in and change the law.

Then Gandhi and his followers protested against the huge tax on salt that the government imposed. They felt the tax was unfair, so Gandhi and his people all walked to the sea, hundreds and hundreds of them, and they collected their own salt. And the law was changed.

All this time, India was ruled by Britain, but the Indian people wanted their independence. They wanted to rule their own country, themselves. Gandhi led many peaceful protests against the British authorities, but when he led a one-day strike throughout the whole of India, violent fighting broke out. Gandhi was horrified. He felt so strongly that all protests should be peaceful. He knew from past experience that peaceful protest worked. You could make changes without resorting to violence and fighting.

Although Gandhi had not taken part in the fighting, he was put in prison for six years for organising the strike. When he came out again, he organised more protests, and he tried to insist that they were peaceful. Finally, in August 1947, India was given her independence.

But almost immediately afterwards, fierce fighting broke out between the Indian Hindus and the Indian Muslims; it was to do with who was going to be in charge, now that India was no longer ruled by Britain. To try and stop the fighting, Gandhi went on a hunger strike.

'I will not eat until the fighting stops,' he said. 'If you do not stop the violence, you will force me to starve to death.'

His plan worked. The people respected him too much to allow him to die, so the fighting stopped. But one man felt angry with Gandhi. He felt Gandhi was not doing enough to help the Hindu people. So he waited, and watched; patiently looking for an opportunity to kill Gandhi.

On 30th January 1948, his chance came. Gandhi was walking to a prayer meeting with a group of people. But just for a second, he was on his own; the others were a little in front of him, or a little behind him. The man seized the opportunity. He ran towards Gandhi and shot him. Mahatma Gandhi, the man who had spent his whole life trying to make conditions better for others, always peacefully, was killed by an act of violence.

Gandhi's methods of peaceful protest worked, and great changes were made to make life fairer and better for the Indian people. Nowadays, campaigners for change, all over the world, still follow Gandhi's example of peaceful protest.

Perhaps we too, can learn something from Gandhi's teaching: to change the things that are wrong, by peaceful means, and to be determined to do what we think is right.

Dear God, help us to accept the things we cannot change. Give us the courage to change the things we can. Grant us the wisdom to know the difference. Amen

Florence Nightingale

Have you ever been to hospital? Perhaps you've been in hospital as a patient, or perhaps you've been there to visit someone. If you have, you'll know how welcoming and warm and clean and comfortable, hospitals are. You'll have seen for yourself how well organised they are and how hard-working and caring the nurses are.

But hospitals weren't always like this. Almost a hundred and fifty years ago, hospitals were dirty, dangerous places, and nurses like the ones we have today were unheard of. But a young lady called Florence Nightingale campaigned for change in the hospitals. Without her, I don't suppose our hospitals would be like they are today.

Florence was born in 1820, in the city of Florence in Italy, when her parents were on a tour of Europe. Mr and Mrs Nightingale were extremely wealthy, and they had Florence's life all planned out for her from the minute she was born. Florence and her sister Parthenope were to be brought up in England. They were to be taught to read and write and to sew and to play the piano. When they were older, they would be allowed to visit their friends and go to parties and dances, where they would meet nice wealthy young men who would marry them. Then they would settle down and live happily ever after.

But Florence had other ideas. She wanted to be a nurse.

Her parents were horrified! The hospitals of those days were dirty, disease-ridden places, and most of the nurses were rough, often drunken, women, with little or no nursing training. It was unheard-of for a well-brought-up young lady to want to be a nurse, and even more unheard-of for her to be allowed to become one.

But Florence was not to be put off. She visited all the hospitals near her home, and studied hospital reports whenever she could. She wrote letters to newspapers and important people saying that hospitals needed properly trained nurses. She travelled abroad with her friends and visited hospitals in other countries. She even managed to work for three months in a hospital in Germany, much to her parents' disapproval. But when a suitable young man asked her to marry him, and she refused because she was more interested in becoming a nurse than in getting married, her parents had to accept the fact that nothing was going to stop Florence doing what she wanted to do, and in 1853, Florence became the matron of a hospital for ladies in London.

The following year, Britain became involved in the Crimean War against Russia, and horrifying reports reached England about the state of the hospital to which the soldiers were being sent. The government minister in charge of the war realised that something would have to be done to improve matters, and he wrote to Florence to ask if she would consider taking some nurses to the hospital in Turkey, to help. Within a week, Florence had gathered together almost forty nurses, and they set off for Turkey.

They arrived at the hospital in November 1854. The conditions were appalling. The huge building they called the hospital was filthy and cold. There was no hot water and no drainage system, so the smell was dreadful. There were no beds, no bedding, no bandages, no medicines. There was not enough food, there were no nurses, no doctors, and only a few untrained people in charge. And in this terrible place, lying on the floor with no sheets or blankets or pillows, were thousands of injured, sick, and dying soldiers. Hundreds of them died every day. Florence felt so angry that these men were dying of simple infections and small injuries; deaths that could be avoided if hospital was better organised and better managed and if the nursing care was better.

No one thought that Florence and her band of nurses would be able to do much to help. But Florence had brought bandages and medicines with her. She had brought money to buy what was needed. And she had brought determination! She was not afraid of hard work, and she was not scared of rules and regulations! Florence set to work.

First she ordered soap and scrubbing brushes. She had the whole building cleaned from top to bottom. She ordered repairs to be carried out to the water supply and the drainage system. She demanded that building repairs and repainting work were carried out. She refitted the kitchens and hired cooks. Then she bought beds and mattresses, blankets, sheets, pillows, shirts. And all the time she was organising the running of the hospital, she was caring for the sick and injured men. She nursed all the worst cases herself. She worked all day and most of the night, only sleeping for a few hours after she had walked round the wards to make sure all the men were comfortable and settled for the night. They became used to seeing her silently walking though the hospital, watching, checking, caring, with her lantern in her hand. The soldiers called her 'The lady with the lamp' and they worshipped her.

Meanwhile, the fighting in the cold Crimean winter grew worse and the soldiers were desperately short of supplies and winter clothing. Thousands of soldiers became ill and were taken to Florence's hospital; soon she was caring for 12 000 men. Almost a year after she arrived in the Crimea, the war stopped. The hospital was to be closed. But Florence refused to leave until every patient had gone.

She returned to England a heroine, but she refused to accept any praise. 'There's work to be done,' she said, and she set about improving the army hospitals in England, even though by now she was ill.

She started to advise people all over the world about nursing care and standards, and in 1860 she set up the first training school for nurses, at St Thomas's Hospital in London. Here, Florence Nightingale set new standards of behaviour, discipline and skill for nurses, and soon, hospitals all over the world were asking for 'Nightingale Nurses' to come and work for them.

During the second part of her life, Florence Nightingale was so ill she rarely left her London house. But she continued to help the hospitals by answering letters that came from every part of the world. She died in 1910, aged ninety.

Florence Nightingale helped not only the men in the Crimean War, but also nurses everywhere. It's due to the changes she made that nursing is as it is today, and due to her that nursing is an acceptable and worthwhile profession for men and women.

Like all campaigners for change, Florence Nightingale was determined to do what she thought was right. And like all campaigners for change, she spent her whole life trying to make the world a better place for people everywhere.

Next time you visit a hospital, remember Florence Nightingale's work, and be glad you're going to hospital now, and not 150 years ago!

Thank you God, for all the people who have worked to change our world for the better. Help us, in our lives, to stand up for what we believe is right; to be determined to do our best for ourselves, for our families, for our world. Amen

Theme 3: Speaking and listening

Onions make your eyes water

Have you noticed how easy it is to jump to conclusions about people? You look at someone, and in just a few seconds you decide all sorts of things about them. The trouble is that you might not be right.

In today's story, some people thought they knew why Len was upset. But not one of them was right.

There was once a man called Len, who had a hot-dog stand at the seaside. One day he ran out of onions, so he went across to the supermarket, bought a huge bagful, and went back to his stall where he began to peel and chop them. Soon Len's eyes were smarting with the vapours from the cut onions. Then his eyes started watering, and in no time at all tears were streaming down his face.

Just then, one of his neighbours happened to walk past, and was astonished to see Len standing behind his hot-dog stall crying.

'What on earth can be the matter with Len?' thought the neighbour to himself. 'Business must be bad if it's making him cry like that. It looks as though he's not making any money and he'll have to sell up. Poor Len! I won't let him see me and then he won't be embarrassed about me knowing that his business is so poor,' and the neighbour hurried away to tell everyone else, having decided that he knew the reason for Len's tears.

A few minutes later one of Len's friends happened to walk by, and was amazed to see Len standing by the hot-dog stall with tears pouring down his face.

'Oh dear me!' thought the friend. 'Whatever can be the matter with Len. I know his daughter was ill last week; she must be really poorly for him to be as upset as that. She must be in hospital, in fact she might even have died! Poor Len! I must go and tell everyone what's happened,' and Len's friend hurried away, having decided that he knew the reason for Len's tears, and determined to tell everyone the sad news.

Only two minutes later Len's brother came past the hot-dog stall, and saw Len standing there with his eyes full of tears.

'Oh dear me!' thought the brother. 'Something terrible has happened. Len's wife must have left him. I know they had an argument the other day. She must have packed her bags and gone. Poor Len! I must go and tell the rest of the family,' and he hurried away, having decided that he knew the reason for Len's tears.

Len had almost finished peeling and chopping the onions when his daughter came past the hot-dog stall. She saw her dad standing there with tears in his eyes.

'Oh, poor dad!' she thought. 'I heard something the other day about a new supermarket being built here. Dad must have heard that he won't be able to keep the hot-dog stand because of the new building. I must go and tell mum what's happened,' and she hurried away, convinced she knew the reason for Len's tears.

Len finished preparing his onions, washed his hands and wiped his streaming eyes on a piece of kitchen roll. Just as he was doing this his father came past and saw his son mopping his eyes. He looked around to see if there were any clues as to why his son was crying, and noticed that Len's car was not in its usual place at the side of the stall.

'Oh dear me!' thought Len's father. 'Poor Len. He's had his car stolen. No wonder he's looking so upset. I must go and tell my wife all about it,' and he hurried away, convinced he knew the reason for Len's tears.

About fifteen minutes later a small group of people met on the street corner near Len's hot-dog stall.

'Isn't it dreadful news about Len's business?' said his neighbour to the others.

'Never mind about the business!' said Len's friend. 'Isn't it dreadful news about his daughter being so ill.'

'What's wrong with his daughter?' asked the friend.

'Yes, what's wrong with me!' asked Len's daughter. 'I'm all right! It's the new supermarket we should be worrying about. Dad must be beside himself with worry about it.'

'I should think he's more worried about the car being stolen, just at the moment,' said Len's father.

'The car's not stolen!' said Len's wife. I've just driven it here, look it's over there.'

'But what are you doing with Len's car?' asked his brother. 'I thought you'd left him!'

'How dare you say that to me!' shouted Len's wife. And in no time at all Len's wife and daughter and father and brother and friend and neighbour were all having the most terrible argument in the middle of the street.

Len heard the noise and came to see what it was all about.

'What on earth are you all doing here?' he said. 'I've never seen such a commotion! What's going on? What's all the shouting about? Why are you all looking so miserable?' and he burst into laughter at the sight of his family and friends all looking so annoyed and gloomy and dejected and glum.

They all turned to him.

'How can you be so cheerful?' they demanded.

'How can you laugh and joke when so many things are wrong?' they said.

'Wrong?' asked Len. 'What's wrong?'

'Everything!' they said, and they all started to talk at once, every one of them telling Len about seeing him crying and deciding the reason for his tears.

Len listened to them all. He waited for them to finish their tales of woe. He waited for them to argue amongst themselves about the reasons for the tears. Then he said quietly 'You are all foolish! You have all gossiped and jumped to conclusions, and you've all come up with your own silly ideas about the tears.

But not one of you bothered to ask me. Not one of you bothered to talk to me about it. Not one of you bothered to speak to me. If you'd asked me... if you'd talked to me... if you'd spoken to me ... and if you'd listened to me... you would have known it was all to do with the onions!'

'Onions?' they said.

'Yes,' said Len. 'Onions! They make your eyes water when you peel and chop them.'

And with that, Len's family and friends understood the real reason for his tears, and they all felt very foolish for having jumped to their own – wrong – conclusions.

None of that fuss and commotion would have happened if Len's family and friends had talked to him. Gossiping about him behind his back wasn't any help at all. Most things in life can be sorted out by talking, and of course by listening, because you can't really have one without the other.

Dear God, help us to understand the importance of speaking and listening. Help us to know when to speak, and when to listen. Help us to know that words are powerful – they can help and they can hurt. Teach us to use words wisely. Amen.

King Midas's ears

Everyone knows how important it is always to tell the truth. But what do you do if a friend wants you to say something to help them, and you know it's not what you believe? This happened to someone in today's story.

The story is also about secrets. They're funny things, secrets! They have a habit of not staying where you put them, and popping up in the most surprising places.

The story is about King Midas; you might have met him already, he's the greedy king who wished that everything he touched would turn into gold, but when it did, he realised how foolish he had been. He was cured of his greed, but unfortunately he was still foolish.

King Midas became friendly with Pan, who was the God of the countryside in Ancient Greece. King Midas made some musical pipes out of wood, and gave them to Pan as a gift. Pan made up wonderful tunes on the panpipes, and everyone liked to listen to his music.

But Pan became conceited about his ability to play and started to tell everyone, 'My music is even better than the music of the great God Apollo. My music is the best, the most tuneful, the most beautiful sound that there has ever been.'

'It certainly is very good,' said King Midas, cautiously, for he didn't want to hurt his friend's feelings. 'But when Apollo plays music on his lyre, the sound is superb; it's magical; and Apollo is the God of music.'

'My music is still better than his, and if you were really my friend, you would say so!' insisted Pan, who was jealous of Apollo's musical ability. 'I'm going to challenge him to a contest to see whose music is best. You have to say it's me!' and with that. Pan went to see Apollo to tell him of the competition.

On the day of the contest Pan and Apollo stood on the riverbank. King Midas and some of their friends sat nearby to listen. Pan took first turn. He played well and everyone enjoyed his cheerful tune. Then Apollo began to play. As soon as he touched the strings of the lyre the music flowed through the air; a smooth liquid golden sound that transported the listeners to a magical place deep in their imagination. Apollo's music was undoubtedly the better of the two, and everyone in the audience said so... except King Midas, who wanted to stand up for his friend.

'I think Pan's music was better,' he said when the applause had died down. 'Pan should be the winner.'

'You can't have been listening,' Apollo answered. 'You can't have heard properly.'

'There's nothing wrong with my ears,' argued King Midas. 'And I'm telling you, Pan's music was better than yours.'

At this, the great God Apollo, the God of music, grew angry.

'If you can't hear better than that, you don't deserve to have human ears,' he shouted. 'There! Have donkey ears and look like the donkey you are!' And Apollo changed King Midas's ears into long, grey-brown, silky, hairy, donkey ears, instead.

King Midas crept away, ashamed of his new ears; ashamed of not being honest about the music, for he knew Apollo's was better than Pan's. He wrapped his head in a turban and tucked his ears inside, so that no one would see them.

Time went by and people forgot about the music contest, and Apollo's anger, and King Midas's donkey ears, but King Midas couldn't forget. And neither could the barber who cut his hair every month.

'How embarrassing for the king to have asses ears,' the barber used to think to himself each time King Midas removed his turban. 'How strange! How dreadful! I wonder how many people know about it?'

Of course, he couldn't tell anyone else the king's secret, but because it was such a strange secret he couldn't keep it to himself either. So the barber went down to the river and dug a hole by the riverbank. He whispered the secret into the hole, then covered it up with earth and stones.

'It's safe there,' he said. 'It's hidden.'

But secrets are never safely hidden. There's always someone ready to tell.

A clump of bulrushes grew where the barber had hidden the secret. Their roots reached down into the hole and found it. And when the wind whispered through their stalks, they whispered back, 'King Midas has asses ears... King Midas has asses ears... asses ears... asssesss earsss...'

People passing the riverbank heard the whispering and gossiped amongst themselves about the strange story.

'Have you heard about the king's ears?'
'Can you believe he's really got the ears of a donkey!'
'How did it happen?'
'They say it was a punishment for something he did wrong. It must have been something very terrible,' and the people gossiped anew about the terrible thing King Midas must have done. Some people said he must have stolen something. Others said must have killed someone to receive such a dreadful punishment. No one bothered to find out what really happened.

King Midas knew his people were gossiping about him, and he felt ashamed. He shut himself in his palace and refused to come out. Years passed by; and eventually, the people heard that he had died of shame.

Poor King Midas! What a pity he didn't tell the truth in the first place; he could have been honest without hurting Pan's feelings. And what a pity people started spreading gossip when they heard the secret. Gossip can be unkind, and very dangerous. I hope you never spread gossip about people, or talk unkindly about them behind their backs.

Help us Lord, to be honest but not unkind, when we are giving our opinions. Help us to be careful with secrets, and never to gossip about people behind their backs. Help each of us to look for the good in people, and to know that good is in everyone. Amen

The Chinese casket

Do you know what rumours are? They are bits of gossip that are spread about by people. The trouble with rumours is that they are usually inaccurate, or even untrue. Rumours can do a lot of damage, and people can become very hurt by them. . There's a saying that goes, 'If you can't say something good about someone, say nothing at all!' I think it's good advice to try and follow.

Today's story is from China, and in it, some people spread rumours about the king's brother. Let's hear what happened.

King Wu was a wise leader and was much loved by his people, but one day he became ill and it seemed that he would die. The king's three brothers were very concerned about him and sent for the best doctors in China, but one of the brothers, the Duke of Chow, went to the temple to pray.

In those days it was the custom to write prayers on pieces of paper, which were then sealed in a beautiful jewelled casket that was kept in the temple. The Duke of Chow wrote down his prayer,

'Please don't let my brother the king die just yet.

He is a good and honest king, and has much work still to do.

If someone must die, then let it be I instead of him.' The Duke then opened the jewelled casket and placed his prayer inside, but as he was doing so, he noticed another piece of holy writing that said 'All living things must die, even kings, but they will be followed by others who must be taught by those who are wise.' The Duke of Chow was puzzled by these words, as he closed the casket and replaced it in the temple.

A few weeks later the king died, and his place was taken by Prince Chang, the king's son. But Chang was young, he was only a boy, and the people said, 'He is too young to be the leader, too young to make decisions, he must have an adviser. He must have someone wise to tell him what to do,' and they chose the Duke of Chow to advise him.

The Duke was kind and caring towards the boy. He was honest and forthright when he gave his advice, and Chang was quick to learn. The people were pleased with the way things were.

'We did well to choose Chow,' they said. 'He's fair and just. He's honest and loyal. He'll be an excellent adviser to Prince Chang until the boy is old enough to be king.'

But the Duke of Chow's brothers was jealous.

'Who does he think he is?' they said.

'Why should he be the one to get chosen?'

'Why not one of us. It really isn't fair!' and they started to spread rumours about the Duke of Chow.

'He gives Prince Chang bad advice,' they said. 'He only says things that are going to be of benefit to himself. He's doing it to get rich and famous,' and the rumours grew and spread until everyone was talking about the Duke.

'I've heard he stole half the Prince's gold,' someone said.

'Well, I've heard he's going to kill the prince and then somehow get to be king himself,' said another.

'He doesn't let anyone else even speak to the prince.'

'I know. He's got him in his power.'

And so it went on. Gossip and rumour all over the country. People who had previously been supportive of the Duke of Chow turned against him. And his brothers were pleased. 'With a bit of luck we'll be able to get rid of him altogether,' they said.

The Duke of Chow first became aware of the rumours and gossip when he noticed that people were being unfriendly towards him. People were no longer greeting him, or talking to him; they were avoiding him. Then he started to overhear what they were saying.

'But it's not true!' he said to his brothers. 'Why are people saying all these things about me? Where have all these lies come from?'

'We have no idea,' lied his brothers.

The Duke of Chow became so unhappy that he decided the only thing for him to do was to leave China and go and live somewhere else. 'One day people will know that these rumours all are lies,' he said as he left.

But almost as soon as he'd gone, things started to go wrong. One of his brothers became ill. The prince fell and broke his leg. A storm blew up and lightening struck the temple. The weather worsened and all the grain that was ready for harvesting was beaten down and ruined. There was a fire at the palace and part of it burned down.

'What is happening?' asked the elders of the temple. 'Why are all these terrible things occurring? We must search in the jewelled casket for answers. The holy writings will tell us what to do,' and they retrieved the casket from the ruins of the temple and opened it. There, on top of the other writings, was the Duke of Chow's prayer. The elders of the temple read it.

'Look!' they said, 'It says, "Please don't let my brother the king die just yet. He is a good and honest king, and has much work still to do. If someone must die, then let it be me instead of him." He wrote this prayer to ask for the king's life to be spared. Chow asked to die instead of the king! What more can anyone offer but their life. Chow was an honest and loyal servant of the king. The rumours and gossip about him must be lies. We have to go and tell Prince Chang.'

The elders of the temple hurried to the palace and told Prince Chang what they had discovered.

'Now we know why so many things have gone wrong since he left,' cried Prince Chang. 'It was a message for us to look in the casket. I knew that Chow was truthful and sincere. I knew he was not plotting against me. I shall go and find him and bring him back. Then I shall search for those who started the rumours and gossip and they will be punished.'

The prince found the Duke of Chow travelling in the east, and told him all that had happened.

'Will you come back and be my adviser?' he asked.

'I will,' said the Duke of Chow.

They returned to China and the prince eventually became king. Under the guidance of the Duke of Chow, the prince became a wise leader and was much loved by his people, just as his father had been. And as for the Duke's brothers, they were forgiven for their gossip and they never spread malicious rumours again.

Do you think the brothers should have been forgiven, or do you think they should have been punished? I wonder, when they started the rumours, if they realised just how much hurt and upset they would cause? I don't suppose they did. When people gossip they don't usually think about the damage they might be causing.

Everyone is perfectly entitled to think what they like about someone else, but no one is entitled to spread rumours and lies about people.

Dear God, help us never to spread rumours and lies about people. Help us to know how harmful gossip can be. Teach us not to use words to hurt others; and if we have nothing good to say about someone, help us to say nothing at all, rather than something unpleasant. Amen

June

Theme 1: Revenge

The rope with three knots

Has anyone ever done something to you that's made you feel so angry you've wanted to get your own back? I wonder how you felt when you tried to get your revenge? Sometimes people get into serious trouble when they try to get their own back. And most people don't feel any happier when they look for revenge; in fact trying to get your own back often makes things even worse.

Anna watched her dad getting the boat ready to go out fishing. It was a new boat. They'd had the naming ceremony only last week and all the family had come to take part. The Marie-Madeleina they called it. They'd all gone down to the quayside and everyone had been given a ride on the new boat, even the baby who was only six months old, and even Anna's great-grandma who was ninety-three. But now it was time for work, Anna's dad said. No more time for messing about, and no more rides. You couldn't go out for rides on a working boat.

Anna had asked her dad if she could go out fishing with him, but her dad had said no. 'You're too young,' he said. 'You're not responsible enough.' So Anna hung around on the quayside looking for something to do. It just wasn't fair that she couldn't go out fishing with her dad. She knew she wasn't too young, other children her age went out on the boats; and she knew that she could be responsible when she tried because they'd told her so at school.

As she stood there kicking some bits of rubbish into the sea, she saw Maurice walking towards her dad. Maurice was an old fisherman who had lived by the harbour forever. Anna liked him because he could tell the most amazing stories – stories about strange sea creatures and far away places, stories about his travels and about magic. But today Anna was feeling too bad-tempered to talk to him, so she hid behind a pile of old lobster pots so that she could listen to what he and her dad were saying.

'Jean-Pierre!' he called. 'Can I have a quick word with you before you set off? I just want to give you this for the new boat,' and he handed Anna's dad an old frayed piece of rope with three knots tied in it.

'What on earth do I want with a bit of old rope?' asked Jean-Pierre.

'This isn't an ordinary rope,' answered Maurice. 'It's magic. It can control the wind. The first knot controls a gentle wind. The second knot controls a strong wind. And the third knot… well you must never ever undo the third knot or you'll have a gale force wind and waves as high as mountains. If you're out on the boat when that happens, you'll be lucky to get back alive.'

'This is one of your sea-stories, Maurice, isn't it?' laughed Jean-Pierre.

'Just keep it with you on the boat,' said Maurice. 'One of these days it might come in useful,' and Maurice walked away down the quayside.

Jean-Pierre stuffed the piece of rope in his pocket and climbed on board the Marie-Madeleina, but as he did so the rope fell out and landed next to the pile of old lobster pots where Anna was hiding. Jean-Pierre didn't notice. He untied the boat from its mooring, started its engine and chugged off across the harbour and out into the open sea.

Anna picked up the rope. She was still feeling angry with her dad for not taking her out on the boat with him, and here seemed a way for her to get her own back. She looked at the knots in the rope, then looked out across the sea. The wind was blowing just enough to make ripples on the sea beyond the harbour wall.

Anna fiddled with the first knot. It was quite loose and almost undid itself.

The wind became a little stronger. It whipped white caps onto the waves beyond the harbour wall. Anna looked for her dad's boat. She could still see it, but it was a tiny dot way out on the waves.

She played with the second knot in the rope. It wasn't a tight knot. One twist... and a turn... pull the end through... and the second knot came undone.

The wind gusted along the quayside. It blew bits of paper about and flapped the flags on the boats in the harbour. Out in the open sea it stirred the water into choppy grey waves and threatened to blow up a storm. Anna looked for the Marie-Madeleina; she thought she could still see it but she wasn't sure. The sea looked so big and so angry. She began to feel scared.

She looked at the third knot. It was hard and tight and round and fast at the end of the piece of rope. She could hear Maurice's voice saying to her dad, 'Never undo the third knot,' but her fingers prodded and poked at it.

The sky grew dark and the rain began. Great fat drops of rain that made holes in the sea in the harbour. Beyond the harbour walls the waves crashed against the rocks and when she looked for her dad's boat Anna couldn't see it at all. She felt really afraid. Perhaps the boat had sunk. Perhaps her dad had drowned. And it was all her fault. She'd undone the knots in the magic rope and made the storm blow up.

The wind howled across the sea and the rain beat down and soaked Anna. The rope was now stiff and wet and impossible to untie, but still Anna's fingers poked and prodded and played with the knot.

Just then Maurice came hurrying past on his way home.

'Whatever are you doing here, Anna, in this weather. Get yourself off home girl before you catch your death of cold.' Anna didn't answer and Maurice noticed the old piece of frayed rope in her hands.

'Is this the rope I gave to your dad, Anna?' he asked.

Anna didn't speak.

'Have you untied the first two knots?'

Again Anna didn't speak.

'Well, at least you haven't untied the third knot. Remember Anna; never, ever undo the last knot on the magic rope. And never try to get your own back; no matter how angry you are, no matter what anyone has done, no matter what you think. When you try to get your own back you end up just being angry for longer. It's just not worth it. Now, let's try to put things right again. Can you retie the knots?'

'"I think so,' said Anna, and she twisted the rope and pulled the end through, twice. As she tied the knots in the rope the storm died down, the rain and wind stopped and the sun broke through the clouds. Then, to her surprise she saw her dad walking towards them along the quayside.

'The strangest thing has happened,' he said. 'I'd no sooner got out of the harbour than a storm blew up, but I've never seen a storm like it. The bad weather was only here – it wasn't round the headland or beyond the rocks or out where the deep water is, it was only near here. So I moored the boat in the shelter of the cove just round the headland, then I walked back over the cliffs. And now the storm has stopped! I've never seen anything like it.'

'Well, maybe you should have looked after this a bit better,' said Maurice, handing Jean-Pierre the piece of rope. 'And then none of this might have happened.'

'I thought it was in my pocket,' said Jean-Pierre.

'No it wasn't, but I think Anna might want to tell you where it was,' said Maurice.

'I'm sorry Dad,' said Anna.

'And I'm sorry too, for not letting you come with me on the boat,' said Jean-Pierre. 'Perhaps next time, eh?'

'YES!' shouted Anna.

Getting your own back doesn't usually work. Trying to get revenge can make you feel bitter and angry and it never puts right what was wrong in the first place. It's better to forgive and forget if you can. But no one says it's easy!

Dear God, Please help us to think before we act. Help us not to do things for spite or revenge or to get our own back. Help us to do what we know is right and sensible and honest. Amen

Two girls and a cockerel

Getting your own back on someone doesn't usually work! Sometimes things don't work out quite as you expect, and instead of making life unpleasant for the other person, you make things worse for yourself.

Today's story is an Aesop's fable, and in it, two girls tried to get their own back on the farmer who employed them. But they soon wished they'd never tried to get their revenge.

The two girls worked for Mrs Billings on her farm. They all three lived on the farm and usually got on well together. The girls enjoyed their work most of the time and they liked working with the animals. But, they hated having to get up early in the morning. And, of course, everyone knows that people who work on farms have to be up at dawn.

'It's not so bad in winter,' grumbled Fiona. 'At least in winter it stays dark until eight o'clock and we can stay in bed until then. But in summer!'

'I know,' said Rowena. 'In summer it gets light so early. Do you know we were up at four o'clock this morning? I can't go on like this, I'm missing all my beauty sleep! It's not fair that she makes us get up so early.'

'It's all that wretched cockerel's fault,' said Fiona. 'It starts to crow just as soon as it gets light, then Mrs Billings hears it, and she shouts to us to get up. If it weren't for that cockerel, we could stay in bed a bit longer.'

'You're right,' said Rowena. 'Listen! I've had an idea. Let's get our own back on Mrs Billings, it'll serve her right for making us get up so early. Let's get rid of the cockerel, then it can't wake us all up at the crack of dawn. Mrs Billings'll never know it was us.'

'Brilliant!' said Fiona. And the two girls went straight out into the farmyard, checked that Mrs Billings was nowhere about, killed the cockerel, buried it in the corner of the orchard, and went back to the barn to get on with their work.

The rest of the day passed smoothly enough. Mrs Billings seemed not to notice that anything was different, and the girls went to bed that night at the usual time.

'Goodnight Mrs Billings,' they called on their way up the stairs.

'Goodnight girls,' answered Mrs Billings. 'Up bright and early in the morning, we've lots to do.'

'Yes, Mrs Billings,' they said.

In the morning the sun rose at around four o'clock. Gradually the countryside awoke. The birds began their dawn chorus, and the animals began to stir. But in the farmyard everything was silent. And in the farmhouse Mrs Billings and the two girls slept on.

The sun rose higher in the sky and the day became warm. The cows began to be restless; it was way past their milking time. The pigs and goats nudged against their pens; it was time they were out in the field. The horses stamped in the stable; it was feeding time. But Mrs Billings and the two girls slept on.

It was eventually around ten o'clock when Mrs Billings woke up. The sun was high in the sky and the day well begun.

'We're late! What's happened? Where's the cockerel? Why aren't you two up?' she shouted. Fiona and Rowena looked at each other and smiled. It was *wonderful* to have had a lie-in until ten o'clock.

'We can do this every morning', whispered Fiona. 'Now we've got rid of that cockerel.'

But things didn't work out quite as the girls had planned.

'I can't understand it,' said Mrs Billings. 'The cockerel has disappeared. I don't know where he can be. He's never disappeared before. What are we going to do? I can't be doing with getting up at ten o'clock every morning. Half the day's gone by that time, and there's work to be done.'

Fiona and Rowena offered no explanation as to what might have happened to the cockerel. But, once again, they smiled at each other.

Mrs Billings worried about the cockerel all day. And she hardly slept a wink that night for worrying about how she would wake up in the morning.

'I mustn't sleep in. I mustn't sleep in,' she said to herself all night. She got up at four o'clock and went to wake the girls.

'Come on,' she said. 'Time to get up.'

'But Mrs Billings, it's only four o'clock,' said Rowena.

'We've work to do,' said Mrs Billings.

The next morning was even worse. Mrs Billings was so worried about sleeping in that she woke up at three o'clock.

'Come on,' she said to the girls. 'Time to get up.'

'But Mrs Billings, it's only three o'clock in the morning,' said Fiona.

'Never mind! We've work to do' said Mrs Billings.

For the rest of that week Mrs Billings woke up at two o'clock, and made the girls get up with her.

At the weekend, Mrs Billings woke at one o'clock, and all the following week she woke at midnight.

'If we go on at this rate, we'll be getting up before we've gone to bed' said Fiona. 'I wish you'd never thought of getting your own back and killing the cockerel. We're much worse off now than we were before.'

'I know,' said Rowena. 'And I've had an idea. Let's go and buy another cockerel and try to get back to normal. It's the last time I try to get my own back on Mrs Billings.'

I wonder if Mrs Billings knew all along what had happened to the cockerel? I wonder if Fiona and Rowena owned up? What do you think they should have done?

Getting your own back hardly ever works. It's much better to try and sort out difficulties and disagreements by meeting and talking than by trying to get your revenge when something goes wrong.

Help us, Lord, to think before we act. Help us to try to sort out disagreements by talking, not fighting. Help us not to retaliate when people upset us. Amen

Urashima's revenge

Wanting to get your own back, or wanting to get your revenge, can take up an awful lot of energy. There are people who spend a whole lifetime trying to get their own back. These people use all their time and energy on looking for revenge, and they don't realise they are wasting their own lives in doing so.

It's far better to try to forgive someone for whatever they've done wrong, and then put the wrong behind you and get on with the rest of your life. But this is extremely difficult to do. In today's story from Japan, someone spent his whole life trying to get his revenge.

A long time ago in ancient Japan, there were two Samurai soldiers. Their names were Harada and Gundara. Both were skilful soldiers, you had to be skilful to be a Samurai; both were good horsemen, and both were excellent swordsmen but Harada was the best swordsman in the whole of Japan.

Gundara was jealous of Harada's skill with the sword, and he used to say that he was just as good as Harada. This caused so many arguments between the two men and their friends, that one day the Emperor said, 'Enough of all this talk about who is better. We'll settle the matter here and now. Fight! We'll soon see who is the better swordsman.'

As expected, Harada won the competition and the Emperor gave him a small golden statue as a prize. Gundara was furious.

'I'll get my own back on him,' he declared.

Gundara spent the whole of the next week plotting and planning how to get his revenge, and by the following week he had decided to kill Harada. The next day Gundara and his gang grabbed hold of Harada as he came home in the evening, they stuffed him into a sack, weighed it down with stones and threw it into the river. Harada drowned.

But as soon as the deed was done, Gundara felt afraid of what would happen to him when everyone found out, so he ran away. He changed his name, went to live in an isolated castle miles away, and got a job as a swordmaker.

Back at home, Harada's son, Urashima, discovered that his father had been killed. He realised that Gundara had disappeared and deduced that the two events were connected. Gundara must have killed his father.

'I will avenge my father's death,' Urashima told everyone. 'I will get my own back on Gundara, on behalf of my father. He won't get away with this.'

'But no-one knows where Gundara is,' said Urashima's friends. 'How can you get your revenge when you don't know where he is?'

'I'll find him,' vowed Urashima. 'No matter how long it takes, I'll find him, and then I'll kill him.'

'But it might take you years and years,' said his friends.

'I don't care,' said Urashima. 'I won't do anything for myself until I have my revenge.'

'But that means no job, no wife, no family, no friends, no leisure, in fact no life,' said his friends.

'I know,' said Urashima. 'But I have to avenge my father's death, and with that, he set off to find Gundara.

Urashima searched all over the country. He asked in every village and town he came to. Wherever a new person had settled, he checked up on who they were and where they were from. Months went by and the search continued. Years went by, and still Urashima looked for Gundara.

By now Urashima was growing old. All the searching and travelling was making him ill. He had no other interests, nothing else in his life except the hatred for Gundara and the search for revenge.

'Give it up now,' said one of the few friends Urashima had left. 'Forget Gundara. It all happened such a very long time ago. Let it go. Settle down and have some peace at the end of your life.'

'Never!' said Urashima. 'I will never give up the search. I will not rest until Gundara is found and I have killed him.'

Later that same day, someone told Urashima of an old old man who'd set up as a swordmaker in an isolated castle in the south of the country, at about the time that Harada had been killed.

'It's him!' said Urashima. 'It's Gundara! I've found him at last.' And he hurried off to the castle he'd been told about.

The old man was there, selling his swords, and there was no doubt that this was Gundara. Urashima pretended to be a customer. He looked at the swords, complimented Gundara on the workmanship, chose one and paid for it.

Then, with the sword in his hand, Urashima turned on Gundara.

'*You* killed my father,' he cried. 'I have searched for you almost all my life, and now I have found you. Now it's time for you to pay for what you did all those years ago. It's *your* turn to die,' and Urashima held the sword aloft, ready to bring it down on the old man and kill him.

But as he stood there with the sword raised, Urashima suddenly stopped.

'What am I doing?' he asked. 'What am I going to achieve by killing this old man? Will killing him bring my father back? Will killing him bring me peace?' And Urashima knew the answer was no.

'Revenge is cruel and bitter,' he said. 'My father's life was wasted because you killed him. But my own life has been wasted because I used it up in looking for revenge.' And Urashima lowered the sword.

'I'm sorry,' said Gundara. 'I was wrong to do what I did, and I have regretted it every day since.'

'I forgive you,' said Urashima. 'I never thought I would look you in the eye and say those words, but it is the only answer to give both of us peace.'

Forgiving someone when they have hurt or upset you is very difficult. But trying to get your own back can make you very unhappy, and it doesn't put right whatever was wrong in the first place. It usually makes things worse.

Someone does something hurtful to you; you do something hurtful back to them; but neither of you is any further forward. Two wrongs don't make a right. The strongest, bravest people are the ones who can forgive. But… it's not easy.

Help us, Lord, to try to forgive, when people are hurtful or unkind. Help us not to look for revenge. Help us to treat other people as we would like them to treat us. Amen

Theme 2: Rights and responsibilities

Manchester United

Do you have a job that's your responsibility in your family, or in your class, or in your school? If so, you'll know how important it is to do the job properly and not let your family or friends or teacher down. If you are responsible for something or someone, you have to put that responsibility before the other things you want to do.

In today's story, a man who was usually sensible and responsible forgot all his responsibilities when he went to a football match. It's a true story!

The man always tried to go to the home matches whenever he could, although he didn't always manage it with being so busy. Mr Brown owned a clothing factory and he had 60 people working for him, making sport and leisurewear - sweatshirts, jogging suits, leotards, that sort of thing. The factory worked Monday to Friday and Saturday morning, but if there was a big order to finish, everyone would work overtime until it was completed. On overtime weekends Mr Brown could never get to the match, and he could never manage to get to any of the away matches because the travelling always took too long.

But this weekend he was determined to be there. Manchester United were playing a championship decider at home against Leeds United. There was no way he was going to miss that, even though the factory had a large order to finish.

On Friday he chivvied the workers all day.

'Come on, this order must be ready for dispatch by tomorrow lunchtime. The shop it's going to wants the goods on display by Monday morning.'

But Mr Brown's workers were not fooled.

'It's nothing to do with sending out the order by lunchtime,' they said. 'He's in a hurry because he wants to lock up at lunchtime and go to the match!'

However, they got on with the work as quickly as they could; they all had things they wanted to do on Saturday afternoon, and they quite liked their boss so they were happy to help him get away early.

By eleven o'clock on Saturday morning the work was almost finished. By twelve o'clock the garments had all been checked and put into bags. By one o'clock everything was packed into big cardboard cartons ready for dispatch. All that remained was for the delivery van to be loaded with the boxes, and for the office staff to finish making out the invoices - these were always posted off separately.

Mr Brown looked at his watch.

'Half past one. Should have everything finished off by two. Yes! Kick-off is at three, so that's just nice timing. I will get to the match.' And he laughed and punched the air with his arm in anticipation of Manchester United scoring winning goals.

By now he was thinking only of the match. It would be good to see his team again, he'd missed their last match. He wondered what the score would be at half time.

As he was thinking about the game, Mr Brown was walking through the factory turning off lights and locking doors.

He was wondering what the final score would be, as he locked up the big double doors of the dispatch bay. And he was thinking about how brilliant it would be if his team won the championship, as he locked the office doors, then the main front door of the factory.

He glanced up at the sign over the door. In huge black and white letters it said BROWN'S SPORTSWEAR, but Mr Brown saw black and white headlines in that night's newspaper instead - MAN UNITED WIN CHAMPIONSHIP.

He arrived at the ground in good time, and settled into his seat. The stadium was full of enthusiastic supporters; the noise was tremendous but not as loud as the thunderous roar he knew would go up when Manchester United scored their first goal. He could hardly wait for the match to begin.

Then, through the noise, Mr Brown became aware of another sound. A woman was speaking over the announcement system. Her voice cracked and echoed but the message was clear enough for everyone to hear.

'Calling Mr Brown. Calling Mr James Brown. Would Mr Brown please return immediately to Brown's sportswear, where he has locked in some secretarial staff? I repeat - would Mr Brown please return immediately to Brown's sportswear where some of his staff are locked in.'

Mr Brown felt so embarrassed as he realised what had happened. He'd been so busy thinking about the match ahead and about getting to the football ground as soon as he could, he'd not checked that everyone was out of the building before he'd locked it. He knew that the workroom was empty and that the machinists had all gone home, and he knew that the dispatch bay was empty - he remembered walking through there and locking the big double doors. But he knew he hadn't checked the offices before he locked them, and he knew there was no other way out of the offices except through the main front door.

He thought of Jane and Sandra, his two invoice clerks. They'd be furious with him for locking them in, even though he hadn't done it on purpose. He realised how thoughtless and selfish he'd been, in thinking only of what he wanted to do and not thinking of his staff and his responsibilities.

Mr Brown left his seat and hurried out of the stadium. As he went, a few people laughed; they realised he was the man who was in such a rush to get to the match he'd locked his staff in.

As he left the football ground, Mr Brown heard the roar of the crowd as the teams ran on to the pitch. He knew that he wouldn't see any of the match now. By the time he'd gone back to the factory, apologised to the two women, and returned to the stadium, the match would be over.

It was a match he wouldn't forget in a hurry, even though he didn't see it!

I wonder what Jane and Sandra said to Mr Brown when he arrived back at the factory to let them out? I wonder if they felt sorry that he'd missed the match? And I wonder how *you* would have reacted if you'd been them?

Help us Lord, to remember our responsibilities. Help us not to become so involved in our own thoughts that we forget the needs of others. Help us to do the jobs were are asked to do, conscientiously and to the best of our ability. Amen

Farmer Brandit's hat

Have you ever been in a situation where you've gone ahead with something *you* wanted to do, but it's ended up not being very good for your friends or someone in your family?

Sometimes it's hard to remember that just about everything we do has an effect on other people. When we live in a family or a neighbourhood or a community of any kind, we have a responsibility to think about the effect our actions have on other people.

The man in today's story never gave a thought to the effects of his actions.

Farmer Brandit found the hat in the hedgebottom early one morning. Of course, he didn't know then that it was magic - well you wouldn't, it was just a battered old straw hat with two holes in it, like donkeys used to wear.

He took it home and put it on the table where Mrs Brandit was making bread.

'Hey, don't you be putting that dirty old thing on my baking table,' she said, picking it up to move it. 'I wish you'd learn to tidy your things away!'

No sooner had she said that, than - whoosh - Farmer Brandit's pipe and slippers, newspaper, walking stick, raincoat, empty tea-cup and wellington boots that he'd left lying around, whizzed into their proper places.

'Well I never!' said Mrs Brandit.

'Here, give that hat to me,' said Farmer Brandit, taking it from his wife. He held it firmly in front of him with both hands.

'I wish... I wish...' he couldn't think of anything to wish for and looked around the kitchen for inspiration. 'I wish your bread was a cherry and walnut cake.'

And - whoosh - the dough that was rising in the baking bowl tipped itself out onto the wooden table and became a newly-baked, piping-hot, cherry and walnut cake.

'Well I never!' said Mrs Brandit.

'This is wonderful,' laughed Farmer Brandit. 'This is brilliant. This is the very best stroke of luck I've ever had in all my long-legged life.'

'I think you should be careful,' warned Mrs Brandit.

'Nonsense!' said Farmer Brandit. 'Just think, with this hat I can get all my work done for me. With this hat I don't need to get up at the crack of dawn any more, and work all hours.'

Now you'll notice that Farmer Brandit wasn't a greedy man. His first thought when he discovered the hat was magic was not to wish for pots of money, big houses and fancy clothes. No, he was a simple man, with simple tastes, and was happy to live his life as he'd always done, just as long as he didn't have to work quite so hard. But because he was a simple man, he didn't think very far ahead.

Farmer Brandit ran out into the yard clutching his hat, and looked around at his farm at all the jobs that were waiting to be done.

He took a deep breath... and began.

'I wish my tractor was mended and would go by itself. I wish the cows would bring themselves in for milking instead of me having to go and get them from the bottom field. I wish...'

'Oh, be careful,' said Mrs Brandit. 'Look!'

The tractor had suddenly leapt into action and was chugging off through the gate, and the cows were heading towards the yard and the milking shed.

'Well I never!' said Mrs Brandit.

'This is great!' yelled Farmer Brandit, really getting into his stride now. 'I wish the stream would flow into that lake I've been going to make. I wish the hay would cut itself. Look! Look Mrs Brandit!' he shouted.

'Well I never,' said Mrs Brandit, as she saw the half-dug hole turn into a wondrous lake; and she saw the doors of the sheep and pig pens open wide; and she watched the hay fall into swathes on the ground then dance into a hay-stack in the corner.

'A whole week's work in half a minute,' said Farmer Brandit. 'And I haven't had to lift a finger. Come on Mrs Brandit, let's go inside for a cup of tea.'

They sat and drank tea, marvelling at the wonderful magic hat. But outdoors the action continued.

The tractor, with no one driving it, crashed into the big oak tree and blocked off the whole lane.

The cows coming in to be milked couldn't get past, and broke down a neighbour's fence and trampled across his vegetables to get to their milking shed.

The sheep and the pigs were everywhere in people's gardens, in the school playground, in the village shop, there was even a pig in the telephone box.

Everyone's hay was being cut, whether they wanted it cutting or not.

And the stream, which had filled the new lake, continued to flow into it, causing a flood on Farmer Brandit's land, and a drought on everyone else's.

It wasn't long before the rest of the neighbourhood realised that things were not right, and they quickly deduced that all the problems came from Farmer Brandit's direction.

They hammered on his door - the local farmers, shopkeepers, neighbours, schoolteachers, policemen; even the man from British telecom.

'What do you think you're doing?' they all shouted. 'You may be solving *your* problems, but for every one of *yours* you've solved, you've caused one for *us*! Everything you do had an effect on someone else, you know!'

'I'm sorry,' said Farmer Brandit. 'I didn't mean any harm. It's just that I had a bit of luck this morning. I never thought it would do any harm to anyone else.'

'Well, it's all right for you, isn't it?' said the man from British telecom. 'A bit of good luck for you, but a bit of bad luck for the rest of us. What are you going to do about it?'

'Oh dear!' said Mrs Brandit, taking the magic hat from her husband. 'I don't like trouble. I wish you'd never set eyes on this.'

And with a whoosh the hat was gone, taking with it the local farmers, shopkeepers, neighbours, schoolteachers, policemen; and even the man from British Telecom.

'Well I never!' said Mrs Brandit, as she turned to get on with her baking. 'I'll go and start the jobs,' said Farmer Brandit. 'There's a lot to do.'

He set off for the fields, but there in the hedgebottom was a battered old straw hat with two holes in it like donkeys used to wear...

I wonder if the hat was magic the second time around? I wonder what happened next in the story? And I wonder what you would have done if you'd been Farmer Brandit?

Dear God, please help us to think ahead and to be aware that what we do affects other people. Help us to be responsible for our actions. Help us to take responsibility for our mistakes and not blame them on other people. Amen

Anansi changes the world

Have you ever been given a job to do, at home or at school, which has given you a special privilege? Perhaps you've been asked to tidy an area of your classroom, and you've been allowed to stay in to do it, at a time when you're not usually allowed to stay in.

If this has happened to you, you'll know that you had a *right* to stay in, but you'll also know that you had a *responsibility* to behave properly in the classroom, and just do the job you'd been asked to do. Rights and responsibilities go together – you can't have one without the other.

In today's story, Anansi is so concerned about his rights, he forgets his responsibilities. You have probably met Anansi before. He is the mischievous spider from African myths, who was God's helper when the world was new.

Way back at the beginning of time when the world was very new, God sent out his chief helper, Anansi, to check with all the animals that they were happy with where everything was. You see, things were not in quite the same place as they are now. For example, God had put the sun at the top of a mountain, and he had hung the moon in the branches of a tree.

'I want you to go everywhere and ask all the animals if they are happy with where everything is,' said God. 'I need to know that everything is in the right place before I finalise all the positions. If you find anything small that needs moving, like a hill or a stream or a rock, just move it to where you think it should be. But don't move anything big; I'll see to the big things when you get back.'

Anansi felt very pleased and proud that God had asked him to do this important job. He set off on his travels straightaway, and soon met the elephants.

'God has asked me to find out if you are happy with where everything is in the world,' said Anansi.

'Everything's fine, thank you,' said the elephants.

'What about your watering hole?' said Anansi. 'Wouldn't it be better a bit further over there?'

'No, we don't think so,' said the elephants. 'We like it just where it is.'

'Well, I have a right to move things if I think fit,' said Anansi. 'And I think the watering hole would be better over there.' So without any further consultation, Anansi moved the watering hole five miles to the south. But what he didn't realise, was that the elephants now had to walk an extra ten miles every day.

Anansi travelled on and met the squirrels.

'God has asked me to find out if you are happy with where everything is in the world,' he said.

'Yes thank you, we like everything just the way it is,' answered the squirrels.

'But what about all those trees?' said Anansi. 'Surely they'd be better at the other side of the valley?'

'We like them where they are,' said the squirrels. 'We keep our store of winter food hidden in those trees.'

'Well I have a right to move things if I think fit, and I think the trees would be better over there,' said Anansi. And without any further consultation, he moved the group of trees to the other side of the valley. But what he didn't realise, was that the squirrels were then unable to find their stores of seeds and nuts, and many of them went hungry.

Anansi travelled on and met the owls.

'God has asked me to find out if you are happy with where everything is in the world,' he said.

'Everything's just right, thank you,' said the owls.

'I notice that you have the moon in the top of your tree,' said Anansi. 'I think the moon would be better in the sea.'

'No, we need...' began the owls, but without any further consultation, Anansi lifted down the moon and dropped it into the deepest part of the sea. But what he didn't realise, because he hadn't given the owls chance to tell him, was that without the moon they couldn't navigate; the owls could not find their way about, and many of them got lost and died.

By now Anansi was feeling very happy. He felt sure he was doing a good job and that God would be pleased with his work. Anansi was also feeling very powerful. The fact that God had given him the right to move things around made him feel strong and important. He forgot that God had told him only to move small things. Anansi continued on his travels and met the sparrows.

'God has asked me to find out if you are happy with where everything is in the world,' he said.

'Yes thank you,' chirped the sparrows. 'We like everything just as it is.'

'I see the top of your tree almost touches the sky,' said Anansi. 'I think the sky would be better a little lower, don't you?'

'Oh no,' said the sparrows. 'You see, we need the space to fly.' But Anansi said 'I have a right to move things if I see fit,' and without any more consultation he put the clouds on the grass and lowered the sky almost down to the ground. But what he didn't realise, was that by moving the sky to the ground, he had removed the flying space of all the flying creatures in the whole world. They had no space in which to move, and were miserable.

Anansi decided not to ask any more of the animals what they thought, but to go ahead and do what he wanted. After all, he'd been given the right to make changes, and God was sure to be pleased with his decisions.

Anansi looked up at the top of the mountain. There sat the sun; a glowing ball of fire. Anansi thought it would be better moved somewhere else, but he couldn't think where to put it. He pulled a bag out of his pocket, caught hold of the sun and stuffed it into the bag. But what he hadn't realised, was that the earth went dark and cold as soon as the sun was hidden.

Anansi looked around him, but it was impossible to see. He listened, but there was no sound. No birds singing, no animals calling, not even the sound of the sea. The waves were still now that the sky was pressing down on them.

Suddenly Anansi heard the voice of God calling out into the darkness and stillness.

'Anansi? Anansi! What have you done to my world? Come here and tell me what you've done.' And suddenly Anansi remembered that he was supposed to move only small things, and he remembered that he was supposed to ask the animals what they thought. He heard anger in God's voice and he felt afraid.

'I'm sorry,' he whispered. 'I didn't mean any harm. I just didn't think about the needs of the others.'

'Well, that's what happens when you don't think,' said God. 'And that's what happens when you have rights without responsibility! If you have a right to do something, you also have a responsibility. You can't have one without the other.'

'I'm sorry,' said Anansi again.

'I think we'd better put things right and get everything back to normal,' said God, as he pushed the sky back to its proper place. 'Give me the sun, Anansi.'

Anansi gave God the bag with the sun in it, and God threw the sun high into the sky. Then he fished the moon out of the sea and threw that into the sky as well.

'I think we'll have those way out of your reach,' said God. And he threw a handful of stars into the sky for good measure.

If you have a right to do something, you have a responsibility that goes with it. Can you think of any rights and responsibilities that you have?

Help us, Lord, to understand that when we have rights, we have responsibilities too. Help us to be aware of the needs of other people. Help us to remember that everything we do has an effect upon someone else. Amen

Theme 3: Wealth, valuables and riches

The golden apple

Have you ever taken part in raising money for something – perhaps for your school or for a charity? Did you notice how the money mounted up as people all added their bit? The total amount raised was due to everyone's efforts; it wasn't just due to one person giving a huge amount. When people are working together to collect for a good cause, everyone's contribution is important. But sometimes this is hard to remember.

There was once a boy called Tom, who lived in a Yorkshire mining village around a hundred and fifty years ago. Tom's family was very poor, and in those days children from poor families had to go out to work from a very young age. Tom worked down the pit with his father and older brothers. Tom had to work a twelve-hour shift. Twelve hours at a time down a cold, wet, dark, dirty, dangerous coalmine, pulling iron trolleys filled with coal along black tunnels. Tom hated it.

Once a month Tom was allowed a day off. It was usually a Sunday and he couldn't wait for his day off to come round. He couldn't wait to get out of the pit and into the fresh air, into the sunshine and light, into the sounds and smells and tastes of life above ground.

'I'm off out for a long walk,' he told his mother one particular Sunday. 'I'm going to walk and walk to see how far I get,' and he set off.

Tom walked out of his village and over the fields. He followed a track through the wood and climbed a hill in the distance. This was as far as he'd ever been before. He stood on the hilltop and looked out across the countryside. The fields were spread out in front on him like a patchwork quilt of shapes and colours. The land here was perfectly flat, no hills, no valleys. He could see for miles.

Over in the distance, almost as far as the horizon, Tom could see what looked like a cathedral. It was made of pale coloured stone and had two tall towers at one end. There were houses clustered round it and a wall encircling the houses. 'York!' breathed Tom to himself. 'It must be York.'

He'd heard of the wonderful city of York with its magnificent minster, but he'd never been there, never seen it for himself. Now was his chance to go.

It took a long time to get there, but eventually Tom reached the city gates. He went inside. The streets were narrow and the houses all pushed close together. There were people everywhere, he'd never seen such crowds. He heard some church music coming from the other end of the street and he walked towards the sound.

Tom found himself in a wide-open space in front of the great west doors of the minster. He walked up to the doors and looked inside. He had never seen such a beautiful building. There was so much space, so much light, so much colour. Sunlight poured through the stained glass windows and made multi-coloured patterns on the worn flagstones of the floor. The pale stone walls were covered in the most intricate carvings. Rich embroideries in gold and coloured threads hung from the roof. People were hurrying in through the doors and taking their places in the polished wooden seats.

Someone pushed him aside. 'Come on, you're blocking the way. Are you coming in or going out? Move along there.' And before Tom realised what was happening he found himself inside the minster, swept along with the surge of the crowd, and sitting in a row near the back.

The service began. Tom had never been to a church service before and didn't know what to do, but he watched the rest of the congregation and did what they did.

The singing was wonderful, the music was beautiful. Tom listened to the prayers that were said and was able to join in with one beginning 'Our Father', that his mother had taught him. He was really enjoying himself, but then something dreadful happened.

A man, who clearly belonged to the church, began to pass round a collection plate, and Tom realised that everyone in the congregation was expected to put some money in it. He watched the plate being passed from person to person along each row. When the collection plate reached the end of a row, the man handed it to the people in the row behind.

Tom began to panic. What should he do? He knew he had no money to give. The collection plate came nearer and nearer, zigzagging along the rows of people. It came to the row where Tom was sitting. The lady at the end of the row put in three golden sovereigns and smiled at the sidesman as if to say 'Look what I've given.' The two children sitting next to her each put in a silver florin, then squabbled over who should pass the plate to their father sitting next to them. He took the collection plate and dropped five golden sovereigns onto the pile of coins. He looked very pleased with himself.

The plate was handed to Tom. What should he do? He had nothing to give. He held the plate with one hand and frantically searched in his pocket with the other. Perhaps there was a penny somewhere in the bottom of his pocket that he'd forgotten about. But no. All he could find was an apple that his mother had given to him as he set off that morning. It was the only thing he had, so he pulled it out of his pocket and placed it very carefully on top of the pile of money on the plate.

He could hear the rustle of disapproval run right round the minster.

'Tut tut tut,' the people said, as they looked at each other and shook their heads.

'What a disgrace,' they muttered.

'How inappropriate,' they said.

'A ragamuffin like him shouldn't be here in the minster,' they whispered.

'Someone should throw him out,' they murmured.

'We don't want the likes of him in our church,' they said.

The sidesman who was in charge of the collection plate said, 'Now then lad, you can't put that in here. Take it out and go into the street where you belong,' and he picked up the apple to give it back to Tom. But no sooner had he touched the apple than it turned into solid gold!

The congregation gasped in astonishment.

'We've never seen anything like it,' they said. 'What does it mean?'

'It means that the child has given all he has,' said the archbishop of York, as he came down the aisle to see what the commotion was about. 'It means that he has given, in fact, more than any of you.'

'But no!' said the lady at the end of Tom's row. 'My family has put more than eight golden sovereigns into the plate today. He has given just an apple!'

'The boy has given what he can,' said the archbishop. 'It is enough that he has come into God's house and has given something. He has nothing to be ashamed of, and perhaps plenty to be proud of,' and the archbishop took Tom by the hand and let him sit next to him for the rest of the service.

Afterwards people said, 'The apple can't really have turned into gold. We must have imagined it.' But whether it did or not, was not important. The people understood that Tom had given everything he could, because he'd given everything he had, and no one can do more than that.

When we join in fundraising and charity events, it doesn't matter if we give more than other people or less than them; but it does matter that we each do what we can to help, and that we each do our best. Fundraising and charity events are successful when everyone works together and when everyone remembers that 'every little helps'.

Dear God, please help us to remember that when we work together on something, everyone's contribution is important. Help us to remember that everyone, from the biggest to the smallest, has a valuable part to play. Amen

The Efflam Rock

On the north coast of Brittany in France, there's a huge boulder called the Efflam Rock. It's been there for thousands of years, ever since the earth heaved and moved and made itself into the shape we now know as Europe.

The rock is huge – as tall as twenty houses and just as wide. One side of it dips into the sea, and just above the place where the high tide reaches, there is a strange arch-shaped cave. The cave looks almost like a doorway except that there's a thick impenetrable wall of rock at the back.

At the other side of the rock, away from the sea, are smaller rocks, all heaped up against the big Efflam Rock as though some enormous giant has thrown them all down in a temper. And everywhere, in all the nooks and crannies and spaces and gaps between the rocks, there are thousands of wild flowers; pink sea-thrift and big ox-eye daisies, prickly sea holly and green sun-spurge.

The people living near the Efflam Rock tell this story about it.

One midsummer day, a man took his boat out to sea near the Efflam Rock, and went fishing. He stayed out in his boat all day – the fishing was good – and it was almost midnight when he came back to the beach. Almost dark. Yet almost daylight too, for this was Midsummer Day, when magic is around.

The man hauled his boat up out of the sea and on to the smooth wet sand. He began to unload his fish. As he did so he glanced up at the massive shape of the Efflam Rock, and he seemed to see something sparkle, glitter, just for an instant, in the arch-shaped cave of the rock.

He stood quite still. He watched. And there it was again. Something shining, shimmering, glinting, deep in the dark of the cave.

The man left his fish and his boat and hurried across the sand. The tide was coming in quickly and the sea was already lapping at the rock just below the cave. He splashed through the water for the last few strides and scrambled up into the mouth of the cave. He climbed into it just as the last of the daylight disappeared, but he didn't need daylight to see what lay before him.

The solid wall of rock at the back of the cave had opened like a huge door, and there inside, glowing in a strange yellow-white light… was treasure. But treasure even beyond the dreams of the fisherman.

The floor and walls and roof of this treasure cave were made of gold and the golden cave was filled with precious stones. Silver stalactites hung from the roof and golden stalagmites grew from the ground. Nuggets of pure gold lay on the floor of the cave, scattered amongst emeralds and diamonds, sapphires and rubies. The walls were studded with amethyst and turquoise, and festooned with strings of coral and pearls.

The man stared for a moment or two in disbelief, and then realised that this treasure was his for the taking.

'I'm rich,' he said aloud. 'I'm rich! No more fishing. I'm rich! No more being poor. I'm RICH!' And he hurried into the golden cave through the open doorway of rock.

Just as he took his first steps into the golden cave, the sea reached the entrance of the outer cave. It lapped against the pebbles of the cave floor and made them move and murmur and shift and sigh.

'Out before daybreak... Out before dawn...' the pebbles whispered. But the message was lost on the fisherman, who was so intent upon his treasure that he didn't hear it.

He could have gone into the cave and taken just a pocketful of treasure. It would have been enough.

He could have gone into the cave and taken just what he could carry. It would have been plenty.

But no! The sight of the treasure made him greedy. The sight of the gold and jewels made all sensible thoughts fly out of his head. The fisherman wasn't content with a pocketful of gold. He wasn't happy with part of the treasure, even though it would have been enough to make him and his family and friends rich for the rest of their lives.

No. He wanted it *all*.

And as he stuffed his pockets and shirt and shoes with gold and jewels, the sea tried to warn him.

'Out before daybreak... Out before dawn...' sang the pebbles.

But the fisherman took no notice. He carried on gathering more and more treasure.

Far away behind him and over the sea the sun began to rise. The first finger of daylight shimmered across the waves and touched the Efflam Rock. The door of the golden cave began to close. Slowly. Silently.

The golden light inside the cave grew dim, and the fisherman looked up from the treasure. He saw the door closing. He saw the pale grey gap of daylight getting smaller and narrower. And he knew then it was time to leave.

But the feeling of greed was too strong.

'Just a bit more,' he said to himself. 'Just a bit more.'

He picked up another handful of jewels, another pocketful of gold, and he looked at the door of the cave again. The gap was even narrower. He knew he had only a few more seconds to get out of the cave, but he wanted to gather just a few more jewels... just a bit more gold...

Far away behind him and over the sea, the sun rose a little higher in the midsummer sky. It touched the tops of the dancing waves and the sea looked as though it was scattered with golden coins. Then a finger of sunlight touched the rocky door of the golden cave and it shut. Tight.

Nowadays, the people living near the Efflam Rock tell the story of the fisherman to their children. They say it serves him right for being so greedy.

They say that the Efflam Rock is still filled with treasure, but they can't agree on when it opens. Some say it opens at the first stroke of midnight on Midsummer's Day. Others say it opens at the first stroke of midnight on

Christmas Eve. But they all agree that anyone still inside the golden cave by the last stroke of midnight will have to stay there forever like the fisherman who was greedy.

Help us, Lord, not to be greedy. Help us to share what we have with others and not want everything for ourselves. Help us to see and appreciate the riches and wealth of the natural world, and to care for the world around us. Amen

The rich man and the well

You will see that I have two things on my table today - I have a glass of water and a can of coke!

If I asked you which you'd like, I think that most of you would choose the can of coke. But what if I ask you which is better? What will you say then? And if I ask you which is more useful? Most people would say the glass of water. After all you can drink water, cook with it, wash in it, water the plants with it, mix paint with it, to name just a few; imagine doing some of those things with coke!

But which is more valuable, the water or the coke? Many of you say the coke because it costs more to buy.

Sometimes we confuse cost with value. They are not the same thing at all. Something that doesn't cost a great deal, can be very valuable.

There was once a man called Abdhul who was immensely wealthy. He had riches beyond the dreams of most ordinary people. He had fine clothes and wonderful jewels, a magnificent palace with beautiful gardens, servants to do anything he asked, and he had a wife, sons, daughters, family and friends.

But he knew that most other people didn't live like he did. He had only to look out of his palace windows each day to see that there were people in his town who were poor. Lots of people. People with no homes, no possessions, no family and no friends.

'I have to do something to help other people,' he said to his wife one day. 'It isn't right that we have so much and others have so little. What can we do to help?'

But his wife was scared that her husband would give away all their riches, and that they'd be left with nothing, so she said 'There's nothing we can do. There are too many poor people in the town for us to be able to make any difference to them. It's no good even trying. Just leave them alone and ignore them. It's not our fault they're poor.'

Abdhul was not happy with his wife's reply, so he went to ask his mother for her advice.

'I have to do something to help the poor,' he said. 'Do you have any ideas?'

'You must help the children,' said his mother. 'Build a house where the street children can live. A house where children who have no mothers or fathers can be looked after.'

Abdhul thought this was a good idea, but he wanted some more advice, so he went to find his father.

'I want to do something to help the poor people of our town,' he said. 'Do you have any ideas?'

'Build a hospital,' said Abdhul's father. 'There are always people who are ill, you could help them. And you could help yourself at the same time – you could have the hospital named after you, then everyone would know how generous you are and you would be remembered forever.'

Abdhul was unsure about this advice. He wanted to help others, not gain recognition for himself. He went to find his children to see what they thought.

'I've been thinking,' he said. 'We have so much and other people in our town have so little, I want to do something to help them. Have you any ideas?'

'Build a kitchen and dining room at the palace gates,' said Abdhul's eldest son. 'Then everyone who is hungry can come along every day and have a good meal. You could put in an appearance every now and then to let them know it's you who's paying for their food. They'll all be grateful to you for ever.'

'I think you should make a park and fill it full of flower gardens,' said Abdhul's eldest daughter. 'The poor people would always have something beautiful to see. And you could name it after me,' she added.

'No, don't do that,' said Abdhul's youngest son. 'Build a park and fill it full of playground stuff – swings and slides and roundabouts – then all the children can come and play there, me included.'

'This is all about people,' said Abdhul's youngest daughter. 'But what about the animals. There are hundreds of animals in our town that need caring for. Poor people haven't enough money to pay for their animals to be looked after, and there are stray cats and dogs and even horses that have been left to fend for themselves. Build an animal hospital and make all the treatment free. You could call it "Abdhul's animal clinic". Everyone would know about it for miles around, and you'd be famous.'

Abdhul listened patiently to his children's ideas, but somehow none of them seemed quite right. He decided to ask someone outside the family, and he went to find his neighbour.

'I want to do something to help the poor people of our town,' he said. 'Do you have any thoughts about what I could do?'

'Why don't you just stand at the gates of your palace, say every Friday, and give away some money to the first hundred people who come along? Word would soon get around, you'd be famous in no time. And when the people got their money, they might come into my shop to spend it,' he laughed.

Abdhul was no more satisfied with this answer than with any of the others he'd received. So he decided to go and ask Mohammed for help. Mohammed was a wise man and would give good advice, he felt sure. 'I don't know why I didn't go to him in the first place,' thought Abdhul.

'I want to do something to help the poor people of my town,' he said. 'I have already asked lots of people for their advice, but I'm not altogether happy with what I've been told.'

'People will always tell you to help the ones *they* think you should help,' said Mohammed.

'That's right,' said Abdhul. 'I've discovered that already.'

'And people will encourage you to do things which will make them, or even you, seem important in the eyes of the world.'

'That's right,' said Abdhul 'I've found that out, too.'

'But that's not really what giving is all about,' went on Mohammed. 'When you give something away, it should be for the person you're giving it to; not for what you might get out of it yourself. Giving should be an unselfish act, not a selfish one.'

'I know,' said Abdhul. 'So what can I do to help all the people of my town?'

'Build a well!' said Mohammed. 'A new well would help everyone, rich and poor, young and old. A new well would help people and animals. A new well would help plants to grow and might help some people to grow their own food. A new well would be valuable, even though it wouldn't cost a great deal to build. Water is one of the most valuable things we have. Build a well!'

'What a brilliant idea,' said Abdhul. 'Thank you for your help,' and off he went to make all the arrangements to build not one, but four, new wells in his town and then to arrange to build new wells in other towns and cities.

Abdhul's family and neighbour all seemed to be trying to do something for themselves when they were telling him how he should help the poor people of their town. Mohammed's idea was very simple, yet very clever, because he knew the value and importance of water. Sometimes we take simple everyday things, like water, for granted. But without water we wouldn't be able to live.

Dear God, thank you for the gift of water. Help us to appreciate its value and to know of its importance in our lives. Help us to understand that there are places on earth where people don't have enough clean water, and places where disasters cause the water to become unusable and contaminated. Help us to do what we can to share the gift of water in our world. Amen

July

Theme 1: Bravery

Superman

Have you seen Superman? I'm sure lots of you will have seen him on the television or on video, or even at the cinema. And I think most of you know that Superman is played by an actor. All heroes and heroines in TV and film adventures are played by actors and actresses.

One famous actor who has played the part of Superman is an American called Christopher Reeve. In the films of course, Superman is always brave. But in real life, Christopher Reeve has been braver than Superman could ever have been.

Christopher Reeve's life changed forever in May 1995 when he was thrown from the horse he was riding. Christopher fell awkwardly; he landed headfirst on hard ground, the nerves in his neck were damaged, he was unable to move any part of his body, and he could hardly breath.

He was taken straight to hospital and intensive care. Five days later he woke up and the doctors gently told Christopher that he had broken the top two bones in his neck. But worse, they told him he would be completely paralysed for the rest of his life. He would never be able to walk or even sit up on his own, and that he would never even be able to breath on his own again, but would always need a machine to help him.

'But you're lucky to be alive,' added one of the doctors.

Christopher was not so sure about that. He was very badly hurt, and knew he would never again be able to do the things he enjoyed. He wouldn't be able to act or ride. He wouldn't be able to go out and see his friends. But more importantly, he wouldn't be able to cuddle or play with his four children. He wouldn't even be able to wash or dress or feed himself. He would be completely dependent upon other people to help him.

He became very depressed. He thought he was going to be a huge burden to his friends and family, and he thought he'd ruined his own life and theirs as well. He thought it would be a lot better all round if he died, and then no one would have to bother about him.

But when he told his wife what he was thinking, she said something that made him change his mind.

'I don't want you to die,' she said. 'You've had an accident, but you're still you. You're still you, and we love you.'

Christopher decided then that he didn't want to die; he wanted to stay around and pick up the pieces of his life. He decided to look for something he was good at; he knew that everyone is good at something, and even though he was paralysed, he knew there must be something he could do.

One day Christopher's three year old son was playing with his toys on the floor, when he suddenly looked up at a nurse and said sadly, 'My daddy can't move his arms any more. And he can't run about any more.' Then he added happily, 'But he can still smile!'

'That's right,' thought Christopher. 'It's only a little thing, but it's something I can do. And if I can smile, perhaps I can do other things too.'

Being good at smiling helped Christopher to be determined to be good at other things. He decided to start with his breathing. This, he thought, was the worst thing about being paralysed. He couldn't breath at all on his own, but had to have a machine called a ventilator to help him. Sometimes the connections on the ventilator would come undone and he would struggle for air until someone came to fix it on again.

Christopher decided to start with just ten breaths on his own. The doctor took him off the ventilator and Christopher breathed in... out, then in... out, then in... but it was so difficult, it was so very hard to do. He managed just four breaths. But he was determined to succeed, so the next day he tried again, and managed six. Then the next day seven, and two days later – ten. He practised every day, and every day his breathing became a little stronger, until one day he managed to breath for fifteen minutes on his own.

'And if I can do fifteen', he thought, 'I can do twenty. And if I can do twenty, then I can do thirty.' And with a great deal of determination and effort, he did.

The next hurdle for Christopher to overcome was to do with going out and facing people again. Christopher had received an invitation to an award ceremony in New York. The awards were to be given to actors and other celebrities who had raised funds for charity. One of Christopher's best friends was to be given an award, and the invitation asked Christopher to present it.

At first Christopher thought it would be impossible for him to go to the ceremony. After all, he was completely paralysed, and still couldn't breathe for more than thirty minutes without his ventilator. But then he thought, 'If I don't try, I won't know whether I can do it or not.'

So on the day of the award ceremony, the nurses dressed him in his best dinner jacket and trousers, and an ambulance took him to the hotel where the ceremony was to be held. By the time he arrived at the hotel he was exhausted and had to rest. But he wasn't going to give up. He was going to present the award to his friend.

The time came for the presentation and Christopher was wheeled onto the stage. In the audience were 700 people, all looking at him. Suddenly Christopher wished he'd never come. What would all these people think when they saw him sitting in his wheelchair, totally paralysed? He didn't like the thought of people staring at him and feeling sorry for him.

But he needn't have worried. These people were his friends and they knew how brave he was. When Christopher appeared on the stage everyone stood up and cheered and clapped. It was their way of saying, 'We're glad you're back with us. We know you're still you, despite your accident, and we're proud of the way you've been so brave in coming here and facing everyone again.' Christopher presented his friend with the award, and he knew he'd overcome another obstacle in his recovery.

The third major hurdle that Christopher wanted to overcome was to go back to work; to begin acting in films again. He knew he would never star in a Superman film again, but perhaps he could act in a different kind of film. He told everyone what he wanted to do, but people said, 'It's impossible. He'll never work again. He's completely paralysed! What could he do?'

But a film director had decided to make a film about a man who was paralysed. In the past, able-bodied actors had always played parts like this, but the director thought it would be better and more real, if someone who really was paralysed played the part. He rang Christopher to ask if he would take the part.

This was what Christopher had been waiting for, and he said he would do it. He learned his lines, and the filming started. He put all his efforts into the film, and even insisted on having his ventilator turned off, so that the breathing difficulties of the character he was playing were real. The doctors had wanted him to act the breathing problems, but Christopher said no, it had to be real.

The film was made and released in 1998. Christopher had overcome another obstacle.

There will no doubt be more difficulties and hurdles for Christopher Reeve to face in the future, but if the past is anything to go by, he will face them positively and bravely.

There are many other people like Christopher Reeve, who face enormous problems in their everyday lives, but who face them with courage. Some people think that in order to be brave, you have to do something really spectacular, like climbing the highest mountain, or flying to the moon, or diving to unknown parts of the sea. But I think that people like Christopher Reeve, who have to struggle to do quite ordinary things every day, are the really brave ones. What do you think?

Dear God, help us to be brave when we are faced with challenges in life. Help us to be positive and cheerful when things are difficult. Amen

Nelly Brennan

There have been so many brave men and women throughout history that it's difficult to single out just a few. Some people's bravery is famous – like Christopher Columbus (who sailed across the ocean blue in fourteen hundred and ninety-two!) not knowing where he was going to end up because there were no maps in those days. But some people's bravery is hardly known about, or is almost forgotten.

Nelly Brennan is one of those people. She lived on the Isle of Man nearly two hundred years ago and risked her own life many times to help other people who were dying of a disease called cholera.

Eleanor was born in 1792, in a tiny house in Factory Lane in the town of Douglas, but everyone called her Nelly. Her mother was desperately poor and her father, who was a sailor, died just before Eleanor was born.

When Nelly was only a few weeks old, her mother spent the last few coins she had on a mangle, then quite a new-fangled invention, and she set up as a laundress, washing and ironing clothes for the rich people of the town. As Nelly grew up she helped her mother to wash and fold the clothes, and to collect and deliver them. But Nelly's mother was weak and frail, and laundry work was hard. Gradually she became able to do less and less and Nelly found herself having to care for her mother and do all their own washing and ironing and housework, and having to do all the laundry work as well. Then, when Nelly was sixteen, her mother died. Nelly had never felt so alone. She had no family, no friends and no money. But she did have her mother's mangle!

So Nelly continued to earn her living by doing other people's washing and ironing, and because she always did her best and worked conscientiously, she had plenty of customers.

The wealthy ladies of the town would walk out on Sundays and show off their fashionable clothes. They would promenade on the Red Pier, or sit under their parasols round the bandstand and listen to the music. And they would recommend their dressmaker or their laundry-woman to their friends. Nelly was recommended by everyone.

'She's the best laundress on the island,' they used to say. 'You should see the care she takes when she irons frills and lace. I've heard it said that she even puts tiny pieces of wood under the hooks of a dress so that the iron doesn't damage the fabric.'

But one Sunday, there was no promenading on the Red Pier. There was no fashion show, no band playing music. Everyone stayed indoors. Everyone was afraid. A terrible disease called cholera had come to the island. People were dying of it. There was no cure, and little anyone could do if they caught it. There was no hospital on the island and only one or two doctors.

Then people started to leave town. Dozens of horses and carriages set out from Douglas to other towns that were still free of the disease. People panicked if their friends or relatives caught cholera, which was highly infectious and contagious. If someone in a family caught it, no one would touch them or even go near them. Hundreds of people died.

But in the midst of all this panic, confusion and chaos, Nelly Brennan stayed calm. She went to see the doctors in the town and offered to help.

'But it's dangerous work,' they said. 'You risk catching the disease yourself, every time you enter a house where there's cholera.'

'I know,' said Nelly. 'But it's a risk I'm prepared to take.'

So Nelly worked with the doctors, bringing comfort and hope to many poor people. She accepted no payment for her work, even though wealthy people offered her money to care for them. She even took in a little girl whose mother and father had died of cholera and brought her up as her own.

Every day Nelly went into the homes of cholera victims, and every day she risked contacting the disease.

'Aren't you afraid?' people asked her.

'Of course,' answered Nelly. 'Everyone is afraid. But this is something I must do, and I pray every day that God will spare me to continue to do his work.'

Now that Nelly was spending all her time helping cholera victims, she was unable to do her laundry work. In any case, her customers were no longer willing to send their laundry to her; they knew she was going into the homes of people with cholera and they were afraid that if she did their washing, the disease would spread to them. Nelly once again became poor and one day found herself without even a pinch of tea in the house. But as always she stayed calm and had faith that God would somehow help her. Sure enough, by the end of the afternoon she had twelve golden guineas in her hand, a gift from a well wisher who wanted to thank her for her good work.

By now, the disease of cholera was beginning to die out and the island was getting back to normal. Building work had started on the new hospital. Nelly wondered what she should do, now that she was no longer needed to look after people with cholera. Once again, she had faith that God would help her.

And within a week she was offered a job. The new hospital needed a matron – a nurse to be in charge – so Nelly went to work at the hospital. But the work was hard and Nelly was no longer strong. Years of laundry work and then years of caring for the sick had weakened her. She left the hospital and moved to a small house by the side of the sea. And although Nelly was poor during the last years of her life, she didn't want for anything as many people gave her gifts as thanks for all her work.

Nelly is buried in St George's churchyard on the Isle of Man, but there is no gravestone, no memorial to say how brave she was. There is only the story, passed down through generations of Manx people, to remember her courage.

There are brave people everywhere, in every country, in the past, and in the present. And just as there are many brave people, so there are many ways of being brave. You can be just as brave doing something small as doing something huge and heroic. Many people do brave things because they feel it's something they must do. They're not brave so that they'll get noticed, or get a reward or a medal, or get written about in the papers. And many people do brave things that no one else ever knows about. We sometimes call people like that, 'unsung heroes'; it means doing something brave without getting any praise for it. A bit like Nelly Brennan really!

Help us Lord, never to be afraid of helping other people. Give us the courage to do what is right, and to do it for its own sake – not for reward or praise. Help us to face difficulties bravely and cheerfully. Amen

Gladys Aylward

There are people in the world who bravely help others, and no one knows about their courage. And there are other people who become very well known because of the acts of bravery. Gladys Aylward became famous and amazed the world, when she saved the lives of over one hundred children, by taking them on a journey that lasted more than three weeks. Her story was even made into a book, and a film called 'The Inn of the Sixth Happiness'. Here's what happened.

Gladys Aylward was born in London in 1904, and when she left school, she worked as a housemaid earning just a few shillings a week.

One evening, on her day off, Gladys went to her local church hall to listen to a missionary talk about her work in China. It was an evening that was to change Gladys's life.

The missionary talked about the poverty in China. She spoke of children who were homeless and hungry. She talked about sick children who died because there was no one to look after them.

By the end of the talk, Gladys had made up her mind that she would go to China and try to help in some way. But travelling to China was expensive, and Gladys had no money. So she worked on all her days off, and did extra work whenever she could. She opened an account at the Post Office, and every week she paid in a little money towards her ticket to China.

Then, quite by chance, she heard of a missionary called Mrs Lawson, who lived in China and who was looking for someone younger to carry on her work. Gladys wrote to Mrs Lawson, who wrote back saying 'Yes, please come!'.

Gladys went to the station to book her ticket. She had saved just enough, and had two pounds ten pence left over. In October 1930 she set off on the Trans-Siberian-Railway, the longest railway in the world, across Europe and Russia. Once in Russia, she had to get on a ship to Japan, then to China, then she travelled by train, bus and donkey to the city of Yangchen in the mountains, near Beijing. What a journey!

When she arrived in China, Gladys and Mrs Lawson rented a big old house, which they turned into an inn where travellers crossing the mountain could stay for the night. In the evenings they would tell the travellers wonderful stories from the bible, and the Chinese, who love stories, would listen carefully, and then retell the stories to their friends in other towns and villages.

Then one day, two things happened which were to change the course of Gladys's life again. Mrs Lawson died, and Gladys found a woman and a child on her doorstep.

The woman was not the child's mother, but she had kidnapped her. Gladys gave the woman ninepence in return for the child. A short time later, 'Ninepence' brought a small boy home to Gladys and said, 'Can he live here too? I'll eat less so that he can have something.' And so 'Less' came to live at the inn as well. Soon, other homeless and hungry children came to Gladys for help. She never turned anyone away, and before long she had more than one hundred children in her care. She became like a mother to them, and they called her Ai-weh-deh, which means the Good One.

Then, in the spring of 1938, a war started. Japanese planes bombed the city of Yangchen. Gladys realised what great danger she and the children were in.

'We must leave,' she said to the children. 'We must go over the mountains and across the river to the city of Sian, where there is no fighting and where it will be safe.'

'But how will we get there?' asked one of the children.

'We'll walk!' said Gladys. She knew the journey would be difficult and dangerous, but she knew she had to get the children to safety somehow.

She collected together blankets and as much food as they could carry, and that night, under cover of darkness, Gladys and her one hundred children, set off to walk over the mountains to safety. In the morning, when it grew light, they huddled together for warmth under trees and bushes, and sheltered from the soldiers and the fighting. At dusk, they set off again. As they climbed higher up the mountain, it became colder and colder. They kept on going for twelve days.

But by then the children, especially the little ones, were exhausted. What had started out as an adventure for them had turned into an ordeal.

'We're so tired,' they said. 'We don't want to go any further. Can we stop now? Can we go back?'

Gladys knew that if they went back to their village they would almost certainly be killed by the Japanese soldiers. But she didn't know what would happen if they went on. Perhaps they could reach Sian and safety. Perhaps not! All she knew was that they had to try. And she knew she had to make the children believe they could walk to safety. She had to be positive. She had to be cheerful.

'We'll stop here and rest,' she said. 'We'll all feel better when we've had a sleep. Then we'll set off again, and we'll *sing*! We'll sing to keep going and we'll sing to keep cheerful.'

And despite the fact that she didn't feel at all like singing, Gladys Aylward led her hundred Chinese children over the mountain and down the other side, singing all the way. They sang every song Gladys could remember, and even some she couldn't remember. They sang nursery rhymes, folk songs, sea shanties and hymns. They sang English songs and Chinese songs and even French and German songs. They sang as they crossed the great wide plain at the bottom of the mountain, and they sang as they reached the Yellow River. And then they stopped.

The great wide expanse of the Yellow River stretched in front of them. But there was no way to cross. The bridges had all been destroyed and the boats burned to stop the Japanese soldiers getting across.

'How are we going to get across?' asked one small child.

'How indeed!' said Gladys, who hadn't the vaguest idea of how they were going to do it.

'We'll sing! God will hear us and help us,' said another child.

So the children sang. Perhaps God heard; but certainly some Chinese soldiers heard, and came to see what was going on.

'I know where there's a boat,' said one of the soldiers. 'But it's only small. It will only carry four at a time.'

'Then there's no problem,' said Gladys, with a twinkle in her eye. 'You can row us over four at a time. About twenty five times should do it!'

So the soldiers took the children over the great wide Yellow River, a few at a time, until they were all safely at the other side.

'Good Luck!' the soldiers called. 'Oh, and there's a railway track down there. You might be able to catch a train if you're lucky!'

'A train!' the children shouted. A train meant no more walking, no more sore feet. But when Gladys and the children arrived at the railway yard, they discovered there were no passenger trains.

'Sorry!' said one of the workmen. 'We've only some coal trucks going to Sian.'

'That's wonderful!' smiled Gladys. 'That'll be perfect!'

So Gladys and her hundred children climbed up onto the railway trucks and hid themselves under the coal. Several hours later, dirty and grimy, stiff and cold, they climbed off the train and walked into the city of Sian, and to safety. Their journey had taken three weeks.

Gladys Aylward's journey to save the children made her famous all over the world. Shortly after the journey she became ill, and came back to England for a while. But she missed China and her children so much that she soon bought another ticket to go back. This time she started a children's home on the island of Formosa, which is now Taiwan, and she lived there for the rest of her life.

Gladys went to China to help people. She didn't go with the thought of becoming famous one day. She led her children to safety because she knew she had to; she didn't do it so that she would become rich or well known. There are many people in our world like Gladys, who put other people's safety before their own, and who act bravely because they feel they must help.

Dear Father God, help us to follow the example of people like Gladys Aylward, who worked hard to help others. Help us to face difficulties positively and cheerfully. Help us to be brave when we are faced with difficult challenges. Amen

Theme 2: Achievements

Tom Peel learns to read

There are many people all over the world, and all through history, who have achieved great things. You'll be able to think of some of them yourselves. For example, there was Edmund Hillary and Sherpa Tensing who were the first men to conquer Mount Everest. There was Alexander Fleming who discovered penicillin; Francis Chichester who sailed round the world single-handed; and Henry Ford who invented the motor car.

These people achieved things that you or I could never do, and the list is endless because so many people have achieved so many things in so many different areas.

But there are many other people who have achieved things that at first glance may seem unimportant or insignificant. Things that may seem easy to you or I, yet the person who achieved them had to struggle in order to succeed. For example, there is the case of Tom Peel, a Yorkshireman who learned to read. So what! you might say. Anyone can learn to read. Maybe! But here's his story.

Tom Peel is a shepherd and lives in Yorkshire. He's been a shepherd all his life and comes from a family of shepherds. His father and grandfather and great-grandfather were all shepherds before him.

Tom lives alone in an isolated house deep in the Yorkshire Dales. He's a very shy, quiet sort of man, not the sort of person who likes to be with a crowd, or who likes to have lots of company. He prefers to be on his own, and he prefers the company of sheep to the company of people.

Tom works long hours, and can go for days without seeing or speaking to another person. His work involves looking after an entire flock of several hundred sheep, and Tom prides himself on knowing each one individually. The sheep are allowed to roam freely over the Yorkshire moors, which is a huge area of heather and bracken, with few trees and hardly any houses. Tom walks over the moors; miles and miles every day, with just his sheep dog for company.

To many people, Tom's life is hard and lonely, but Tom is satisfied with his way of life; he's used to it and it suits him. Except for the paper work! He has an ever-increasing amount of paperwork to do; forms to fill in and letters to write, and the problem is, he can't read or write. Or at least he couldn't, until a couple of years ago.

Tom realised that his inability to read and write was beginning to stop him doing his job properly.

'There's only one thing for it,' he said to himself one day. 'I'll have to learn.'

So, at the age of fifty, Tom joined an adult literacy class, and began to learn to read and write.

It can't have been easy for him. For a start, the nearest class was at a college in Skipton, his nearest town, but three miles from his house and not on a bus route. He walked the six mile round trip three times every week. In the summer it was a pleasant walk, but in winter it was a struggle through the snow and ice and wind and rain.

Tom found it difficult having to sit still in a classroom. He was used to working outdoors, not sitting inside at a desk. He found it difficult working alongside other people, this was something else he wasn't used to. He found the actual work quite hard. When he was small he'd hardly ever been to school, so he'd not learned much in the way of reading and writing, so he didn't have much previous knowledge to work on.

In fact, the whole business was so difficult that it would have been the easiest thing in the world for Tom to give up the whole idea. But he didn't. He stuck at it. He worked hard. He did his best even when he knew his best wasn't very good. He persevered.

The people in charge of the adult literacy course were so impressed by Tom's hard work and by the progress that he was making, that they put his name forward for an award. Tom knew nothing about it until a letter was delivered to his house.

In the old days he used to hide any letters that came behind the clock on the mantelpiece, because he knew he couldn't read them, but not any more. He read the postmark on the envelope.

'London! Who's writing to me from London?'

He slit open the envelope and read the letter.

'Dear Mr Peel, You are invited to attend the Literacy Course Award Ceremony, here in London, on July 20th. We are pleased to tell you that you were a regional finalist, and now are a national finalist for an award to be given to the student making the most progress during the last year. We hope you will be able to attend.'

Tom could hardly wait to go to college and find out more about the event.

'I've never been to London before,' he said. 'In fact I've never travelled outside Yorkshire.'

The arrangements were made and Tom, together with two friends from the college, travelled to London for the award ceremony.

There were six finalists, who were each given a prize and a certificate in recognition of the progress they'd made. Afterwards, press and television reporters interviewed the six award winners.

'And what about you, Mr Peel?' they said to Tom. 'How did you do so well? What is the secret of your success?'

'It's no secret,' said Tom. 'Anyone can do it if they have the will and the perseverance.'

So Tom succeeded in doing something that might sound on the surface quite easy, yet for him it was a big step to take and was difficult to do. He did so well because he stuck at it. He didn't give up. It's surprising what can be achieved when people stick at things and don't give up.

There's a saying that goes 'success is one per cent inspiration, and ninety nine per cent perspiration'. It means that everything successful is made up of the idea, and the hard work. The idea is only a tiny part of the success, the main part is the hard work! We could all do with remembering that next time we try to do something.

Dear God, help us to understand that we can achieve a great deal if we want to, and if we work hard. Help us to have perseverance, to be able to stick at things, and not to give up as soon as something becomes difficult. Amen

Miranda's painting

Do you enjoy painting and drawing? Most children do, and a great many adults draw and paint as a hobby. Professional artists, of course, earn their living by painting and drawing. In today's true story, someone who enjoyed painting was told she'd probably never be able to do anything like that again, but she decided she was going to, no matter how difficult it might be. You see, she had a special reason for wanting to paint again.

Miranda felt happy! Everything was going well for her and her husband Chris. They'd been married for a couple of years, they had a house and a job, and now they'd just found out they were going to have a baby. Miranda and Chris decorated the small bedroom ready for the baby, and Miranda, who was very good at drawing and painting, painted animals and teddy bears all round the walls. Life could not have been better!

And then one day as Miranda was out shopping, there was a terrible accident. A lorry ran out of control and crashed into the pedestrian precinct. Several people were slightly injured, but Miranda was seriously hurt. She was rushed to hospital, and whilst she was there, her baby was born.

He was a beautiful baby boy. Chris held him in his arms and said to Miranda, 'Shall we call him Ben?' but Miranda didn't reply.

'I'm afraid she can't talk,' said the doctor. 'I'm sorry to have to tell you, but Miranda has had something called a stroke. She isn't going to die, but part of her brain is damaged and she can't walk or talk or even see properly. I'm afraid she won't be able to do much for herself, and she won't be able to look after the baby.'

'Then I'll look after him,' said Chris. 'But will Miranda get better?'

'It's difficult to say,' answered the doctor. 'She might make some improvement, but it's going to be hard for her, and it will take a long long time.'

Miranda stayed in hospital for about two months, and had physiotherapy - exercises to help her to move again - and some speech therapy to try and help her to talk again. And then she came home. But there were so many things she still couldn't do. She couldn't bath Ben, because she couldn't hold him. Her left hand just wouldn't work. She couldn't dress him, because when she held up a piece of clothing she couldn't tell which was the top or the bottom or the right or the left. The part of her brain that would normally help her to understand what she could see, was damaged. But she was beginning to be able to talk again.

'I *will* get better,' she said over and over again. 'I will look after Ben myself.'

One day when Ben was about two, Miranda watched him playing on the rug in front of her chair. 'He's so beautiful,' she thought. 'I wonder if I could draw him. I used to be able to draw.' She went to the cupboard where her pencils and crayons and paints were kept. She took out a sketchbook and some charcoal pencils. Then she started to draw. Picture after picture after picture. She was still drawing when Chris came home.

'Look!' she said happily. 'What do you think?'

Chris looked at the drawings. But it was impossible to tell what they were. The pages were covered with scribbly lines and squiggles and dots and dashes, yet to Miranda they were pictures of Ben. Chris remembered the wonderful drawings that Miranda used to be able to do, and he felt very sad.

'I don't think you can draw any more,' he said gently. Miranda looked at the pictures and realised that they were just scribbles. They weren't the lovely pictures she had in her head, in her imagination.

'I *will* draw again,' she said.

Every day after that, Miranda got out her sketchbook and practised drawing. But somehow her brain wouldn't make her fingers go where she wanted them to, and she drew strange houses with windows in the gardens instead of in the walls, and roofs floating in the sky instead of fastened to the house. She drew peculiar stick-people with disconnected heads and arms and legs that weren't attached. When she tried to write down words, only half the letters appeared and the writing looked like some strange ancient foreign language. And when she tried to read, the words seemed to dance and jump about on the page so that she couldn't read them in the right order.

Friends and family said to her, 'Why do you keep on trying? It's too hard for you. Just give up and be thankful that you can walk and talk.' But Miranda was determined to be able to do again all the things she'd been able to do in the past.

'Ben will be starting school soon,' she said. 'I want to be able to help him with reading and writing and drawing. I will learn to do those things again.'

So Miranda kept on trying. She was determined to be able to help Ben, but she could only help him if she was able to do the things herself. Every day she struggled to write a few words. Every day she tried to draw something in her sketchbook. And every day she tried to read something. Adult books were too difficult for her, so she practised on Ben's baby books. Most of them had just a word or two on each page, and she learned all over again how to read and write.

When Ben was five he started school. Miranda by then could walk him to school, talk to the other mums, and more importantly, read him stories when he came home.

Whilst Ben was at school all day, Miranda found she had spare time, so she decided to join an art class. By now she was able to draw recognisable shapes, and had even tried painting again. At first Miranda was nervous about joining the class. The people there were not disabled in any way, and some of them were extremely skilful artists. But, once more Miranda persevered. She bravely faced her difficulties and worked hard and did her best.

At the end of the year, the art class put on an exhibition. It was to be held in the city art gallery. Several well-known local professional artists were also exhibiting there, and a famous art critic from London was coming to award the top prize. The students each chose the picture they wanted to exhibit. Miranda chose a painting of Ben, lying on the floor with his chin in his hands, watching television.

Two days later, Miranda, Chris and Ben went back to the gallery to see the exhibition and to find out which picture had won. But as soon as they walked into the gallery they were surrounded by people.

'Congratulations Miranda.'

'Well done!'

'You deserved to win. Your painting was the best of all of them.'

Miranda looked puzzled at first, and then she realised that she had won. Her painting had been awarded first prize, not because she'd been ill, not because anyone felt sorry for her, but because her painting was the best. She went to look at it. It had a small gold circle in the corner, indicating that it was the winner.

'Is it for sale?' someone asked her. 'I'd like to buy it.'

'I'm sorry; it's not for sale,' said Miranda, who knew she would never part with the painting. It would always remind her of her struggle to beat her disability, and her success in overcoming the problems.

Miranda's achievement would have been exceptional even if she'd not had an accident. But to win the art prize so soon after being unable to draw or paint anything, was remarkable. She was successful because she persevered. She kept on trying even when things were difficult. She didn't give up.

Help us Lord, to persevere when things are difficult. Help us to have the will to continue and determination to succeed. Help us to face difficulties with courage. Amen

Daley Thompson goes for gold

When you look at some people who are very successful, you can see how they came to achieve what they did. Most people who succeed have the same qualities of motivation, determination, and perseverance. That means they want to succeed, and they're prepared to stick at something until they do. But no one says it's easy! Whether you can do it or not depends on how badly you want it!

Today's story is about a sporting achievement. Daley Thompson has gone down in history as the best decathlete in the world. But I bet his primary school teachers didn't think he would!

Daley was always in trouble! He was never sitting in his place, never where he should be, always clowning around and showing off, usually looking for attention, and often in fights with other boys. His teachers despaired of him.

'He'll never make anything of himself,' they used to say.

Daley wanted to be a footballer when he grew up, but, as anyone who plays football knows, you have to be a good team member to be a good footballer, and Daley was no good in a team. He used to get the ball to himself and refuse to pass it to others. He wanted to score all the goals himself. In fact he wanted to be the only man on the team! Daley needed a sport he could do on his own, and he found one quite by chance one day, when his coach sent him to the local athletic club to get some running practice.

Daley discovered he liked athletics. He could run fast. And it was a brilliant feeling when he came in first in a race. But when he was entered for his first competition, Daley came in fourth.

'That's it! I'm quitting!' he said. 'I'm only going to do it if I'm good enough to win.'

'Then you'd better work hard and make sure you are good enough to win,' said his coach.

Daley tried many different athletics. He tried long jump and high jump. He had a go at throwing the discus, the hammer and the javelin. He tried pole vaulting and hurdling. He was good at them all.

'So which are you going to choose?' asked his coach. 'Which are you going to concentrate on?'

'All of them,' said Daley. 'I'm going to do them all. I'm going to be the best all round athlete in the whole world.' So he began to train for the decathlon.

Decathlon is a Greek word and it means 'ten struggles'. In the Olympic Games, the decathlon is a gruelling competition in which the athletes take part in ten different events, spread over two days. They have to be good at all ten events. They are awarded points for each event, and the winner is the decathlete with the most points all together.

On the first day the athletes do a 100 metre sprint and a 400 metre run. They do the long jump, the high jump and a shot putt. On the second day they throw the discus and the javelin, they do the pole vault, and a 1500 metre run. You can imagine how fit they have to be to do all that.

Daley put his training before everything else in his life. He knew that serious training for any sport involved motivation and determination. But he had both. He wanted to be the best, and he knew he could only be the best with real hard work.

There were times when he felt like giving up. Like when he went in for competitions and didn't win. Like when he had a training session that went badly. Like when he just felt so tired he wanted to sleep and sleep for a week. But Daley didn't give up. He didn't quit. He kept on training, working, working, training, week in, week out, training, working.

The single-minded, attention-seeking behaviour which had got him into so much trouble at school, now started to pay off. The crowds loved him. And he loved showing off to them. He'd wave and they'd cheer at the start and end of a race.

The 1980 Moscow Olympic Games drew near. Daley trained harder than ever. He'd taken part in the 1976 Games, but not with any thought of winning gold; just to learn what it was like to take part in the Olympics. But this time it was for real. This time he was taking part to win. And being Daley, he wanted to win well. He wanted to win all ten events and come out as champion decathlete.

The Games opened. The athletics began. Still Daley trained, never letting up. The day of the decathlon arrived. Daley did well in the sprint and the 400 metres. He scored high points in the long jump and high jump. His shot putt was terrific. The crowd roared and cheered.

Day two started. Daley threw his best ever discus and javelin throw. He cleared the high hurdles in record time and cleared the pole vault. He ran through the finishing tape of the 1500 metres run to huge applause from the crowd. Then there was the wait for the points to be announced.

'Daley Thompson. 8495 points. Gold for Britain.' And the crowd went wild. He was the best decathlete in the world.

He could have stopped then. He'd achieved his aim and won Olympic gold. But Daley Thompson had the 1984 Olympics in sight. He kept on training. At the 1984 Los Angeles Olympics, he did it again. Another Gold for Britain. A double decathlon Olympic champion. What an achievement!

Daley Thompson has retired now from Olympic athletics, but he was double Olympic decathlon champion for only the second time in history and was an unbeaten world champion for nine years. I suppose this record will be beaten one day, and who knows, it might be one of you who does it! I don't suppose Daley thought he would be an Olympic champion, when he was your age.

Daley was successful because he was talented, but also because he had the motivation and determination to succeed. If you want to, and if you're prepared to work hard, you can succeed at whatever you're good at. I'm going to keep my eye on the newspapers of the future, to see if any of you become famous achievers!

Help us God, to find what we are good at, to use out talents well, and to have the motivation and determination to succeed at what we do. Help us to know that everyone is good at something. Amen

Theme 3: Journeys

Teriak's journey

We're almost at the end of another school year, so it's a good time to think about endings and beginnings and journeys. We're all on a journey through life, and every so often one part ends and another one begins. Just now, this school year is ending and another one will start after the holiday.

One day, when you're older, your school journey will end altogether, and you'll start the next bit of your life. Perhaps you'll go on to college or university or start a new job. Maybe you'll stay here in the house you live in now, or perhaps you'll travel somewhere else.

Whatever you do on your journey through life, and wherever you go, it's important to make the most of every experience. In today's story, a man was so busy searching all the time for something better, he didn't really enjoy living his life.

Many years ago, in the frozen north of the Arctic Circle, lived two young Inuit men with their families. Their names were Teriak and Kasaag. They followed the old traditional ways, in the days before the white man came to their land of snow and ice.

In the summer time, when the ice melted and the days were long, the men used to take their tents and travel inland to hunt for rabbits, foxes and bears. In the wintertime when snow fell every day and ice gripped the land, and when the sun rarely rose above the horizon, they hunted for fish, seals and small whales. Their wives stayed behind and cared for the children, made clothes out of sealskin or caribou, and prepared meals for the evenings, when the two families would gather together and tell stories of times gone by, or adventures, or of magic. Life was difficult in that cold harsh environment, but the families were settled in their ways and contented… except for Teriak, who always wondered what lay beyond.

'I wonder what is over the ice, at the other side of the world?' he used to say. 'I wonder what is across the sea? I wonder what it would be like to live somewhere else?'

'But you don't live somewhere else. You live here,' Kasaag would reply. 'What does it matter what lies beyond?'

'It matters to me,' Teriak would answer. 'Because I want to know.'

One day, Teriak made a decision. He would take his family and travel to the other side of the ice mountain. They would set up home there instead.

'It's bound to be better than here,' he said to Kasaag. 'Why don't you come too?' But Kasaag didn't want to leave.

'My family has always lived here,' he said. 'And yours has too. Why do you want to leave? Why do you always think somewhere else will be better?'

'I just think it will,' answered Teriak, and he began to pack all his family's things on the sledges. Soon they were ready to leave. The two families said goodbye.

'When will we see you again?' cried Kasaag's wife. 'I wish you weren't leaving. I shall miss you.'

'We'll come back. One day soon I hope,' said Teriak's wife, but little did they know how long it would be before they saw each other again.

Teriak and his family set off with the dogs pulling the sleds. They travelled all that day, and slept in the tent at night.

'How will we know when we get there?' asked one of the children.

'I shall just know,' answered Teriak.

After three day's travelling, the family came to a small settlement at the far side of the ice mountain.

'This looks a good place to live,' said Teriak, and he unpacked the tent. The next day, he and some of the men from the settlement built a snow house. Teriak's wife and children made friends with the other people in the settlement and they soon began to feel as though this place was home.

But soon, Teriak's questions started again.

'I wonder what's over there? I wonder what it would be like to live somewhere else?' And after only a few months of living at the settlement, he told his wife and children that it was time to move on. Time to find another home. Time to see what somewhere else was like.

Once again, the sledge was packed with their belongings, and once again they set off. This time the family travelled for seven days before Teriak found the place he felt was right. They quickly settled in and made friends with some people who lived nearby. Teriak's family stayed there for the rest of the winter, but as spring and the longer days came, Teriak's questions started again.

'I wonder what it's like over the sea? I wonder what it would be like to live somewhere else?' And before his wife and family had time to think about it, they were on the move again.

'We have to go now,' explained Teriak. 'I want to see what it's like at the other side of the sea. We must travel now whilst the sea is still frozen. In a few weeks the ice floes will melt and we won't be able to cross.'

Teriak's family spent the next thirty *years* travelling from place to place, trying to answer Teriak's question - 'What is it like over there?' But wherever they went, wherever they lived, the question was always there, because there was always somewhere else that might be better, or more interesting, or more exciting. By now, Teriak's children were grown up and had left their parents to set up families of their own. Teriak and his wife were alone and growing old.

'We're too old now, to travel,' she would say. 'Why don't we settle down and stay here for the rest of our days,' but Teriak would say 'Let's just see what it's like over there. If we like it, perhaps we'll stay,' and they'd set off on their travels again.

One day they arrived at a place that looked vaguely familiar. There were several snow houses grouped round a central area where some children were out playing.

'Have we been here before?' asked Teriak's wife.

'I don't think so,' said Teriak. 'We've always travelled east, following the sun, so I don't see how we can have been here before.'

Just then an old man came out of one of the snow houses. He looked across the snow at the strangers, and was about to call out a greeting when something about them seemed familiar to him. He peered at them again, more intently this time.

'I don't believe it,' he said. 'It's you! It's my old friend Teriak. I never thought I'd see you again.'

'Kasaag?' said Teriak. 'Is it really you? What are you doing here?'

'Doing here?' said Kasaag. 'I live here! I've always lived here. I've never moved from here. You're the one who went travelling, so what are you doing here? Come in and tell me all about your adventures.'

When they started talking, they realised that Teriak had spent his entire life travelling in a huge circle, only to end up where he began in the first place. But he had many stories to tell his friend. Kasaag, on the other hand, had spent all his life in one place. But he knew every rock and boulder, every path and every animal. He had children and grandchildren living around him. He was now head of a large family, and he, too, had many stories to tell.

Teriak and his wife stayed in the place where Kasaag lived.

In the daytime they watched the younger men hunt for rabbits and foxes, seals and whales. In the evening the two families gathered together and told tales of their lives and their adventures. Life was difficult in that cold harsh environment, especially for the old people, but they were contented… even Teriak, because he now knew what lay beyond.

I wonder what you think of that story? Who do you think had the better journey through life – Teriak who travelled, or Kasaag who stayed at home? Maybe neither of them was right or wrong. Perhaps they each did what was right for them. But I wonder if Teriak wasted a lot of his life in always searching for something better, and never being satisfied with what he had. What do you think?

Help us, Lord, on our journey through life. Help us to make the right choices and to travel the right way. Make us always find time to help other people as we travel on our journey. Help us not to be too busy with our own lives that we haven't time to help other people in theirs. Amen

The Lynmouth lifeboat launch

There have been many remarkable journeys through the years, but one of the most spectacular and memorable, was a journey the Lynmouth lifeboat made, a hundred years ago. You might expect it to be a sea journey, but it was in fact a journey over land that the boat made, in one of the worst storms people could remember.

The journey took place in the days when lifeboats had no motors to drive them, and no tractors to pull them. The lifeboats were moved by 'people-power' using oars at sea and ropes on land.

Here's the story.

At 7 o'clock in the evening, on January 12th 1899, a message was sent to the Lynmouth lifeboat that a large ship was in trouble just off the coast at Porlock, about fourteen miles away.

The weather was atrocious; there was a gale force wind blowing with beating rain, and to make matters worse there was an extra-strong high tide that night. The lifeboatmen looked at the beach at Lynmouth where they normally launched the lifeboat when it was needed. But the beach couldn't be seen. The sea was already over the sea wall and the road along the sea front was a metre under water.

'It's impossible to launch the boat from here,' said one of the men.

'But there's nowhere else to launch it from,' said another.

'The only place we could do it, is at Porlock,' said the skipper.

The men stared at him. Porlock was fourteen miles away, at the other side of Countisbury Hill, and over the moor.

'We'll never drag the boat that distance overland,' said the men.

'Well, it's that or nothing!' said the skipper. 'If we don't get the lifeboat to them, those men in the ship will surely drown.' And as he said that, the decision was made.

'We'll go!' they all said.

And so began a very unusual journey.

They sent for all the horses of the people in the village, and asked for as many men and women as possible to come along and help. Then they sent six men out in advance with picks and shovels, to dig out the banking at the side of the road, so that the carriage the lifeboat was resting on, could get through. They fastened ropes to the carriage and pulled the lifeboat out of the boathouse. They harnessed six horses to the carriage and set off. It was now eight o'clock.

The wind and rain were worse than ever and constantly blew out the lanterns. The villagers could hardly see where they were going, and were soaked to the skin within minutes of setting off. A few people went home, but most carried on.

At the bottom of Countisbury Hill, they harnessed ten more horses to the lifeboat carriage. The hill had a gradient of 25% and they didn't want to risk the carriage slipping back. Sixteen horses pulled, and all the available people pushed. They made it! But no sooner had they reached the top, than disaster struck. One of the wheels came off the carriage because of the constant scuffing against the sides of the narrow muddy lane.

'We'll never get there,' someone said.

'Yes we will!' said a lifeboatman, and he set to and fastened the wheel back on. The journey continued.

They were now 500 metres above sea level, and up on the top of Exmoor.

The wind and rain were driving into them, and it was impossible to keep the lanterns lit. Many of the helpers turned back.

'You'll never do it. It's impossible in these conditions.'

'It's an impossible journey in any conditions!' they said.

But the Lynmouth lifeboatmen had come this far and were not going to turn back. They struggled on. Wet, cold and hungry. It was now eleven o'clock.

Part way across the moor, they came to a narrow gate. They couldn't get through so they took down the gateposts. Then they reached a section of the lane, about a mile long, that was also too narrow for the carriage to go through. They divided men and horses into two teams. One team pulled the carriage over the moor, whilst the other team put down planks of wood on the mud of the lane, and pulled the boat over those, constantly taking the planks from the back and placing them in front so the boat could move forwards.

By now it was two o'clock in the morning and the storm was as bad as ever, but they'd come over Hawkcombe Head and could see Porlock in the distance. Nearly there! But there was the steep lane down Porlock Hill still to negotiate.

They untied the horses and re-harnessed them to the back of the carriage. Going downhill meant they needed to hold the carriage back to stop it running out of control to the bottom. Then the men tied more ropes and chains to the lifeboat, and tied themselves to the ropes. Slowly, centimetre by centimetre they guided the boat and carriage down the hill. Safely. To the bottom. Where the cottages were!

One corner of one of the cottages jutted out into the lane. The gap between that cottage and the one opposite was just too narrow for the carriage to go through.

'Take the boat off the carriage. We'll push it through on its own,' said the skipper. They lifted the boat off but it wouldn't go through; the gap was too narrow.

'What do we do now?' asked one of the crew.

'Only one thing we can do,' answered the skipper, and they all waited for him to admit defeat and say they'd have to turn back. But no.

'We'll have to take the wall down!' he said. So they did.

'What do you think you're doing, waking good people at four o'clock in the morning, and knocking their houses down?' demanded the woman who lived in the cottage. But when the skipper explained, she gave them her blessing, (but asked that someone repair her wall the next day!)

Round the corner and past the cottages. Almost there. The ship was in sight, floundering in the bay, its distress flags flapping in the wind. But the men faced another problem.

'You can't get through,' someone shouted. 'The sea's brought down the wall and washed the road away.

'Well, we're not turning back now,' said the skipper, and once again they pulled the boat and carriage off the roadway and onto the fields, round the back of the washed-away road, cutting down trees and branches that got in their way.

At six o'clock in the morning they arrived at Porlock Beach. Then, without thinking of how tired and hungry they felt, they launched the lifeboat and rowed for an hour and a half over the stormy sea, to the damaged ship. With the help of a small tugboat, which had also come to the rescue, they towed the stricken ship into the safety of Barry Harbour, on the south coast of Wales. It was seven o'clock in the evening when they arrived, on Friday the 13th January, exactly twenty-four hours since the Lynmouth lifeboat had set off on its remarkable journey.

What a journey! Nowadays, with engines and tractors and modern technology, the journey wouldn't be nearly so difficult. But what an achievement it was in those days, a hundred years ago.

The lifeboatmen didn't give up, even though the odds were against them. They didn't say, 'It's too difficult. We can't do it. It's too hard.' They persevered and overcame each obstacle as they came to it, and succeeded in the end.

I hope that you, on your journey through life, will try to be like the Lynmouth lifeboatmen: I hope you will stick to things that are worthwhile, even when it's hard, so that you find success, just as they did.

Dear God, help us on our journey through life to cope when things are difficult. Help us to face challenges bravely, and not to give up when the going gets tough. Help us always to be prepared to help other people as we travel through life. Amen

Journey on a dustcart

I wonder what's the most unusual journey you've ever been on? Perhaps some of you have been on unusual kinds of boats or planes, or on an unusual kind of car or even bicycle. It's amazing how many different kinds of journeys there are, and how many different ways of travelling there are.

In today's true story, a woman had a journey to hospital, but not in an ambulance, as you might expect.

One of Jean Cusworth's favourite activities was walking. Since she'd retired from her job in the post office, she'd joined the local rambling association, and most weekends she met her friends from the walking group and they hiked for miles, enjoying the fresh air and the beautiful Yorkshire countryside.

On this particular Saturday about ten of them had set off to walk over the fields and past the reservoir to a small village pub, where they were going to have lunch before walking back. Some of the group were up ahead, in front of Jean, laughing and chatting together. Two of her friends were way back, straggling behind because they'd stopped to talk to someone they'd met, who turned out to be a friend of someone they knew. Jean was somewhere in the middle of the walkers, and for the time being she was on her own.

Jean was in fact quite grateful for a bit of peace and quiet and solitude. She'd had a busy week, what with one thing and another, and the following week didn't look as though it was going to be any quieter. For one thing it was her sixty-eighth birthday in a few days, and she was going to have a small party for her friends. As she walked along, it was a good opportunity to plan the party and to think about what baking she'd need to do, and the things she'd need to buy.

'I think I'll go into town on Monday,' she thought. 'Then I can do the supermarket shopping on Tuesday, bake on Wednesday, and be all ready for the party on Thursday.' The plans all seemed to be falling into place rather well. But suddenly, the birthday party plans became unimportant.

Jean felt a strange pain in her shoulder. She walked a few more steps then felt a terrible pain in her chest. She collapsed against a wall but was in too much pain to call for help. None of the walkers had seen there was a problem. The ones up ahead were still laughing and talking, and the people behind were so engrossed in conversation they hadn't noticed either.

Jean lay against the wall, gasping for breath.

The path she was on was near a road, and traffic was going past in both directions. The driver of one car slowed down.

'What's the matter with her?' he asked his passenger.

'I don't know, but it's nothing to do with us,' the passenger replied, so the car drove away.

Another car came by. The driver stared at Jean as she lay on the path, but it didn't seem to occur to him that she might need help. He drove on.

A van drove past. Two workmen inside didn't see Jean by the wall.

A lorry rumbled by. The driver glanced across at the path and saw what looked like a pile of clothes on the ground. He never thought it could be a person. 'Some people'll throw their rubbish anywhere,' he said to himself.

Another car sped by. A young woman was driving. She slowed down and looked at Jean, then sped off again. Perhaps she thought Jean was a bag lady, or maybe she thought she was drunk. Anyway, whatever the reason, she didn't stop.

Jean by now was unconscious, and knew nothing of what happened next.

A dustcart came by, with binmen Scott and Richard in the cab. They'd just finished emptying the bins in one village and were going on to the next.

'What's that, there by the side of the road?' said Scott.

'It's a woman!' said Richard. 'She looks as though she's ill. She's collapsed.' He stopped the dustcart and got out. He gently felt Jean's pulse.

'She's alive, but I think she's had a heart attack,' he said.

'We'd better get her to hospital,' said Scott. 'I'll go and find the nearest phone and ring 999.'

'No, there isn't time,' said Richard. 'When someone's had a heart attack every second counts. You have to get them to hospital as quickly as possible.'

'But we can't take her on the cart!' said Scott.

'We have to,' answered Richard, already gently lifting Jean up and carrying her to the cab.

They carefully lifted her onto the seat, then Richard set off, driving as fast as the traffic would allow. He drove straight up to the accident and emergency doors of the nearest hospital and ran inside to get a doctor. Within fifteen minutes of the attack starting, Jean was in the intensive care unit, having life-saving treatment.

'You two did a good job,' the doctor said. 'You were right. She had a heart attack, and if you hadn't acted as quickly as you did and got her here as soon as you did, she might not be alive now. Well done!'

Later, the doctors allowed Scott and Richard to visit Jean in intensive care.

'Thank you,' she said. 'I think you saved my life. When I go home, I'm going to have a birthday party. It'll be a few weeks later than the one I was planning to have, but will you come?'

'Certainly will!' said Scott and Richard, and they did, taking with them the most enormous birthday cake Jean had ever seen.

Jean's walking trip certainly didn't turn out as she expected, but what a good job the two binmen noticed that Jean had a problem, and bothered to do something about it. The story would have ended very differently if they hadn't. Scott and Richard, by the way, were hailed as heroes, and later given certificates and diamond stickpins by the local newspaper and radio station, as a reward for their quick thinking efforts.

And why am I telling you this story of a woman you don't know, and two dustbinmen you've never met, on the last day of the school year? Because I hope that in your journey through life you will never be too busy or too selfish or too proud, to stop and help someone who needs help.

Happy holiday everyone, and I wish you all well on the next bit of your journey!

On our journey through life, Lord, help us always to find time to help other people. Help us never to be too busy, or too selfish, or too proud to give help when it's needed. Help us to be generous of spirit. Amen

Alphabetical index of stories

Acrobat, The **167**
Anansi changes the world **95**
Angel Falls **63**
Autumn leaves **19**

Broken plate, The **106**

Charlie's new bag **101**
Chinese casket, The **181**
Cross-Channel ferry, The **13**

Daley Thompson goes for gold **218**
Dare, The **146**

Eagle and the beetle, The **159**
Efflam Rock, The **201**

Evacuee, The **110**
Excalibur **93**

Farmer Brandit's hat **193**
Firework maker, The **42**
Flight of the beasts, The **156**
Florence Nightingale **174**
Fourth wise man, The – and the ruby **76**
and the sapphire **78**
and the pearl **80**
From tomorrow on **113**

Giant chopsticks, The **15**
Gladys Aylward **211**
Golden apple, The **198**
Graffiti **130**
Great council of rats, The **118**

Harvest anagram **26**
Hopes and dreams **87**
How corn came to America **28**
How Coyote made the first people **3**
How fire learned to run **47**
How much is he worth? **7**
How the jellyfish lost its bones **51**

I am going to advance **90**

Joshua saves his dad **99**
Journey on a dustcart **226**

Katie-Lee's treat **38**
Kimoto and the rice harvest **31**
King Midas's ears **179**

Lynmouth lifeboat launch, The **223**

Making jelly **97**
Manchester United **191**
Marmoset on holiday, A **123**
Martin Luther King **169**
Miranda's painting **216**
Mohandas Gandhi **172**
Mr Storten builds a house **1**
Mr Watson and the garden party **103**

Nelly Brennan **208**
Noah's choices **143**

Obstacle course, The **17**
Odd one out, The **112**
Onions make your eyes water **177**
Oona McCool and the Giant Cahoolin **58**
Orion **69**
Otter who came back, The **134**

Petsearch **125**
Planet Earth **66**
Pleiades, The **71**
People of Chelm, The **35**

Rainforests and burgers **132**
Rabbi and the emperor, The **61**
Recipes **145**
Remarkable victory, A **116**
Remembrance Day **44**
Rich man and the well, The **203**
Robin escapes **56**
Rope with three knots, The **184**

Saint Kevin and the King's goose **108**
Saint Nonmiricordo and the fish **40**
Servant girl, The – in the city **136**
in the garden **138**
on the hill **140**
Severed head, The **164**
Shoeboxes **23**
Small brown dog, The **127**
Snow spirit, The **49**
Soup from a stone **21**
Sparrows' gifts, The **154**
Sponsored spell, The **162**
Spreading the news **82**
Superman **206**
Sword in the stone, The **54**

Teriak's journey **221**
Three shoemakers in Baghdad **149**
Tom Peel learns to read **214**
Tony Bullimore **95**
Trickster tricked, The **33**
Twenty eighty **152**
Two brothers **120**
Two girls and a cockerel **186**
Two sides to every story **148**

Urashima's revenge **188**
Ursa Major **74**

William conquers England **85**

Vital difference **9**

What's in a name? **10**
Wotsis, The **5**

Story source index

'Action' assemblies
Broken plate, The **106**
Harvest anagram **26**
Making jelly **97**
Obstacle course, The **17**
Odd one out, The **112**
Recipes **145**
Two sides to every story **148**

Fables
Anansi changes the world **195**
Eagle and the beetle, The **159**
Flight of the beasts, The **156**
Great council of rats, The **118**
Remarkable victory, A **116**
Sparrows' gifts, The **154**
Two girls and a cockerel **186**

Fantasy stories
Farmer Brandit's hat **193**
Rope with three knots, The **184**
What's in a name? **10**

Fiction
Charlie's new bag **101**
Dare, The **146**
Evacuee, The **110**
Graffiti **130**
Hopes and dreams **87**
I am going to advance **90**
Mr Watson and the garden party **103**
Mr Storten builds a house **1**
Noah's choices **143**
Onions make your eyes water **177**
Otter who came back, The **134**
Planet Earth **65**
Rainforests and burgers **132**
Small brown dog, The **127**
Sponsored spell, The **162**

Folk stories
Giant chopsticks, The **15**

People of Chelm, The **35**
Severed head, The **164**
Soup from a stone **21**
Teriak's journey **221**
Trickster tricked, The **33**
Two brothers **120**
Wotsis, The **5**
Vital difference **9**

Legends
Chinese casket, The **181**
Efflam Rock, The **201**
Excalibur **93**
Kimoto and the rice harvest **31**
King Midas's ears **179**
Oona McCool and the giant Cahoolin **58**
Robin escapes **56**
Sword in the stone, The **54**
Urashima's revenge **188**

Stories from the major religions
Fourth wise man – and the ruby **76**
and the sapphire **78**
and the pearl (Christianity) **80**
Rabbi and the emperor, The (Judaism) **61**
Rich man and the well, The (Muslim) **203**
Saint Kevin and the King's goose (Christianity) **108**
Saint Nonmiricordo and the fish (Christianity) **40**
Servant girl, The – in the city **136**
in the garden **138**
on the hill (Christianity) **140**
Spreading the news (Christianity) **82**

Traditional tales
Acrobat, The **167**
Golden apple, The **198**
Three shoemakers in Baghdad **149**

True stories
Angel Falls **63**
Cross-Channel ferry, The **13**
Daley Thompson goes for gold **218**
Firework maker, The **42**
Florence Nightingale **174**
From tomorrow on **113**

Gladys Aylward **198**
How much is he worth? **7**
Joshua saves his dad **99**
Journey on a dustcart **226**
Katie-Lee's treat **38**
Lynmouth lifeboat launch, The **223**
Manchester United **191**
Marmoset on holiday, A **123**
Martin Luther King **169**
Miranda's painting **216**
Mohandas Gandhi **172**
Nelly Brennan **208**
Petsearch **125**
Remembrance Day **44**
Shoeboxes **23**
Superman **206**
Tom Peel learns to read **214**
Tony Bullimore **95**
Twenty eighty **152**
William conquers England **85**

Myths
Autumn leaves **19**
How corn came to America **28**
How Coyote made the first people **3**
How fire learned to run **47**
How the jellyfish lost its bones **51**
Snow spirit, The **49**
Orion **69**
Pleiades, The **71**
Ursa Major **74**

Theme index – other than main themes listed in contents

Awareness

How corn came to America **28**
Hopes and dreams **87**
Joshua saves his dad **99**
Rainforests and burgers **132**
Flight of the beasts, The **156**
Farmer Brandit's hat **193**
Anansi changes the world **195**
Efflam Rock, The **201**
Journey on a dustcart **226**

Bravery/Courage

How corn came to America **28**
Kimoto and the rice harvest **31**
Robin escapes **56**
Angel Falls **63**
Planet Earth **65**
Fourth wise man, The **76**
Spreading the news **82**
Tony Bullimore **95**
Joshua saves his dad **99**
From tomorrow on **113**
Remarkable victory, A **116**
Dare, The **146**
Eagle and the beetle, The **159**
Martin Luther King **169**
Mohandas Gandhi **172**
Florence Nightingale **174**
Superman **206**
Nelly Brennan **208**
Gladys Aylward **211**
Tom Peel learns to read **214**
Miranda's painting **216**
Lynmouth lifeboat launch, The **223**

Bullying

Robin escapes **56**
Oona McCool and the Giant Cahoolin **58**
Ursa Major **74**
Great council of rats, The **118**
Two brothers **120**
Recipes **145**
Chinese casket, The **181**

Caring for animals

Charlie's new bag **101**
Saint Kevin and the King's goose **108**
Two brothers **120**
Marmoset on holiday, A **123**
Petsearch **125**
Small brown dog, The **127**
Otter who came back, The **134**
Noah's choices **143**
Sparrows' gifts, The **154**

Caring for the environment

How corn came to America **28**
Rabbi and the emperor, The **61**
Angel Falls **63**
Planet earth **65**
Hopes and dreams **87**
Graffiti **130**
Rainforests and burgers **132**
Otter who came back, The **134**

Caring for others

Vital difference **9**
Shoeboxes **23**
Harvest anagram **26**
Kimoto and the rice harvest **31**
Katie-Lee's treat **38**
Saint Nonmiricordo and the fish **40**
Saint Kevin and the King's goose **108**
Evacuee, The **110**
Great council of rats, The **118**
Two brothers **120**
Recipes **145**
Twenty eighty **152**
Martin Luther King **169**
Mohandas Gandhi **172**
Florence Nightingale **174**
Chinese casket, The **181**
Nelly Brennan **208**
Gladys Aylward **211**
Lynmouth lifeboat launch, The **223**
Journey on a dustcart **226**

Caring for things
Graffiti **130**
Rope with three knots, The **184**

Cheating
How Coyote made the first people **3**
Trickster tricked, The **33**
How the jellyfish lost its bones **51**
Sword in the stone, The **54**
William conquers England **85**
Sponsored spell, The **162**

Cheerfulness
Trickster tricked, The **33**
People of Chelm, The **35**
Recipes **145**
Superman **206**
Gladys Aylward **211**

Complacency
Remarkable victory, A **116**
Great Council of rats, The **118**
Golden apple, The **198**

Conceit
How Coyote made the first people **3**
Remarkable victory, A **116**
Great council of rats, The **118**
King Midas's ears **179**

Consideration for others
Mr Storten builds a house **1**
Vital difference **9**
Autumn leaves **19**
Shoeboxes **23**
Kimoto and the rice harvest **31**
Katie-Lee's treat **38**
Fourth wise man, The **76**
From tomorrow on **113**
Great council of rats, The **118**
Two brothers **120**
Graffiti **130**
Twenty eighty **152**
Two sides to every story **148**
Martin Luther King **169**

Mohandas Gandhi **172**
Florence Nightingale **174**
Anansi changes the world **195**
Nelly Brennan **208**
Lynmouth lifeboat launch, The **223**
Journey on a dustcart **226**

Co-operation
Cross-Channel ferry, The **13**
Obstacle course, The **17**
Soup from a stone **21**
Shoeboxes **23**
People of Chelm, The **35**
Katie-Lee's treat **38**
Evacuee, The **110**
Marmoset on holiday, A **123**
Two sides to every story **148**
Martin Luther King **169**
Lynmouth lifeboat launch, The **223**

Determination
Two brothers **120**
Eagle and the beetle, The **159**
Martin Luther King **169**
Mohandas Gandhi **172**
Gladys Aylward **211**
Daley Thompson goes for gold **218**

Differences
How Coyote made the first people **3**
Wotsis, The **5**
What's in a name? **10**
Two brothers **120**
Teriak's journey **221**

Doing your best
How corn came to America **28**
Kimoto and the rice harvest **31**
Angel Falls **63**
Tony Bullimore **95**
Making jelly **97**
Joshua saves his dad **99**
Marmoset on holiday, A **123**
Petsearch **125**
Sponsored spell, The **162**

Martin Luther King **169**
Mohandas Gandhi **172**
Florence Nightingale **174**
Superman **206**
Nelly Brennan **208**
Gladys Aylward **211**
Tom Peel learns to read **214**
Miranda's painting **216**
Daley Thompson goes for gold **218**
Lynmouth lifeboat launch, The **223**
Journey on a dustcart **226**

Duty
How corn came to America **28**
Kimoto and the rice harvest **31**
Remembrance Day **44**
Spreading the news **82**
Hopes and dreams **87**
Excalibur **93**
Evacuee, The **110**
Great council of rats, The **118**
Marmoset on holiday, A **123**
Small brown dog, The **127**
Dare, The **146**

Fairness
Mr Storten builds a house **1**
Shoeboxes **23**
Harvest anagram **26**
Trickster tricked, The **33**
Robin escapes **56**
William conquers England **85**
Saint Kevin and the King's goose **108**
Great council of rats, The **118**
Two sides to every story **148**
Martin Luther King **169**
Mohandas Gandhi **172**
Chinese casket, The **181**

Forgiveness
Sword in the stone, The **54**
Pleiades, The **71**
Excalibur **93**
Two brothers **120**
Chinese casket, The **181**

Friendship

Giant chopsticks, The **15**
Soup from a stone **21**
Pleiades, The **71**
William conquers England **85**
Excalibur **93**
Mr Watson and the garden party **103**
Broken plate, The **106**
Saint Kevin and the King's goose **108**
From tomorrow on **113**
Recipes **145**
Dare, The **146**
Acrobat, The **167**
King Midas's ears **179**
Teriak's journey **221**

Generosity

Autumn leaves **19**
Soup from a stone **21**
Shoeboxes **23**
Kimoto and the rice harvest **31**
Katie-Lee's treat **38**
Pleiades, The **71**
Fourth wise man, The **76**
Mr Watson and the garden party **103**
Petsearch **125**
Sparrows' gifts, The **154**
Acrobat, The **167**
Florence Nightingale **174**
Golden apple, The **198**
Nelly Brennan **208**

Gossip

Onions make your eyes water **177**
King Midas's ears **179**
Chinese casket, The **181**

Greed

Giant chopsticks, The **15**
Harvest anagram **26**
How fire learned to run **28**
Great council of rats, The **118**
Sparrows' gifts, The **154**
Efflam Rock, The **201**

Helpfulness
Obstacle course, The **17**
Kimoto and the rice harvest **31**
Katie-Lee's treat **38**
Marmoset on holiday, A **123**
Petsearch **125**
Recipes **145**
Sparrows' gifts, The **154**
Florence Nightingale **179**
Nelly Brennan **208**
Lynmouth lifeboat launch, The **223**
Journey on a dustcart **226**

Honesty
How much is he worth? **7**
Trickster tricked, The **33**
Snow spirit, The **49**
Sword in the stone, The **54**
Excalibur **93**
Three shoemakers in Baghdad **149**
Two sides to every story **148**
Sponsored spell, The **162**
King Midas's ears **179**
Chinese casket, The **181**

Humility
Sparrows' gifts, The **154**
Mohandas Gandhi **172**

Insincerity
Trickster tricked, The **33**
William conquers England **85**
Two brothers **120**
Dare, The **146**
Chinese casket, The **181**

Jealousy
Orion **69**
King Midas's ears **179**
Chinese casket, The **181**

Jumping to conclusions
Remarkable victory, A **116**
Twenty eighty **152**
Flight of the beasts, The **156**
Onions make your eyes water **177**

Keeping your word

Mr Storten builds a house **1**
How Coyote made the first people **3**
How much is he worth? **7**
Trickster tricked, The **33**
Snow spirit, The **49**
William conquers England **85**
Excalibur **93**
Saint Kevin and the King's goose **108**
Marmoset on holiday, A **123**
Severed head, The **164**

Kindness

Autumn leaves **19**
Shoeboxes **23**
Katie-Lee's treat **38**
Fourth wise man, The **76**
Two brothers **120**
Petsearch **125**
Small brown dog, The **127**
Recipes **145**
Sparrows' gifts, The **154**
Acrobat, The **167**
Florence Nightingale **174**
Golden apple, The **198**
Nelly Brennan **208**
Journey on a dustcart **226**

Laziness

Making jelly **97**
Great council of rats, The **118**
Graffiti **130**
Two girls and a cockerel **186**
Farmer Brandit's hat **193**

Loyalty

Kimoto and the rice harvest **31**
Snow spirit, The **49**
Robin escapes **56**
Spreading the news **82**
William conquers England **85**
Excalibur **93**
Saint Kevin and the King's goose **108**
Dare, The **146**
Martin Luther King **169**

Chinese casket, The **181**
Lynmouth lifeboat launch, The **223**

Obedience
Snow spirit, The **49**
Sword in the stone, The **54**
Excalibur **93**
Making jelly **97**
Noah's choices **143**
Dare, The **146**
Severed head, The **164**
Rope with three knots, The **184**
Anansi changes the world **195**

Patience
How corn came to America **28**
Tony Bullimore **95**
Saint Kevin and the King's goose **108**
Two brothers **120**
Martin Luther King **169**
Superman **206**
Miranda's painting **216**

Perseverance
Mr Storten builds a house **1**
Saint Nonmiricordo and the fish **40**
Angel Falls **63**
Fourth wise man, The **76**
Tony Bullimore **95**
Two brothers **120**
Martin Luther King **169**
Mohandas Gandhi **172**
Florence Nightingale **174**
Superman **206**
Gladys Aylward **211**
Tom Peel learns to read **108**
Miranda's painting **216**
Daley Thompson goes for gold **218**
Teriak's journey **221**
Lynmouth lifeboat launch, The **223**

Power
How Coyote made the first people **3**
Wotsis, The **5**
How fire learned to run **47**

How the jellyfish lost its bones **51**
Remarkable victory, A **116**
Great council of rats, The **118**
Two brothers **120**
Anansi changes the world **195**

Repentance
Sword in the stone, The **54**
Rabbi and the emperor, The **61**
Excalibur **93**

Responsibility
Kimoto and the rice harvest **31**
Firework maker, The **42**
Snow spirit, The **49**
How the jellyfish lost its bones **51**
Hopes and dreams **87**
I am going to advance **90**
Excalibur **93**
Tony Bullimore **95**
Joshua saves his dad **99**
Evacuee, The **110**
Great council of rats, The **118**
Marmoset on holiday, A **123**
Small brown dog, The **127**
Graffiti **130**
Rainforests and burgers **132**
Dare, The **146**
Lynmouth lifeboat launch, The **223**
Journey on a dustcart **226**

Retaliation
Oona McCool and the Giant Cahoolin **58**
Ursa Major **74**
Broken Plate, The **106**
Eagle and the beetle, The **159**
Mohandas Gandhi **172**
Urashima's revenge **188**

Safety
Kimoto and the rice harvest **31**
Firework maker, The **42**
How fire learned to run **47**
Planet earth **65**
Tony Bullimore **95**

Joshua saves his dad **99**
Evacuee, The **110**
Otter who came back, The **134**
Gladys Aylward **211**
Lynmouth lifeboat launch, The **223**

Selfishness
Mr Storten builds a house **1**
Giant chopsticks, The **15**
How fire learned to run **47**
Ursa Major **74**
Mr Watson and the garden party **103**
Great council of rats, The **118**
Two brothers **120**
Recipes **145**
Sparrows' gifts, The **154**
Manchester United **191**
Rich man and the well, The **203**
Teriak's journey **221**

Setting an example
Vital difference **9**
Shoeboxes **23**
Kimoto and the rice harvest **31**
Petsearch **125**
Small brown dog, The **127**
Martin Luther King **169**
Mohandas Gandhi **172**
Florence Nightingale **174**
Superman **206**
Nelly Brennan **208**
Miranda's painting **216**
Daley Thompson goes for gold **218**
Lynmouth lifeboat launch, The **223**
Journey on a dustcart **226**

Sharing
Vital difference **9**
What's in a name? **10**
Shoeboxes **23**
Harvest anagram **26**
How corn came to America **28**
Kimoto and the rice harvest **31**
Katie-Lee's treat **38**
Mr Watson and the garden party **103**

Evacuee, The **110**
Sparrows' gifts, The **154**

Taking for granted
Mr Storten builds a house **1**
Wotsis, The **5**
Hopes and dreams **87**
Remarkable victory, A **116**
Graffiti **130**
Rainforests and burgers **132**
Rich man and the well, The **203**

Temptation
Sword in the stone, The **21**
Excalibur **93**
Charlie's new bag **101**
Dare, The **146**
Sponsored spell, The **162**

Thinking
How much is he worth? **7**
Kimoto and the rice harvest **31**
Oona McCool and the Giant Cahoolin **58**
Excalibur **93**
Tony Bullimore **95**
Joshua saves his dad **99**
Charlie's new bag **101**
Remarkable victory, A **116**
Small brown dog, The **127**
Rainforests and burgers **132**
Dare, The **146**
Two sides to every story **148**
Flight of the beasts, The **156**
Severed head, The **164**
Martin Luther King **169**
Lynmouth lifeboat launch, The **223**
Journey on a dustcart **226**

Thoughtlessness
Mr Storten builds a house **1**
How fire learned to run **47**
Making jelly **97**
Charlie's new bag **101**
Great council of rats, The **118**
Graffiti **130**

Otter who came back, The **134**
Twenty eighty **152**
Flight of the beasts, The **156**
Manchester United **191**
Farmer Brandit's hat **193**
Anansi changes the world **195**

Tolerance
Mr Storten builds a house **1**
Mr Watson and the garden party **103**
Odd one out, The **112**
Three shoemakers in Baghdad **149**
Two sides to every story **148**

Trust
How much is he worth? **7**
Trickster tricked, The **33**
Robin escapes **56**
William Conquers England **85**
Excalibur **93**
Tony Bullimore **95**
Evacuee, The **110**
Great council of rats, The **118**
Small brown dog, The **127**
Otter who came back, The **134**
Sponsored spell, The **162**
King Midas's ears **179**
Nelly Brennan **208**

Unselfishness
Vital difference **9**
Soup from a stone **21**
Shoeboxes **23**
Kimoto and the rice harvest **31**
Katie-Lee's treat **38**
Fourth wise man, The **76**
Two brothers **120**
Petsearch **125**
Sparrows' gifts, The **154**
Martin Luther King **169**
Nelly Brennan **208**
Gladys Aylward **211**
Lynmouth lifeboat launch, The **223**
Journey on a dust cart **226**

Value of natural things
Rabbi and the Emperor, The **61**
Angel Falls **63**
Planet earth **65**
Orion **69**
Pleiades, The **71**
Hopes and dreams **87**
Rainforests and burgers **132**
Otter who came back, The **134**
Efflam Rock, The **201**
Rich man and the well, The **203**

Working together
Obstacle course, The **17**
Shoeboxes **23**
People of Chelm, The **35**
Katie-Lee's treat **38**
Hopes and dreams **87**
Great council of rats, The **118**
Marmoset on holiday, A **123**
Petsearch **125**
Graffiti **130**
Noah's choices **143**
Martin Luther King **169**
Mohandas Gandhi **172**
Florence Nightingale **174**
Lynmouth lifeboat launch, The **223**